The Pantheon, Representing the Fabulous Histories of the Heathen Gods and Most Illustrious Heroes

Pl. I.

To face the title.

H. Moses del. et sculp.

THE

PANTHEON,

REPRESENTING

THE FABULOUS HISTORIES

OF THE

HEATHEN GODS

AND MOST ILLUSTRIOUS HEROES,

IN A PLAIN AND FAMILIAR METHOD.

BY ANDREW TOOKE, A.M.

THE

THIRTY-FOURTH EDITION, REVISED AND CORRECTED.

ILLUSTRATED BY TWENTY-EIGHT PLATES, ENGRAVED FROM NEW AND ORIGINAL DESIGNS.

LONDON:

PRINTED FOR F. C. AND J. RIVINGTON; SCATCHERD AND LETTERMAN; LACKINGTON, HUGHES, HARDING, AND CO.; LONGMAN, HURST, AND CO.; BALDWIN, CRADOCK, AND JOY; J. RICHARDSON; G. AND W. B. WHITTAKER; J. MAWMAN; W. GINGER; J. ROBINSON; E. WILLIAMS; AND R. SCHOLEY.

1819.

LONDON:
PRINTED BY THOMAS DAVISON, WHITEFRIARS.

TO THE READER.

IT is confessed that there are already many books published on the present subject, two or three of which are in our own tongue; and those, without doubt, will, by some men, be thought enough. But since this can be the opinion but of a few, and those unexperienced people, it has been judged more proper to regard the advice of many grave persons of known skill in the art of teaching; who, though they must acknowledge that Goodwin, in his Antiquities, has done very well in the whole, yet cannot but own that he has been too short in this point: that Rosse also, though he deserves commendation for his Mythology, is yet very tedious, and as much too large; and that Galtruchius, as D'Assigny has translated and dished him out to us, is so confused and artless in his method, as well as unfortunate in his corrections, that it in nowise answers the purpose it was designed for; and hereupon this work was recommended to be translated, being first well approved by learned gentlemen, as is above mentioned, for its easy method and agreeable plainness. Besides, it having been written by so learned a person, and that for the use of so great a prince, and so universally received in our neighbour nations, as to have sold several impressions in a short time, there was no room to doubt of its being well received here. As for the quotations out of the Latin poets, it was considered awhile, whether they should be translated or not: but it was, at last, judged proper to print them in English, either from those who already rendered them well, or, where they could not be had, to give a new translation of them, that so nothing of the whole work might be out of the reach of the young scholar's understanding, for whose benefit chiefly this version was intended. In this impression, care has been taken, not only to move the citations to the ends of the pages, sections, or chapters, which before lying in the body of the discourse, and making part of it, the sense was greatly interrupted, the connexion disturbed, and thereby a confusion often created in the understandings of some of those younger scholars, into whose hands it was put, by such an undue and improper mixture of English and Latin, of prose and verse; but further, to make it still more plain and familiar, and thereby better suited to their capacity, and more proper for their use, such ambiguous expressions and obscure phrases have been removed, and such perplexed periods rectified, as had been found either to cause misunderstanding of the author's meaning, or to lead the scholar into barbarism, in rendering any part of it into Latin, when such translations have been imposed as a task. And lastly, a complete and significant Index, instead of a verbal one before, has been added to this impression, whereby any thing material in the whole book may be readily found out; the usefulness of which need not be mentioned here, since the want of it, in all former editions, has been much complained of by most of those many masters who have made use hereof in their schools.

ANDREW TOOKE.

CHARTERHOUSE,
June 30, 1713.

⁎ In this thirty-second edition, the citations are all placed at the bottom of the pages, and several errors and omissions rectified, by referring to the different authors.

ADVERTISEMENT

TO THE

THIRTY-THIRD EDITION.

IT is now more than a century since THE PANTHEON was first published. During this period, it has maintained a high reputation in our public schools, and other places devoted to classical erudition, as the most extensively useful introduction to ancient Mythology. Its superiority over every other work of the kind is derived as well from the vast fund of knowledge which it contains, as also on account of the perpetual references to, and large quotations from, the principal works of antiquity, which are the objects of our youthful and more mature studies. In this view, THE PANTHEON has ever been regarded not only as a capital introduction to, but companion and illustrator of the writings of Homer, Horace, Virgil, Ovid, &c. &c.

The Proprietors, in return for the liberal patronage, which their work has so long experienced, feel anxious that it may still merit the public approbation, and lay just claim, by improvements in its style and embellishments, to that eminence which it has hitherto maintained. They have accordingly spared no expense in rendering it at once an interesting and practically useful school-book.

It will be seen, that for this edition, a set of new and beautiful out-lined plates have been drawn from antique statues, and engraved by an artist of considerable reputation, to supersede others that were much worn, and in the execution of which there was certainly a deficiency of taste, that ill corresponded with the improved state of the arts.

The letter-press has undergone a complete and diligent revision: numerous alterations, corrections, and additions, have been made throughout: obsolete, coarse, and indelicate phrases and expressions, have been obliterated, and others substituted, which may accord with modern usage, and which will neither administer fuel to youthful passions, nor excite the blush of female innocence.

THE PANTHEON, then, in its present corrected state, is equally adapted to persons of every age, and of each sex; which was the more desirable, because classical literature has of late become an object of considerable importance in female education.

In conformity with the wishes of many of the preceptors in our best schools, the Editor has laid aside the form of dialogue, which was ill supported, and, in its stead, has introduced, at the end of each section or chapter, a series of questions, by means of which the assiduity and improvement of the pupils, either individually or in classes, may be ascertained without any additional labour to the teacher.

LONDON, *May* 1, 1810.

CONTENTS.

THE

FABULOUS HISTORIES

OF THE

HEATHEN GODS.

INTRODUCTION.

CHAPTER I.

THE APPROACH TO THE PANTHEON.—THE ORIGINAL OF IDOLATRY.

THE Fabulous *Pantheon* is, as its name imports, the *Temple of all the Gods*, which the superstitious folly of men have feigned, either through a gross ignorance of the true and only GOD, or through a contempt of him.

It may be right, in the outset of our description, to give some account of the Pantheon, of which you have a view in the plate that faces the title-page. It is uncertain by whom this beautiful edifice was erected: some suppose it to have been built by Agrippa, the son-in-law of Augustus; but others contend that he only enlarged and adorned it, and added to it a magnificent portico. Its body is cylindrical, and its roof or dome spherical: its inner diameter was 144 feet, and the height from the pavement to the grand aperture on its top was also 144 feet. Its exterior was built after the Corinthian order of architecture. The inner circumference is divided into seven grand niches, six of which are flat at the top, but the seventh, which is opposite to the entrance, is arched. Before each niche are two columns of antique yellow marble, fluted, and of one entire block. The whole wall of the temple, as high as the grand cornice inclusive, is cased with different kinds of precious marble, in compartments. The frieze is entirely of porphyry. Above the grand cornice rises an attic, in which are wrought, at equal distances, fourteen oblong square niches, between each of which were four marble pilasters, and between the pillars marble tables of various kinds. This attic had a complete entablature; but the cornice projected less than that of the grand order below. The sperical roof springs from the cornice, which is divided by bands, that cross each other like the meridians and parallels of an artificial terrestrial globe. The spaces between the bands decrease in size as they approach the top of the roof, to which they do not reach, there being a considerble space left plain between them and the great opening.

The walls below were formerly decorated with works of carved brass or silver, and the roof was covered on the outside with plates of gilded bronze. The portico is composed of sixteen columns of granite, four feet in diameter, eight of which stand in front, with an equal intercolumniation. To these columns is a pediment, whose tympanum, or flat, was ornamented with bas-reliefs in brass: the cross beams, which formed the ceiling of the portico, were covered with the same metal, and so were the doors. Such *was* the Pantheon, the richness and magnificence of which induced Pliny and others to rank it among the wonders of the world.

The eruption of Mount Vesuvius, in the reign of Tiberius, did much damage to this fine edifice, which was, however, repaired by Domitian; and the temple subsisted in all its grandeur till the incursion of Alaric, who plundered it of its precious metals. The building continues to this day; but it was, in the beginning of the seventh century, converted, by Boniface IV., into a christian church, and dedicated to the "Virgin Mary and all the Saints:" thus the same place that was eminent for heathen idolatry of the worse kind has been equally notorious for a species of worship as absurd and idolatrous as that which it superseded.

The causes which have chiefly conduced to the establishment and continuance of idolatry are thus enumerated.

1. *The first cause of Idolatry was the extreme folly*[a] *and vainglory of men*, who have denied to Him, who is the inexhausted fountain of all good, the honours which they have attributed to muddy streams: "Digging,"[b] as the prophet complains, "to themselves broken and dirty cisterns, and neglecting and forsaking the most pure fountain of living waters." It ordinarily happened after this manner. [c] If any one excelled in stature of body, if he were endued with greatness of mind, or noted for clearness of [d] wit, he first gained to himself the admiration of the ignorant vulgar; this admiration was by degrees turned into a profound respect, till at length they paid him a greater honour than men ought to receive, and ranked the man among the number of the gods: while the more prudent were either carried away by the torrent of the vulgar opinion, or were unable, or afraid, to resist it.

2. *The sordid flattery of subjects toward their princes was a second cause of Idolatry.* To gratify their vanity, to flatter their pride, and to soothe them

[a] Sap. xiv. 14. [b] Jerem. ii. 13. [c] Diodor. l. 17. Plut. in Lysand. [d] Val. Max. l. 8. c. ult. Cic. de Rep. apud Aug. de Civ. Dei. 3.

in their self-conceit, they erected altars, and set the images of their princes on them; to which they offered incense, in like manner as to the gods; [e] and not unfrequently while they were still living.

3. *A third cause of Idolatry was an [f] immoderate love of immortality in many,* who studied to attain it, by leaving effigies of themselves behind them; imagining that their names would still be preserved from the power of death and time, so long as they lived in brass, or in statues of marble, after their funerals.

4. [g] *A desire of perpetuating the memories of excellent and useful men to future ages was the fourth cause of Idolatry.* [h] For, to make the memory of such men eternal, and their names immortal, they made them gods, or rather called them so.

The contriver and assertor of false gods was Ninus, the first king of the Assyrians, who, to render the name of his father [i] Belus, or Nimrod, immortal, worshipped him with divine honour after his death, which is thus accounted for.

After Ninus had conquered many nations far and near, and built the city called, after his name, Nineveh; in a public assembly of the Babylonians he extolled his father Belus, the founder of the empire and city of Babylon, beyond all measure, representing him, not only worthy of perpetual honour among all posterity, but also of an immortality among the gods above. He then exhibited a statue of him, curiously and neatly made, to which he commanded them to pay the same reverence that they would have given to Belus while alive: he also appointed it to be a common sanctuary to the miserable, and ordained, " that if at any time an offender should fly to this statue, it

[e] Athen. l. 6. deipnosoph. c. 6. de Demetrio Poliorcete. Sueton. in Julio. c. 76 & 84. [f] Pontan. l. 1. c. de Saturn. [g] Thucyd. l. 7. Plutarch. Apopht. Lacon. 4. Cic. de Nat. Deor. 1. 1. Sap. 14, 15. [h] Vid. Annal. Salian. anno 2000. [i] Hier. in Ezech. & in Oseam.

should not be lawful to force him away to punishment." This privilege easily procured so great a veneration to the dead prince, that he was thought more than a man, and therefore was created a god, and called Jupiter, or as others write, Saturn of Babylon; where a most magnificent temple was erected to him by his son.

After this beginning of Idolatry, several nations formed to themselves gods; receiving into that number not only mortal and dead men, but brutes also; and even the most mean and pitiful inanimate things. For it is evident, from the authority of innumerable writers, that the Africans worshipped the heavens, as a god; the Persians adored fire, water, and the winds; the Libyans, the sun and moon; the Thebans, sheep and weasels; the Babylonians of Memphis, a whale; the inhabitants of Mendes, a goat; the Thessalians, storks; the Syrophœnicians, doves; the Egyptians, dogs, cats, crocodiles, and haw[illegible] leeks, onions, and ga[illegible]; wh[illegible] [illegible]ary to [illegible] Juvenal [illegible] [illegible] April [illegible]

> "O sanctas gentes, quibus hæc nascuntur in hortis
> Numina"——
>
> Religious nations sure, and bless'd abodes,
> Where ev'ry orchard is o'errun with gods.

The ancient Romans, who were so superior in arms, in arts, in eloquence, and in almost every thing that can adorn human nature, were plunged into the grossest idolatry. They reckoned among their gods, not only beasts and things void of all sense, but, which is a far greater madness, they sometimes worshipped as gods the very worst of mankind.

Besides their own country gods and family gods, they worshipped all strange deities that came to the city, and which were made free of it. Whence it came to pass, in time, that when they saw their precincts too narrow to contain so many, necessity forced them to send their gods into colonies, as they did their men..

QUESTIONS FOR EXAMINATION ON THE FOREGOING CHAPTER.

What is meant by the fabulous Pantheon?

Give some account of the Pantheon at Rome.

Write a description of it from memory.

By what accident was it injured?

To what purpose was it devoted by Pope Boniface?

What causes have conspired to the establishment of idolatry?

Who was the contriver of false gods, and how is the circumstance accounted for?

Whom or what did the Africans, Persians, and others worship as gods?

Did the ancient Romans exhibit more wisdom in this respect?

To what had they recourse when their deities became very numerous?

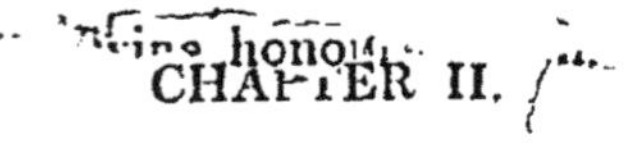

CHAPTER II.

THE ENTRANCE INTO THE PANTHEON. A DISTRIBUTION OF THE GODS INTO SEVERAL CLASSES.

NOTWITHSTANDING the crowd of *dead deities*, whose figures you see painted and described upon the walls, this is the smallest part of them. For the very walls of the city, although it be so large, much less the walls of this temple, can scarcely contain even their *titles*. But these gods were not all of the same order and dignity.

As the *Roman people* were distributed into three ranks; namely, of [k] *senators* or *noblemen*, *knights* or *gentlemen*, *plebeians* or *citizens*; as also into [l] *noble*, *new-raised*, and *ignoble* (of which the *new-raised*

[k] Patricii, equites, et plebeii. [l] Nobiles, novi, et ignobiles. Cic. pro Muræn.

were those who did not receive their nobility from their ancestors, but obtained it themselves by their own virtue); so the *Roman gods* were divided, as it were, into three classes.

The *first* class is of [m]*superior gods,* for the people paid to them a higher degree of worship; because they imagined that these gods were more eminently employed in the government of this world. These were called also [n]*select,* because they had always the title of *celestial* gods, and were famous and eminent above others, of extraordinary authority and renown. Twelve of these were styled [o]*consentes;* because, in affairs of great importance, *Jupiter* admitted them into his council. The images of these were fixed in the Forum at Rome: six of them were males, and six females; commonly, without other additions, called *The Twelve gods;* and whose names Ennius comprises in a [p]distich.

These *twelve gods* were believed to preside over the *twelve months;* to each of them was allotted a month; *January* to *Juno, February* to *Neptune, March* to *Minerva, April* to *Venus, May* to *Apollo, June* to *Mercury, July* to *Jupiter, August* to *Ceres, September* to *Vulcan, October* to *Mars, November* to *Diana, December* to *Vesta.* [q]They likewise presided over the twelve celestial signs. If to these twelve *Dii Consentes,* you add the eight following, *Janus, Saturnus, Genius, Sol, Pluto, Bacchus, Tellus,* and *Luna,* you will have twenty, that is, all the *select gods.*

The *second* class contains the gods of lower rank and dignity, who were styled *Dii Minorum Gentium;*

[m] Dii Majorum Gentium. [n] Selecti. [o] Consentes, quasi consentientes. Senec. l. 2. Quæst. Nat. Lucian. dial. de Deorum concil. Plaut. in Epidico.

[p] Juno, Vesta, Minerva, Ceres, Diana, Venus, Mars,
Mercurius, Neptunus, Jupiter, Vulcanus, Apollo.
Dempster paralip. ad c. 3.

In posteriore hoc versu alii legunt Jovis, non Jupiter; et meliùs meo judicio, olim enim Jovis in nominativo dicebatur; elisâ, metri gratiâ, ultimâ literâ. Rosin Antiq. l. 2. [q] Manilii Astron. l. 2.

because they shine with a less degree of glory, and have been placed among the gods, as [r]Cicero says, by their own merits. Whence they are called also [s]*Adscriptitii Minuscularii*, [t]*Putatii*, and [u]*Indigetes:* because now they wanted nothing; or because, being translated from this earth into heaven, they conversed with the gods; or being fixed, as it were, to certain places, committed peculiarly to their care, they dwelt in them, to perform the duty entrusted to them. [w] Thus Æneas was made a god, by his mother Venus, in the manner described by Ovid[x].

The gods of the *third* and *lower* class are sometimes called [y]*Minuti, Vesci*, and *Miscellanei*, but more usually [z]*Semones*, whose merits were not sufficient to gain them a place among the *celestial gods;* yet their virtues were such, that the people thought them superior to mortal men. They were called [a]*Patellarii*, from certain small [b]dishes, in which the ancients offered to the gods their sacrifices, of which [c]Ovid makes mention.

To these we ought to adjoin the gods called [d]*Novensiles*, which the Sabines brought to Rome by the command of king Tatius; and which were so named,

[r] De Nat. Deor. 2. [s] Var. apud August. [t] Lucian dial. de Deor. concil. [u] Indigetes quòd nullius rei indigerent, quòd in Diis agerent, vel quòd in iis (sc locis) degerent. Serv. in Æn. 12. [w] Liv. l. 1.

[x] "Lustratum genitrix divino corpus odore
Unxit, et ambrosiâ cum dulci nectare mixta.
Contigit os, fecitque Deum, quem turba Quirini
Nuncupat Indigetem, temploque, arisque recepit." Met. 14.

His better parts by lustral waves refined,
More pure and nearer to etherial mind;
With gums of fragrant scent the goddess strews,
And on his features breathes ambrosial dews.
Thus deified, new honors Rome decrees,
Shrines, festivals; and styles him Indiges.

[y] Hor. Carm. 3. [z] Semones vulgò dicebantur quasi semi homines, antiqui enim *hominem* dicebant *hemonem*. Ap. Guther. de jur. Man. l. 1. c. 4. Lips. l. 2. ante lect. 2. 18. [a] Plaut. in Cistell. [b] Fulgent. Placid. ad Chalcid.

[c] "Fert missos Vestæ pura patella cibos." Fast. 6.
To Vesta's deity, with humble mess,
In cleanly dish served up, they now address.

[d] Liv. l. 8. Varro de linguâ Lat.

as some say, because they were [e] latest of all reckoned among the gods; or because they were [f] presidents over the changes, by which the things of this world subsist. Circius believes them to have been the strange gods of conquered nations; whereof the numbers were so vast, that it was thought fit to call all in general [g] *Novensiles,* lest they should forget any of them. And lastly, to this class also we must refer those gods and goddesses by whose help and means, as [h] Cicero says, men are advanced to heaven, and obtain a place among the gods; of which sort are the principal virtues, as we shall show in the proper place.

QUESTIONS FOR EXAMINATION.

Were the heathen gods all of one degree of rank; if not, into how many classes were they divided?

What is said of the first class?

Why were they called *select?*

Why were some of them called *consentes?*

Over what did the Twelve Gods preside? Enumerate them.

Which others make up the twenty Select Gods?

Which is the second class of gods, and why are they so styled?

Repeat the lines from Ovid, and translation.

What are they denominated, and why?

What are the gods of the third class, and how are they denominated?

What are the "Novensiles?"

Who are they supposed to have been?

[e] Quod novissimi omnium inter Deos numerati sint. [f] Novitatum præsides, quòd omnia novitate constent aut redintegrentur. Apud. Gyr. synt. 1. [g] Arnob. 3. adv. Gentes. [h] De Nat. Deor. 2.

CHAPTER III.

A SUPPOSED VIEW OF THE PANTHEON. A MORE COMMODIOUS DIVISION OF THE GODS.

HAVING already described to you the structure and ornaments of this wonderful building, within the niches of which the statues of the gods were placed, it is right you should be informed, that the three classes, mentioned above, are here divided into six, and painted upon the several parts of the Pantheon. 1. The *celestial* gods and goddesses are upon an arch. 2. The *terrestrial*, upon the wall on the right hand. 3. The *marine* and *river* gods upon the wall on the left. 4. The *infernal*, upon the lower compartment by the pavement. 5. The *minuti* or *semones*, and *miscellanei*, before you. 6. The *adscriptitii* and *indigetes* behind you. Our discourse shall likewise consist of six parts; in each of which I shall lay before you whatever I have found most remarkable among the best authors upon this subject. Let us, however, first sit down together awhile; and, as the place is free from company, we will take a deliberate view of the whole army of gods, and inspect them one after another; beginning, as is fit, with the *celestial*, and so with *Jove*, according to the direction of the poet:

> "Ab Jove principium Musæ: Jovis omnia plena."
> Virg. Ecl. 3.

> From the great father of the Gods above
> My Muse begins: for all is full of Jove.

QUESTIONS FOR EXAMINATION.

Into how many classes are the gods in the Pantheon divided?
How are they ranged?
Whence does the description begin?
Repeat the line from Virgil, and translation.

PART I.

OF THE CELESTIAL DEITIES.

CHAPTER I.

SECT. 1.—JUPITER. HIS IMAGE.

THE Gods commonly called Celestials are Jupiter, Apollo, Mars, Mercury, and Bacchus. The celestial Goddesses are Juno, Vesta, Minerva or Pallas, Venus, Luna, and Bellona.

We will begin with Jupiter, the king of them all, who is [a] the father and king of gods and men, whom you see sitting in a throne of ivory and gold, under a rich canopy, with a beard, holding thunder in his right hand, which he brandishes against the giants at his feet, whom he formerly conquered. His sceptre, they say, is made of cypress, which is a symbol of the eternity of his empire, because that wood is free from corruption [b]. On his sceptre sits an eagle, either because he was brought up by it [c], or because an eagle resting upon his head portended his reign, or because in his wars with the giants [d] an eagle brought him his thunder, and thence received the title of *Jupiter's armour-bearer* [e].

He wears golden shoes, and an embroidered cloak, adorned with various flowers and figures of animals.

[a] Divûm pater atque hominum rex. Virg. Æn. 1. Pausan. in Eliac. Lucian. de Sacrif. [b] Apud Laert. l. 8. [c] Mæro ap. Nat. Com. [d] Serv. in Æn. 1. [e] *Jovis Armiger.* Virg. Æn. 5.

This cloak, it is reported, Dionysius the tyrant took from him in Sicily, and giving him a woollen cloak instead of it, said, "[f] That would be more convenient for him in all seasons, since it was warmer in the winter, and much lighter in the summer." Yet you must not be surprised, if by chance you should see him in another place and in another dress: for he is wont to be decked in several fashions, according to the various names he assumes, and according to the diversity of the people among whom he is worshipped. You may see him among the [g] Lacedæmonians without ears; whereas the Cretans are so liberal to him in this particular, that they give him four. So much for the figure of Jupiter: for, if it were my design to speak of his statue, I should repeat here what [h] Verrius says, that his face upon holydays ought to be painted with vermillion; as the statues of the rest of the gods used to be smeared with ointments, and adorned with garlands, according to an observation of [i] Plautus.

The learned [k] Hetrurians teach us, that the power of hurling thunder and lightning was committed to nine gods; but to which of them it does not plainly appear. Some, beside Jupiter, mention Vulcan and Minerva; whence the phrase *Minervales manubiæ* signifies thunder (as the books of those ancient Hetrusci called strokes of thunder *manubias*), because the noxious constellation of Minerva is the cause of tempests in the vernal equinox. [l] Others say, that thunder was also attributed to Juno, to Mars, and to the south wind; and they reckon up several kinds of thunders; "fulmina [m] peremptalia, pestifera, popularia, perversa, renovativa, ostentatoria, clara, familiaria, bruta, consiliaria." But the Romans commonly took notice of no more than two; the [n] diurnal thunder,

[f] Cic. de Nat. Deor. 3. [g] Plaut. de Osir. & Isid, [h] Ap. Guther. de Jur. Man. Plin. l. 33. c. 7. [i] In Asinar. [k] Plin. l. 2. c. 51. Serv. in Æn. l. 2. [l] Serv. in Æn. 8. [m] Plin. l. 2. c. 43, 51, 52. Amm. Marcel. l. 2. [n] Κεραυνοβολια νυκτερικα, κεραυνοβολια ἡμερικα.

which they attributed to Jupiter; and the [o]nocturnal, which they attributed to Summanus, or Pluto.

QUESTIONS FOR EXAMINATION.

Which are the celestial gods?
Who is Jupiter?
Of what is his sceptre the symbol?
What does the eagle on his sceptre denote?
What happened to him with respect to his cloak?
How was he represented by the Lacedæmonians and Cretans?
To whom was the power of hurling thunder given? What is the phrase for thunder?
Mention the several kinds of thunder.
To whom did the Romans attribute the diurnal and nocturnal thunder?

SECT. 2.—JUPITER'S DESCENT AND EDUCATION.

[p]Those who were skilled in the Heathen Theology, reckon up three Jupiters; of which the first and second were born in Arcadia. The father of the one was Æther; from whom Proserpine and Liber are said to be born. The father of the other was Cœlus: he is said to have begot Minerva. The third was a Cretan, the son of Saturn, whose tomb is yet extant in the isle of Crete. [q]But Varro reckoned up three hundred Jupiters; [r]and others mention a much larger number; for there was hardly any nation that did not worship a Jupiter of their own, and suppose him to be born among themselves. But of all these, the most famous Jupiter, according to the general opinion, is he, whose mother was Ops, and whose father was Saturn; to whom therefore all that the poets fabulously wrote about the other Jupiters is usually ascribed.

He was educated at the place where he was born,

[o] Ap. Guther. de jur. Man. l. 1. c. 3. [p] Cic. de Nat. Deor. 3.
[q] Apud Aug. de Civ. Dei. [r] Euseb. Cæs. l. 2. præp. Evang.

that is, upon the mountain Ida in Crete, but it is not agreed by whom he was brought up. [s]Some affirm, that he was educated by the Curetes and Corybantes; some say, by the Nymphs, and some, by Amalthæa, the daughter of Melissus, king of Crete. Others, on the contrary, have recorded, that the bees fed him with honey; and some maintain, that a goat gave him milk. Not a few say, that he was nourished by doves; some, by an eagle; many, by a bear. And further, it is the opinion of some, concerning the aforesaid Amalthæa, that she was not the daughter of Melissus, as we now mentioned; but the very goat which suckled Jupiter, whose [t]horn he gave afterward to his nurses, with this admirable privilege, "that whoever possessed it should immediately obtain every thing that he desired." They add besides, that after this goat was dead, Jupiter took the skin and made a shield of it; with which he singly combated the giants; whence that shield was called *Ægis*[u], from a Greek word that signifies a *she-goat*, which at last he restored to life again, and, giving her a new skin, placed her among the celestial constellations:

QUESTIONS FOR EXAMINATION.

How many Jupiters were there, and whence do they derive their origin?

Which was the most famous Jupiter?

What is ascribed to him?

Where was he educated?

What do authors say of those who brought him up?

What is said of the horn of the goat which is thought to have suckled Jupiter?

Why was his shield called the Ægis?

[s] Vid. Nat. Com. in Jove. [t] Cornu Amalthææ.

[u] Απο της αιγος.

SECT. 3.—EXPLOITS OF JUPITER.

He overcame, in war, the Titans and the Giants, of whom we shall say more when we speak of Saturn. He also delivered his father Saturn from imprisonment; but afterwards deposed him from the throne, and banished him for a conspiracy, and then divided the paternal inheritance with his two brothers, Neptune and Pluto. In fine, he so assisted and obliged all mankind by the great favours which he did, that he not only thence obtained the name of [w]Jupiter, but he was advanced also to divine honours, and was esteemed the common father both of gods and men. Among some of his most illustrious actions, we ought to remember the story of Lycaon. For, when Jupiter had heard a report concerning the wickedness and great impiety of men, it is said that he descended from heaven to the earth, to know the real truth of it; and, that being come into the house of Lycaon, king of Arcadia, where he declared himself to be a god, while others were preparing sacrifices for him, Lycaon derided him: nor did he stop here, but added an abominable wickedness to his contempt; for, being desirous to try whether Jupiter was a god, as he pretended, he kills one of his domestic servants, roasts and boils the flesh of him, and sets it on the table as a banquet for Jupiter; who, abhorring the wretch's barbarity, [x]fired the palace with lightning, and turned Lycaon into a wolf.

His other exploits are dishonourable and highly criminal; for there was scarcely any kind of lewdness of which he was not guilty, or any mark of infamy that is not branded upon his name. I will only mention a few actions of this sort among many.

1. In the shape of a crow[y] he ruined his sister Juno,

[w] Jupiter, quasi juvans Pater. Cic. de Nat. Deor. 2. [x] Ovid. Met. 1. [y] Doroth. 2. Metam.

deluding her with promises of marriage. 2. He violated the chastity of Danae, the daughter of Acrisius, king of the Argives, though her father had shut her up in a tower; because the oracle had foretold, that he should be slain by his grandson. For, changing himself into a [z]*shower of gold*, he slid down through the roof and tiles of the place into the lady's lap. 3. He corrupted [a]Leda, the wife of Tyndarus, king of Laconia, in the similitude of a *swan*. 4. He abused [b]Antiope, the wife of Lycus, king of Thebes, in the likeness of a *satyr*. 5. He defiled [c]Alcmena, the wife of Amphytrion, in her husband's absence, in the likeness of Amphytrion himself. 6. He inflamed [d]Ægina, the daughter of Æsopus, king of Bœotia, with love, in the similitude of *fire*, and robbed her of her chastity. 7. He acted the same part with [e]Clytoris, a virgin of Thessalia, a great beauty, by turning himself into an *ant*. 8. He debauched [f]Calisto, the daughter of Lycaon, king of Arcadia, counterfeiting the modesty and countenance of Diana: and yet he did not protect her from the disgrace that afterwards followed. She was then changed into a *bear*, advanced to heaven, and made a constellation; which by the Latins is called Ursa Major, and by the Greeks, Helice. 9. He sent an [g]eagle to snatch away Ganymede, the son of Tros, as he hunted upon the mountain Ida: or rather he himself, being changed into an eagle, took him into his claws, and carried him up to heaven. He offered the same violence to Asteria, the daughter of Cœus, a young lady of the greatest modesty, to whom he [h]appeared in the shape of an eagle, and, having accomplished his foul purpose, carried her away in his talons. 10. He abused [i]Europa, the daughter of Agenor, king of Phœnicia, in the form of a beautiful white *bull*, and carried her into

[z] Ovid. Met. 4. [a] Arat. in Phænom. [b] Ovid. Met. 6. [c] Idem ibid. [d] Idem ibid. [e] Arnod. ap. Gyr. [f] Bocart. de Gen. Deor. 6. [g] Virg. Æn. 5. Ovid. Met. 10. [h] Fulgent. Plan. [i] Ovid. Met. 6.

Crete with him. The bull is supposed to have been the ship upon which a bull was painted, in which Europa was carried away. In like manner the horse Pegasus, which was painted upon Bellerophon's ship, and the ram, which was painted on that of Phryxus and Helle, created ample matter of fiction for the poets. But to return to our fable: Agenor immediately ordered [k] his son Cadmus to travel, and search every where for his sister Europa, which he did, but could nowhere find her. Cadmus dared not to return without her, because, [l] by a sentence not less unjust to him than kind to his sister, his father had banished him for ever unless he found her. Wherefore he built the city of Thebes, not far from the mountain Parnassus; and as it happened that his companions who were with him were devoured by a certain serpent, while they went abroad to fetch water; he, to avenge their death, slew that serpent; whose teeth he took out, and by the advice of Minerva, sowed them in the ground; and suddenly sprouted up a harvest of armed soldiers, who, quarrelling among themselves, with the same speed that they grew up, mowed one another down again, excepting five only, by whom that country was peopled afterward. At length Cadmus and his wife Hermione, after much experience, and many proofs of the inconstancy of fortune, were changed into serpents.

He is said to have [m] invented sixteen of the letters of the Greek alphabet; α, β, γ, δ, ε, ι, κ, λ, μ, ν, ο, ϖ, ρ, σ, τ, υ, which, in the time of the judges of Israel, he

[k] Ovid. Met. 3.

[l] "Cum pater ignarus Cadmo perquirere raptam
Imperat, et pœnam, si non invenerit, audit
Exilium, facto pius et sceleratus eodem." Ovid. Met. 3.

When now Agenor had his daughter lost,
He sent his son to search on ev'ry coast;
And sternly bad him to his arms restore
The darling maid, or see his face no more,
But live an exile in a foreign clime:
Thus was the father pious to a crime.

[m] Pl. l. 5. c. 39. Cæs. 39. 24.

brought out of Phœnicia into Greece: two hundred and fifty years after this, Palamedes added four more letters, namely, ξ, θ, φ, χ, in the time of the siege of Troy; although some affirm that Epicharmus invented the letters θ and χ: and six hundred and fifty years after the siege of Troy, Simonides invented the other four letters, namely, η, ω, ζ, ψ. Cadmus is also said to have taught the manner of writing in prose; and he was the first among the Greeks who consecrated statues to the honour of the gods.

QUESTIONS FOR EXAMINATION.

Mention some of the exploits of Jupiter.
How did he derive his name and honours?
What did he to Lycaon, and why?
What were his other exploits?
What happened to Calisto?
What circumstance occurred to Ganymede and Asteria?
Explain the fable respecting Europa.
What did Agenor do to recover his daughter?
Repeat the lines from Ovid, and the translation.
What city did Cadmus build, and what exploit did he perform on a serpent?
Which of the letters of the Greek alphabet did Cadmus invent?
Who added the others, and when?
What besides did Cadmus do for the benefit of mankind?

SECT. 4.—THE NAMES OF JUPITER

Can hardly be numbered; so many did he obtain, either from the places where he lived and was worshipped, or from the things that he did. The most remarkable shall be given alphabetically.

The Greeks called him [a] Ammon, or Hammon,

[a] Arenarius ἄμμος ab Arena Plut. in Osir. V. Curt. l. 4.

which name signifies *sandy*. He obtained this name first in Libya, where he was worshipped, under the figure of a ram; because when Bacchus was athirst in the fabulous deserts of Arabia, and implored the assistance of Jupiter, Jupiter appeared in the form of a ram, opened a fountain with his foot, and discovered it to him. But others give this reason, because Jupiter in war wore a helmet, whose crest was a ram's head.

The Babylonians and Assyrians, whom he governed, called him [o] Belus, who was the impious author of idolatry; and because of the uncertainty of his descent, they believed that he had neither father nor mother; and therefore he was thought the first of all gods. In different places and languages he was afterwards called Beel, Baal, Beelphegor, Beelzebub, and Belzemen.

Jupiter was called [p] Capitolinus, from the Capitoline hill, upon the top of which he had the first temple that ever was built in Rome; this Tarquin the Elder determined to build, Tarquin the Proud did build, and Horatius, the consul, dedicated.

He was also called Tarpeius, from the Tarpeian rock, on which this temple was built. He was likewise styled [q] Optimus Maximus, from his power and willingness to profit all men.

He was also called [r] Custos. There is in Nero's coins an image of him sitting on his throne, which bears in one hand thunder, and in the other a spear, with this inscription, *Jupiter Custos*.

In some forms of oaths he was commonly called [s] Diespiter, the father of light; as we shall further remark presently under the word *Lapis;* and to the same purpose he was by the [t] Cretans called Dies.

[o] Beros. l. 4. Euseb. l. 1. præp. Evang. Hier. l. in Oseam. [p] O Capitolino, quem, propter beneficia, populus Romanus Optimum, propter vim, Maximum appellavit. Cic. de Nat. Deor. l. [q] Plin. Liv. Plut. Tacit. 19. [r] Apul. de mundo. Senec. 2. qu. nat. [s] Quasi diei pater. Var. de lingua Latina. [t] Macrob. in Saturn. ep. Bochart. in Geogr.

The title of Dodonæus was given him from the city Dodona in Chaonia, which was so called from Dodona, a nymph of the sea. Near to this city there was a grove sacred to Jupiter, which was planted with oaks; and famous, because it was the most ancient oracle of all Greece. Two doves delivered responses there to those who consulted it: or, as others used to say, [u] the leaves of the oaks themselves became vocal, and gave forth oracles.

He was named [w] Elicius, because the prayers of men may bring him down from heaven.

The name Feretrius is given him, because [x] he smites his enemies; or, because he is the [y] giver of peace; for when peace was made, the sceptre by which the ambassadors swore, and the flint-stone on which they confirmed their agreement, were fetched out of his temple: or lastly, because, after they had overcome their enemies, they [z] carried the grand spoils *(spolia opima)* to his temple. Romulus first presented such spoils to Jupiter, after he had slain Acron, king of Cænina; and Cornelius Gallus offered the same spoils, after [illegible] conquered Tolumnius, king of Hetruria; and [illegible] Marcellus, when he had vanquished Viridomarus, king of the Gauls, as we read in [a] Virgil. Those spoils were called *opima*, which one general took from the other in battle.

Fulminator, or [b] Ceraunius, in Greek Κεραυνιος, is

[u] Alex. ab Alex. c. 2. [w] Quod cœlo precibus eliciatur, sic Ovid.

"Eliciunt cœlo te Jupiter; unde Minores
Nunc quoque te celebrant, Eliciumque vocant." Fast. 3.

Jove can't resist the just man's cries,
They bring him down e'en from the skies;
Hence he's Elicius call'd.

[x] A feriendo, quod hostes feriat. [y] Vel à ferenda pace. Fest.

[z] Vel à ferendis spoliis opimis in ejus Templum. Plut. in Rom. Dion. 2.

[a] "Tertiaque arma Patri suspendet capta Quirino."
And the third spoils shall grace Feretrian Jove.
Æn. 6. Serv. ibid.

[b] Hor. Carm. 5.

Jupiter's title, from hurling thunder, which is thought to be his proper office, if we believe the [c] poet.

In Lycia they worshipped him under the name of [d] Gragus, Γραψιος [*Grapsios*] and Genitor.

In Ægium, about the sea-coast, he is said to have had a temple, with the name of [e] Homogynus.

At Præneste he was called Imperator. [f] There was a most famous statue of him at that place, afterward translated to Rome.

He was called Latialis, [g] because he was worshipped in Latium, a country of Italy; whence the Latin [h] festivals are denominated, to which all the inhabitants of those cities of Italy resorted, who desired to be partakers of the solemnity; and brought to Jupiter several oblations: particularly, a bull was sacrificed at that time, in the common name of them all, of which every one took a part.

The name Lapis, or, as others write, Lapideus, was given him by the Romans, who believed that an oath [i] made in the name of Jupiter Lapis was the most solemn of all oaths. And it is derived either from the stone which was presented to Saturn by his wife Ops, who said it was Jupiter, in which sense [k] Eusebius says, that Lapis reigned in Crete; or from the flint-stone, which, in making bargains, the swearer held in his hand, and said, "[l] If knowingly I deceive, so let Diespiter, saving the city and the capitol, cast me away from all that is good, as I cast away this stone;" upon which he threw the stone away. The Romans had another form, not unlike to this, of making bargains,

[c] "——— O qui res hominumque Deûmque
Æternis regis imperiis, et fulmine terres." Virg. Æn. 1. 229.
O king of gods and men, whose awful hand
Disperses thunder on the seas and land;
Dispensing all with absolute command.

[d] Lycophron. [e] Virg. Æn. 1 & 4. [f] Pausan. et Hesych. Liv. 6. [g] Cic. pro Milone, 86. Dion. l. 4. [h] Latinæ Feriæ. [i] Juramentum per Jovem Lapidem omnium sanctissimum, Cic. 7. ap. 12. [k] In Chron. [l] Si sciens fallo, me Diespiter, salvâ urbe arceque, bonis ejiciat, ut ego hunc lapidem. Fest ap. Lil.

which may be mentioned here: "[m] If with evil intention I at any time deceive; upon that day, O Jupiter, so strike thou me, as I shall this day strike this swine; and so much the more strike thou, as thou art the more able and skilful to do it:" he then struck down the swine.

In the language of the people of Campania, he is called Lucetius, from *lux;* and among the Latins [n] Diespiter, from *dies.* Which names were given to Jupiter, "[o] because he cheers and comforts us with the light of the day, as much as with life itself:" or, because he was believed to be the father of light[p].

The people of Elis used to celebrate him by the title of [q] Martius.

He was also called [r] Muscarius, because he drove away the flies: for when the religious exercises of Hercules were interrupted by a multitude of flies, he immediately offered a sacrifice to Jupiter, which being finished, all the flies flew away.

He was styled [s] Nicephorus, that is, carrying victory: and by the oracle of Jupiter Nicephorus, emperor Adrian was told, that he should be promoted to the empire. Livy often mentions him; and many coins are extant, in which is the image of Jupiter bearing victory in his hand.

He was called [t] Opitulus, or Opitulator, the *helper,* and Centipeda; from his stability; because those things stand secure and firm which have many feet. He was called Stabilitor and Tigellus, because he supports the world: Almus and Alumnus, because he cherishes all things: and Ruminus, from Ruma, which signifies the nipple, by which he nourishes animals.

[m] Si dolo malo aliquando fallam, tu illo die, Jupiter, me sic ferito, ut ego hunc porcum hodie feriam; tantoque magis ferito, quanto magis potes, pollesque. Liv. l. 1. [n] Serv. in Æn. 9. [o] Quod nos die ac luce, quasi vitâ ipsâ afficeret ac juvaret. Aul. Gell. [p] Festus. [q] Ἀρειος, Ζευς, Jupiter pugnax. Plut. in Pyrrho. [r] Απομυιος, muscarum abactor. Pausan. 5. Eliac. [s] Νικηφορος, i. e. Victoriam gestans. Ælius Spart. in Adriani vita. [t] Quasi opis later. Fest. Aug. de Civ. Dei. 7.

He was styled [u] Olympius, from Olympus, the name of the master who taught him, and of the heaven wherein he resides, or of a city which stood near the mountain Olympus, and was anciently celebrated far and near, because there a temple was dedicated to Jupiter, and games solemnized every five years. [w] To this Jupiter Olympus the first cup was sacrificed in their festivals.

When the Gauls besieged the capitol, an altar was erected to Jupiter [x] Pistor; because he put it into the minds of the Romans to make loaves of bread, and throw them into the Gauls' tents; upon which the siege was raised.

The Athenians erected a statue to him, and worshipped it upon the mountain Hymettus, giving him in that place the title of [y] Pluvius; this title is mentioned by [z] Tibullus.

Prædator was also his name; not because he protected robbers, but because, out of all the booty taken from the enemy, one part was due to him. [a] For, when the Romans went to war, they used to devote to the gods a part of the spoil that they should get, and for that reason there was a temple at Rome dedicated to Jupiter Prædator.

He was styled Quirinus, as appears by that verse of Virgil, cited above, when we spoke of the name Feretrius.

Rex and Regnator are his common titles in [b] Virgil, Homer, and Ennius.

[u] Pausan. in Attic. et Eliac. Liv. l. 4. [w] Pollux. [x] A pinsendo. Ovid. Fast. 6. Lact. l. 22. Liv. l. 5. [y] Phurnut. in Jov.

[z] "Arida nec Pluvio supplicat herba Jovi."
Nor the parch'd grass for rain from Jove doth call.

[a] Serv. in Æn. 5.

[b] "Divum pater atque hominum rex." Æn. l. 10.
The father of the gods, and king of men.
"Summi regnator Olympi" Æn. 7.
Ruler of the highest heaven.

Jupiter was also called [c] Stator, which title he first had from Romulus on this occasion: When Romulus was fighting with the Sabines, his soldiers began to fly; upon which Romulus, as [d] Livy relates, thus prayed to Jupiter: "O thou father of the gods and mankind, at this place at least drive back the enemy, take away the fear of the Romans, and stop their dishonourable flight. And I vow to build a temple to thee upon the same place, that shall bear the name of Jupiter Stator, for a monument to posterity, that it was from thy immediate assistance that Rome received its preservation." After this prayer the soldiers stopped, and, returning again to the battle, obtained the victory; upon which Romulus consecrated a temple to Jupiter Stator.

The Greeks called him Σωτηρ [*Soter*] Servator [e], the *saviour*, because he delivered them from the Medes. Conservator also was his title, as appears from divers of Dioclesian's coins, on which were his effigies, with thunder brandished in his right hand, and a spear in his left; with this inscription, *Conservatori*. In others, instead of thunder, he holds forth a little image of victory, with this inscription, *Jovi Conservatori Orbis, To Jupiter the conservator of the world.*

The augurs called him [f] Tonans and Fulgens. And emperor Augustus dedicated a temple to him so called; wherein was a statue of Jupiter, to which a little bell was fastened [g]. He is also called Βρονταιος [*Brontaios*] by Orpheus; and [h] Tonitrualis, the thunderer, by Apuleius; and an inscription is to be seen upon a stone at Rome, *Jovi Brontonti*.

[i] Trioculus, Τριοφθαλμος [*Triopthalmos*] was an epi-

[c] A stando vel sistendo. [d] Tu pater Deûm hominumque, hinc saltem arce hostem, deme terrorem Romanis, fugamque fœdam siste. Hic ego tibi templum Statori Jovi, quod monumentum sit posteris tuâ præsenti ope servatam urbem esse, voveo. Liv. l. 1. [e] Strabo, l. 9. Arrian. 8. de gest. Alex. [f] Cic. de Nat. Deor. 1. [g] Dio. l. 5. [h] Ap. Lil. Gyr. synt. 2. [i] Pausan. ap. eundem.

Pl. II. p. 21.

H. Moses del. et sculpt.

JUPITER

Published by Wilkie & Robinson, Paternoster Row, May 1. 1810.

thet given him by the Grecians, who thought that he had three eyes, with one of which he observed the affairs of heaven, with another the affairs of the earth, and with the third he viewed the sea affairs. There was a statue of him of this kind in Priamus' palace, at Troy; which, beside the two usual eyes, had a third in the forehead.

[k] *Vejovis*, or *Vejupiter*, and *Vedius*, that is, "little Jupiter," was his title when he was described without his thunder, viewing angrily short spears which he held in his hand. The Romans accounted him a fatal and noxious deity; and therefore they worshipped him, only that he might not hurt them.

Agrippa dedicated a pantheon to Jupiter Ultór, "the avenger," at Rome, according to [l] Pliny.

He was likewise called [m] Xenius, or Hospitalis, because he was thought the author of the laws and customs concerning hospitality. Whence the Greeks call presents given to strangers *xenia*, as the Latins called them *lautia*.

[n] Ζευς [*Zeus*] is the proper name of Jupiter, because he gives life to animals.

QUESTIONS FOR EXAMINATION.

Had Jupiter many names?
What did the Greeks call him?
What name did he obtain in Lybia?
By whom and on what account was he called Belus?
Why was he called Capitolinus?
Why was he called Tarpeius, and why Optimus Maximus?
How did he obtain the title of Diespiter?
Why was he styled Dodonæus?
Why was he named Elicius?
Repeat the lines.
Explain the reason why the name Feretrius was given him?
Why was he called Fulminator?

[k] Cic. de Nat. Deor. 5. Gell. l. 5. Ovid. in Fast. [l] Plin. 36. 15.
[m] Serv. in Æn. 1. pro Deiot. Plut. qu. Rom. Demost. Or. de legation. [n] Ἀπο της ζωης, Phurnut. de Jove.

Repeat the lines from Virgil.
What was he called at Præneste?
Why was he called Latialis?
How did he obtain the name Lapis, and from what is it derived?
What was the Roman form of making bargains?
Why was he called Lucetius?
Why was he styled Muscarius, and why Nicephorus?
Why was he denominated Opitulator, Centipeda, Almus, and Ruminus?
On what account was he denominated Olympius, Pistor, Pluvius, and Prædator?
What are his titles in Virgil, Homer, and Ennius?
How did he obtain the title Stator?
Why, and by whom was he called Soter?
What was he called by the augurs?
Why was he called Trioculus?
Why was he called Xenius, and why Zeus?

SECT. 2—THE SIGNIFICATION OF THE FABLE, AND WHAT IS UNDERSTOOD BY THE NAME JUPITER.

Natural philosophers many times think that [o]heaven is meant by the name Jupiter: whence many authors express the thunder and lightning, which came from heaven, by these phrases; *Jove tonante, fulgente,* &c. and in this sense [p]Virgil used the word Olympus.

[q]Others have imagined that the air, and the things that are therein contained, as thunder, lightning, rain, meteors, and the like, are signified by the same name. In which sense [r]Horace is to be understood, when he says, *sub Jove,* that is, "in the open air."

Some, on the contrary, call the air Juno; and the fire Jupiter, by which the air being warmed becomes fit for the production of things. [s]Others, again, call the sky Jupiter, and the earth Juno, because out of the earth

[o] Cic. de Nat. Deor. 2.
[p] "Panditur interea domus omnipotentis Olympi." Æn. 10.
Meanwhile the gates of heaven unfold.
[q] Theocr. Ecl. 4. [r] Jacet sub Jove frigido, id est, sub Dio, ὑπὸ τοῦ Διός. Hor. Od. 1. [s] Lucret. l. 1.

all things spring; which Virgil has elegantly expressed in the second book of his [t]Georgics.

[u]Euripides thought so, when he said that the sky ought to be called *Summus Deus*, "the Great God." [w]Pluto's opinion was different, for he thought that the sun was Jupiter; and [x]Homer, together with the aforesaid Euripides, thinks that he is fate; which fate is, according to [y]Cicero's definition, "The cause from all eternity why such things, as are already past, were done; and why such things as are doing at present, be as they are; and why such things as are to follow hereafter, shall follow accordingly." In short, others by Jupiter understand the [z]soul of the world; which is diffused not only through all human bodies, but likewise through all the parts of the universe, as [a]Virgil poetically describes it.

Jupiter is usually represented by the ancients as governing the world by his providence; and is described as viewing from an eminence the pursuits and contentions of mankind, and weighing in his scales their fortunes and their merits. He is the moderator of the differences of the gods, and whenever any of the in-

[t] "Tum pater omnipotens fæcundis imbribus æther
Conjugis in gremium letæ descendit, et omnes
Magnus alit, magno commistus corpore, fœtus."
Ether, great lord of life, his wings extends,
And on the bosom of his bride descends;
With showers prolific feeds the vast embrace,
That fills all nature, and renews her race.

[u] Apud Cic. de Nat. Deor. [w] In Phæd. [x] Odyss. 24.

[y] Æterna rerum causa; cur ea, quæ preterierint, facta sint; et ea, quæ instant, fiant; et ea, quæ consequentur, futura sint. Cic. de Divin. 1.

[z] Arat. init. Astron.

[a] "Principio cœlum, ac terras, composque liquentes,
Lucentemque globum Lunæ. Titaniaque astra
Spiritus intus alit, totamque infusa per artus,
Mens agitat molem, et magno se corpore miscet." Æn. 6.
——— The heaven and earth's compacted frame,
And flowing waters, and the starry frame,
And both the radiant lights, one common soul
Inspires, and feeds, and animates the whole.
This active mind, infused through all the space,
Unites and mingles with the mighty mass.

ferior deities asked him a favour, he was disposed to nod his assent.

> He, whose all-conscious eyes the world behold,
> Th' eternal thunderer, sat enthroned in gold;
> High heav'n the footstool for his feet he makes,
> And, wide beneath him, all Olympus shakes.
> He spake; and awful bends his sable brows,
> Shakes his ambrosial curls, and gives the nod;
> The stamp of fate and sanction of the god:
> High heav'n, with trembling, the dead signal took,
> And all Olympus to the centre shook. Homer.

All heaven is represented as shaken with his terrors, and neither men nor gods had the temerity to oppose his will.

> Then spake th' almighty father, as he sat
> Enthroned in gold; and closed the great debate.
> Th' attentive winds a solemn silence keep;
> The wond'ring waves lie level on the deep;
> Earth to his centre shook; high heav'n was aw'd,
> And all th' immortal pow'rs stood trembling at the god.
> Virgil.

QUESTIONS FOR EXAMINATION.

What do philosophers understand by the word Jupiter?
What meaning do others give of it?
What is the example from Horace?
How does Virgil understand it in the Georgics?
Repeat the original and translation.
Give me the opinions of Euripides, Plato, and Homer.
Repeat the lines from the sixth Æneid, and point out the application.
How is Jupiter represented by the ancients?
Repeat the lines from Homer.
How is he represented by Virgil?

CHAPTER II.

SECT. I.—APOLLO. HIS IMAGE AND DESCENT.

APOLLO is represented as a [b]beardless youth, with long hair, comely and graceful, who wears a laurel crown, and shines in garments embroidered with gold, with a bow and arrows in one hand, and a harp in the other. [c]He is at other times described holding a shield in one hand, and the Graces in the other. And because he has a threefold power; in heaven, where he is called Sol; in earth, where he is named Liber Pater; and in hell, where he is styled Apollo; he is usually painted with these three things, a harp, a shield, and arrows. The harp shows that he bears rule in heaven, where all things are full of harmony; the shield describes his office in earth, where he gives health and safety to terrestrial creatures; his arrows show his authority in hell, for whoever he strikes with them, he sends them into hell.

Sometimes he is painted with a crow and a hawk flying over his head, a wolf and a laurel tree on one side, and a swan and a cock on the other; and under his feet grasshoppers creeping. The crow is sacred to him, because he foretels the weather, and shows the different changes of it by the clearness or hoarseness of his voice. The swan is likewise endued with a divination, [d]because foreseeing his happiness in death, he dies with singing and pleasure. The wolf is not unacceptable to him, not only because he spared his flock when he was a shepherd, but the sharpness of his eyes represents the foresight of prophecy. The laurel-tree is of a very hot nature, always flourishing, and conducing to divination and poetic raptures; and the leaves of it put under the pillow, was said to produce true dreams. The hawk

[b] Hor. ad Callimach.

[c] Porphyr. de sole.

[d] Cygni non sine causâ Apollini dicati sunt, quod ab eo divinationem habere videantur; quia prævidentes quid in morte boni sit, cum cantu et voluptate moriuntur. Cic. Tuscul. 1.

has eyes as bright as the sun; the cock foretels his rising; and the grasshoppers so entirely depend on him, that they owe their rise and subsistence to his heat and influence.

There were four Apollos: the first and most ancient of them was born of Vulcan; the second was a Cretan, a son of one of the Corybantes; the third was born of Jupiter and Latona; the fourth was born in Arcadia, called by the Arcadians, Nomius. [e] But though, as Cicero says, there were so many Apollos, yet the rest of them are seldom mentioned, and all that they did is ascribed to one only, namely, to him that was born of Jupiter and Latona: which is thus represented.

Latona, the daughter of Cœus the Titan, conceived twins by Jupiter: Juno, incensed at it, sent the serpent Python against her; and Latona, to escape the serpent, [f] fled into the island of Delos; where she brought forth Apollo and Diana at the same birth.

QUESTIONS FOR EXAMINATION.

How is Apollo represented?

With what things is he painted, and why?

Why are the crow, hawk, wolf, swan, and laurel, consecrated to him?

How many Apollos were there, and which is the principal?

Where was Apollo born, and what was the occasion of his birth at Delos?

SECT. II.—ACTIONS OF APOLLO.

Apollo was advanced to the highest degree of honour and worship by these four means; *viz.* by the invention of physic, music, poetry, and rhetoric, which is ascribed to him; and therefore he is supposed to preside over the Muses. It is said, that he taught the arts of foretelling events, and shooting with arrows; when

[e] Atque, cum tot Apollines fuerint, reliqui omnes filentur, omnesque res aliorum gestæ ad unum Apollinem, Jovis et Latonæ filium, referuntur. Cic. de Nat. Deor. 3.

[f] Hesiod.

therefore he had benefited mankind infinitely by these favours, they worshipped him as a god. [g] Hear how gloriously he himself repeats his own accomplishments of mind and nature, where he magnifies himself to the flying nymph, whom he passionately loved:

His principal actions are as follow:

1. He destroyed all the Cyclops, the forgers of Jupiter's thunderbolts, with his arrows, to revenge the death of Æsculapius his son, whom Jupiter had killed with thunder, because by the help of his physic he revived the dead. [h] For this act Apollo was cast down from heaven, and deprived of his divinity, exposed to the calamities of the world, and commanded to live in banishment upon the earth. In this distress he was compelled by want to look after Admetus' cattle: where, it is said, he first invented and formed a harp. After this, Mercury got an opportunity to drive away a few of the cattle of his herd by stealth; and while Apollo complained and threatened to punish him, un-

[g] ——————" Nescis, temeraria, nescis
Quem fugias, ideoque fugis.——————
Jupiter est genitor. Per me quod eritque, fuitque,
Estque, patet. Per me concordant carmina nervis;
Certa quidem nostra est, nostra tamen una sagitta
Certior, in vacuo quæ vulnera pectore fecit.
Inventum medicina meum est, opiferque per orbem
Dicor; et herbarum est subjecta potentia nobis." Ov. Met. 1.
Stay, nymph, he cry'd, I follow not a foe;
Thus from the lion darts the trembling doe:
Thou shunn'st a god, and shunn'st a god that loves.
But think from whom thou dost so rashly fly,
Nor basely born, nor shepherd's swain am I.
——————What shall be,
Or is, or ever was, in fate I see.
Mine is the invention of the charming lyre;
Sweet notes and heavenly numbers I inspire.
Sure is my bow, unerring is my dart,
But ah! more deadly his, who pierced my heart.
Med'cine is mine; what herbs and simples grow
In fields, and forests, all their powers I know,
And am the great physician call'd below.

[h] Lucian Dial Mort. [i] Pausan. in Eliac.

less he brought the same cattle back again, his harp was also stolen by the same [k] god; so that his anger was changed to laughter.

2. He raised the walls of the city of Troy, by the music of his harp alone; if we may believe the [l] poet.

Some say [m] that there was a stone, upon which Apollo only laid down his harp, and the stone by the touch became so melodious, that whenever it was struck with another stone, it sounded like a harp.

3. By misfortune he killed Hyacinthus, a boy that he loved. For, while Hyacinthus and he were playing together at quoits, Zephyrus was enraged, because Apollo was better beloved by Hyacinthus than himself; and, having an opportunity of revenge, he blew the quoit that Apollo cast, against the head of Hyacinthus, by which blow he fell down dead. Apollo caused the blood of the youth, that was spilt upon the earth, to produce flowers called *violets*, as [n] Ovid finely expresses it.

Besides, he was passionately fond of Cyparissus, another boy, who, when he had unfortunately killed a fine deer, which he exceedingly loved and had brought up from its birth, was so melancholy for his misfortune, that he constantly bewailed the loss of his

[k] Hor. Carm. 1.

[l] "Ilion aspicies, firmataque turribus altis
Mœnia, Apollineæ structa canore lyræ." Ovid. Ep. Parid.
Troy you shall see, and walls divine admire;
Built by the music of Apollo's lyre.

[m] Pausan. in Attic.

[n] "Ecce cruor, qui fusus humi signaverat herbam,
Desinit esse cruor; Tyrioque nitentior ostro
Flos oritur, formamque capit, quam lilia; si non
Purpureus color huic, argenteus esset in illis." Met. 10.
Behold the blood, which late the grass had dy'd,
Was now no blood; from which a flower full blown,
Far brighter than the Tyrian scarlet, shone,
Which seem'd the same, or did resemble right
A lily, changing but the red to white.

deer, and refused all comfort. [o] Apollo begged of the god that his mourning might be made perpetual, who in pity changed him into a cypress-tree, the branches of which were always used at funerals.

4. He fell violently in love with the virgin Daphne, so famous for her modesty. He pursued her, but while she fled to secure her chastity from the violence of his passion, she was changed into a laurel, which remains always flourishing, always pure.

5. He courted also a long time the nymph Bolina, but never could gain her; for she chose rather to throw herself into the river and be drowned, than yield to his wishes. Thus she gained to herself an immortality, by sacrificing her life in the defence of her honour; and not only overcame Apollo, but the very powers of death.

6. Leucothoe, the daughter of Orchamus, king of Babylon, was not so tenacious of her chastity; for she yielded at last to Apollo's desires. [p] Her father could not bear this disgrace brought on his family, and therefore buried her alive. [q] Apollo was greatly grieved at this, and though he could not bring her again to life,

[o] ——" munusque supremum,
Hoc petit à superis, ut tempore lugeat omni.—
Ingemuit, tristisque Deus, lugebere nobis,
Lugebisque alios, aderisque dolentibus, inquit." Ov. Met. 10.
Implores that he might never cease to mourn,
When Phœbus sighing, I for thee will mourn,
Mourn thou for others, herses still adorn.

[p] ————————" defodit altè
Crudus humo, tumulumque super gravis addit arenæ."
Interr'd her living body in the earth,
And on it raised a tomb of heavy sand,
Whose pond'rous weight her rising might withstand.

[q] " Nectare odorato spargit corpusque locumque,
Multaque præquestus, tanges tamen æthera, dixit.
Protinus imbutum cœlesti nectare corpus
Delicuit, terramque suo madefecit adore;
Virgaque per glebas, sensim radicibus actis,
Thurea surrexit; tumulumque cacumine rupit." Ov. Met. 4.
He mourn'd her loss, and sprinkled all her herse
With balmy nectar, and more precious tears.

he poured nectar upon the dead body, and thereby turned it into a tree that drops frankincense. These amours of Leucothoe and Apollo had been discovered to her father by her sister Clytie, whom Apollo formerly loved, but now deserted: which she seeing, pined away, with her eyes continually looking up to the sun, and at last was changed into a [r] flower called a sun-flower, or *heliotrope.*

7. Apollo was challenged in music by Marsyas, a proud musician; and when he had overcome him, [s] Apollo flayed him for his temerity, and converted him into the river of that name in Phrygia.

8. Midas, king of Phrygia, having foolishly determined the victory to Pan, when Apollo and he sang together, [t] Apollo stretched his ears to the length and shape of asses' ears. Midas endeavoured to hide his disgrace by his hair: but since it was impossible to conceal it from his barber, he prevailed with him, by great promises, not to divulge what he saw. But the [u] barber went and dug a hole, and putting his mouth to it, whispered these words, "King Midas has asses' ears;" and the reeds that grew out of that hole, if they were moved by the least blast of wind, uttered the same words, *viz.* "King Midas has the ears of an [w] ass."

Then said, since fate does here our joys defer,
Thou shalt ascend to heav'n and bless me there.
Her body straight embalm'd with heav'nly art,
Did a sweet odour to the ground impart,
And from the grave a beauteous tree arise,
That cheers the gods with pleasing sacrifice.

[r] Ovid. Met. 4. [s] Ovid. Fast 6.

[t] ——" partem damnatur in unam;
Induiturque aures lentè gradientis asellì." Ovid. Met. 6.
Punish'd in th' offending part, he bears
Upon his skull a slow-paced ass's ears.

[u] ——" Secedit, humumque
Effodit, et domini quales conspexerit aures,
Voce refert parvâ." Ovid. Met. 15.
He dug a hole, and in it whispering said,
What monstrous ears sprout from king Midas' head!

[w] Aures asinas habet rex Midas.

QUESTIONS FOR EXAMINATION.

How was Apollo advanced to honour?
Repeat the description of himself, as given by Ovid.
What occurred to Apollo with regard to the Cyclops?
What is said of the music of his harp?
How did he kill Hyacinthus, and what was the effect of it?
Repeat the lines from Ovid.
What is the story of Cyparissus?
Repeat the lines from Ovid.
What was his connexion with Daphne?
What is related of Bolina?
What happened to Leucothoe?
Repeat the story from Ovid.
What became of Marsyas?
What is the story respecting Midas?

SECT. 3.—NAMES OF APOLLO.

As the Latins call him [x] Sol, because there is but one sun; so some think the Greeks gave him the name Apollo for the same reason. Though [y] others think that he is called Apollo, either because he drives away diseases, or because he darts vigorously his rays.

He was called [z] Cynthius, from the mountain Cynthus, in the island of Delos; whence Diana also was called Cynthia.

And Delius, from the same island, because he was born there: or, as some [a] say, because Apollo (who is the sun), by his light, makes all things manifest; for which reason he is called [b] Phanæus.

He was named Delphinius, [c] because he killed the serpent Python, called Delphis: or else, because when

[x] Ab ἀ particula privativa, et πολλοὶ quemadmodum Sol, quòd sit solus. Chrysip. apud Gyr.

[y] Synt. 7. p. 219. ἀπὸ τῦ ἀπαλλάττειν νόσυς, ab abigendis morbis, vel ἀπὸ τῦ πάλλειν τὰς ἀκτίνας.

[z] Varr. de Ling. Lat. Plut. apud Phurnut.

[a] Festus cuncta facit δῆλα, i. e. manifesta.

[b] Ἀπὸ τυ φαίνειν, apparere, Macrob. et Phurnut.

[c] Pausan. in Attic.

Castilius, a Cretan, carried men to the plantations, Apollo guided him in the shape of a dolphin.

His title Delphicus comes from the city Delphi, in Bœotia, which city is said to be the [d] navel of the earth; because when Jupiter, at one time, had sent for two eagles, the one from the east, and the other from the west, they met together by equal flights exactly at this place. [e] Here Apollo had the most famous temple in the world, in which he [f] uttered the oracles to those who consulted him; which he first received from Jupiter. They say, that this famous oracle became dumb at the birth of our Saviour, and when Augustus, who was a great votary of Apollo, desired to know the reason of its silence, the oracle answered him, [g] that in Judea a child was born, who was the son and image of the supreme God, and had commanded him to depart, and return no more answers.

Apollo was likewise called [h] Didymæus, which word in Greek signifies *twins*, by which are meant the two great luminaries of heaven, the sun and the moon, which alternately enlighten the world by day and night.

He was also called [i] Nomius, which signifies either a shepherd, because he fed the cattle of Admetus; or because the sun, as it were, feeds all things that the earth generates, by his heat and influence. Or perhaps this title may signify [k] *lawgiver;* and was given him, because he made very severe laws, when he was king of Arcadia.

He was styled Pæan, either from [l] allaying sorrows,

[d] Pausan. ομφαλὸς της γης, i. e. umbilicus terræ.

[e] Phurnut. Lactant. [f] Æscul. in Sacerd.

[g] Me puer Hebræus, divos Deus ipse gubernans,
Cedere sede jubet, tristemque redire sub orcum;
Aris ergo dehinc nostris abscedito, Cæsar.

[h] A verbo διδυμοι, gemelli. Macrob. apud Gyr. synt. 7.

[i] Νομιὸς, i. e. Pastor, quod pavit Admeti gregem, vel quod quasi pascat omnia. Phurnut. Macrob. [k] Νόμος, Lex. Macrob. Cic. de Nat. Deor. 3. [l] Παρὰ τὸ παύειν τὰς ἀνίας, à sedando molestias, vel παρὰ τὸ παίειν, à feriendo. Festus.

or from his exact skill in striking; wherefore he is armed with arrows. And we know that the sun strikes us, and often hurts us with his rays, as with so many darts.

He is accordingly referred to in this character by Homer:

> Bent was his bow, the Grecian hearts to wound;
> Fierce as he moved his silver shafts resound.
> Breathing revenge, a sudden night he spread,
> And gloomy darkness roll'd around his head:
> The fleet in view, he twang'd his deadly bow,
> And hissing fly the feather'd fates below.
> On mules and dogs th' infection first began;
> And last the vengeful arrows fix'd on man. Iliad.

By this name Pæan, his mother Latona, and the spectators of the combat, encouraged Apollo, when he fought with the serpent Python, crying frequently, "[m] Strike him, Pæan, with thy darts." By the same name the diseased invoke his aid, crying, "[n] Heal us, Pæan." And hence the custom came, that not only all hymns in the praise of Apollo were called *Pæanes*, but also, in all songs of triumph in the celebration of all victories, men cried out, "Io Pæan." After this manner the airy and wanton lover in [o] Ovid acts his triumph too. And from this invocation Apollo himself was called Ιειος [*Ieios*].

He was called Phœbus, [p] from the great swiftness of his motion, or from his method of healing by purging, which was Apollo's invention.

He was named Pythius, not only from the serpent Python, which he killed, but likewise from [q] asking and consulting; for none among the gods was more consulted, or delivered more responses, or spake more

[m] Ιε παιὰν, jace vel immitte, Pæan; nempe tela in feram.

[n] Ἰε παιάν, medere Pæan.

[o] " Dicite Io Pæan, et Io, bis discite, Pæan!
Decidit in casses præda petita meos." Art Am. 2
Sing Io Pæan twice, twice Io say:
My toils are pitch'd, and I have caught my prey.

[p] Ἀπὸ τȣ φοιταν, quod vi feratur, vel à φοιβάυ, purgo. Lil. Gyr. synt. 7.

[q] Ἀπό τȣ πυνθάνεσθάι, ab interrogando vel consulendo. Hygin. in Fab. c. 50.

oracles than he; especially in the temple which he had at Delphi, to which all sorts of nations resorted, so that it was called "the oracle of all the [r]earth." The oracles were first given out by a young virgin; afterwards it was determined that an old woman should give the answers, in the dress of a young maid, who was therefore called Pythia, from Pythius, one of Apollo's names, and sometimes Phœbas from Phœbus, another of them. But as to the manner by which the woman understood the god's mind, men [s] differ.

There are also different opinions respecting the tripos on which the oracle sat. Some say that it was a table with three feet, on which she placed herself when she designed to give forth oracles. [t] But others say, that it was a vessel, in which she was plunged before she prophesied; or rather, that it was a golden vessel, furnished with ears, and supported by three feet, whence it was called tripos; and on this the lady sat down. It happened that this tripos was lost in the sea, and afterward taken up in the nets of fishermen, who contended among themselves which should have it: the Pythian priestess being asked, gave answer that it ought to be sent to the wisest man of all Greece. Whereupon it was carried to Thales of Miletus; who sent it to Bias, as to a wiser person; Bias referred it to another, and that other referred it to a fourth; till, after it had been sent backward and forward to all the wise men, it returned again to Thales, who dedicated it to Apollo at Delphi.

The seven wise men of Greece were, "Thales of Miletus," "Solon of Athens," "Chilon of Lacedæmon," "Pittacus of Mytilene," "Bias of Priene," "Cleobulus of Lindi," and "Periander of Corinth." I will add some remarkable things concerning them.

Thales was reckoned among the wise men, because he was believed to be the first that brought geometry into Greece. He first observed the courses of the times,

[r] Cic. pro Font. Diodor. 1 Stat. Theb. Vide Orig. adv. Cels. l. 7.
[s] Cic. de Divin. l 14. apud Lil. Cyr. [t] Plut. in Solon.

the motion of the winds, the nature of thunder, and the motions of the sun and the stars. Being asked what he thought the most difficult thing in the world, he answered, "To know one's self." This perhaps was the occasion of the advice written on the front of Apollo's temple, to those that were about to enter, [u] "Know thyself."

When Solon visited Crœsus, king of Lydia, the king showed his vast treasures to him, and asked him whether he knew a man happier than he: "Yes," says Solon, "I know Tellus, a very poor, but a very virtuous man at Athens, who lives in a little tenement, and he is more happy than your majesty: for neither can those things make us happy, which are subject to the changes of the times; nor is any one to be thought truly happy till he dies." [w] It is said, when king Crœsus was afterward taken prisoner by Cyrus, and laid upon the pile to be burnt, he remembered this saying of Solon, and often repeated his name; so that Cyrus asked why he cried out Solon, and who the god was whose assistance he begged. Crœsus said, "I now find by experience that to be true, which he told me;" and he then related the story. Cyrus, on hearing it, was so touched with the sense of the vicissitude of human affairs, that he preserved Crœsus from the fire, and ever after had him in great honour.

Chilo had this saying continually in his mouth, [x] "Desire nothing too much." Yet, when his son had got the victory at the Olympic games, the good man died with joy, and all Greece honoured his funeral.

Bias, a man no less famous for learning than nobility, preserved his citizens a long time. And when at last, [y] says Cicero, his country Priene was taken, and the rest of the inhabitants, in their escape, carried away with them as much of their goods as they could; one advised him to do the same, but he made answer, "[z] It is what

[u] Γνῶθι σεαυτὸν, Nosce teipsum. Laert. [w] Plutarch. Herodotus.
[x] Ne quid nimium cupias. Plin. l. 7. c. 32. [y] De Amicitia.
[z] Ego vero facio, nam omnia mea mecum porto. Val. Max. 7. c. 2.

I do already; for all things that are mine I carry about me" He often said, "[a]that friends should remember so to love one another, as persons who may sometimes hate one another." A sentiment very unworthy of a wise and good man.

Of the rest, nothing extraordinary is reported.

QUESTIONS FOR EXAMINATION.

What is the origin of the name Apollo?
Why was he called Cynthius, Delius, and Delphinius?
From what did he derive his title Delphicus?
When did the oracle become dumb?
Why was he called Didymæus and Nomius?
Why was he styled Pæan?
Repeat the lines from Homer.
On what account was he named Phœbus and Pythius?
What is said of the tripos?
Who were the seven wise men of Greece?
On what account was Thales celebrated?
For what is Solon celebrated?
What was the famous saying of Chilo?
Why is Bias reckoned among the seven wise men?

SECT. 4.—THE SIGNIFICATION OF THE FABLE.
APOLLO MEANS THE SUN.

Every one agrees, that by [b]Apollo the Sun is to be understood; for the four chief properties ascribed to Apollo were, the arts of prophesying, of healing, of darting, and of music; of all which we may find, in the sun, a lively representation and image.

It may be observed that Apollo's skill in music seems to agree with the nature of the sun, which, being placed in the midst of the planets, makes with them a kind of harmony, and as it were, a concert: and because the sun is thus placed the middlemost of the seven planets,

[a] Amicos ita amare opertere, ut aliquando essent osuri. Laert.
[b] Cic. de Nat. Deor. 3.

H. Moses del. et sculp.

APOLLO

Published by Wilkie & Robinson Paternoster Row Mar 1. 1810.

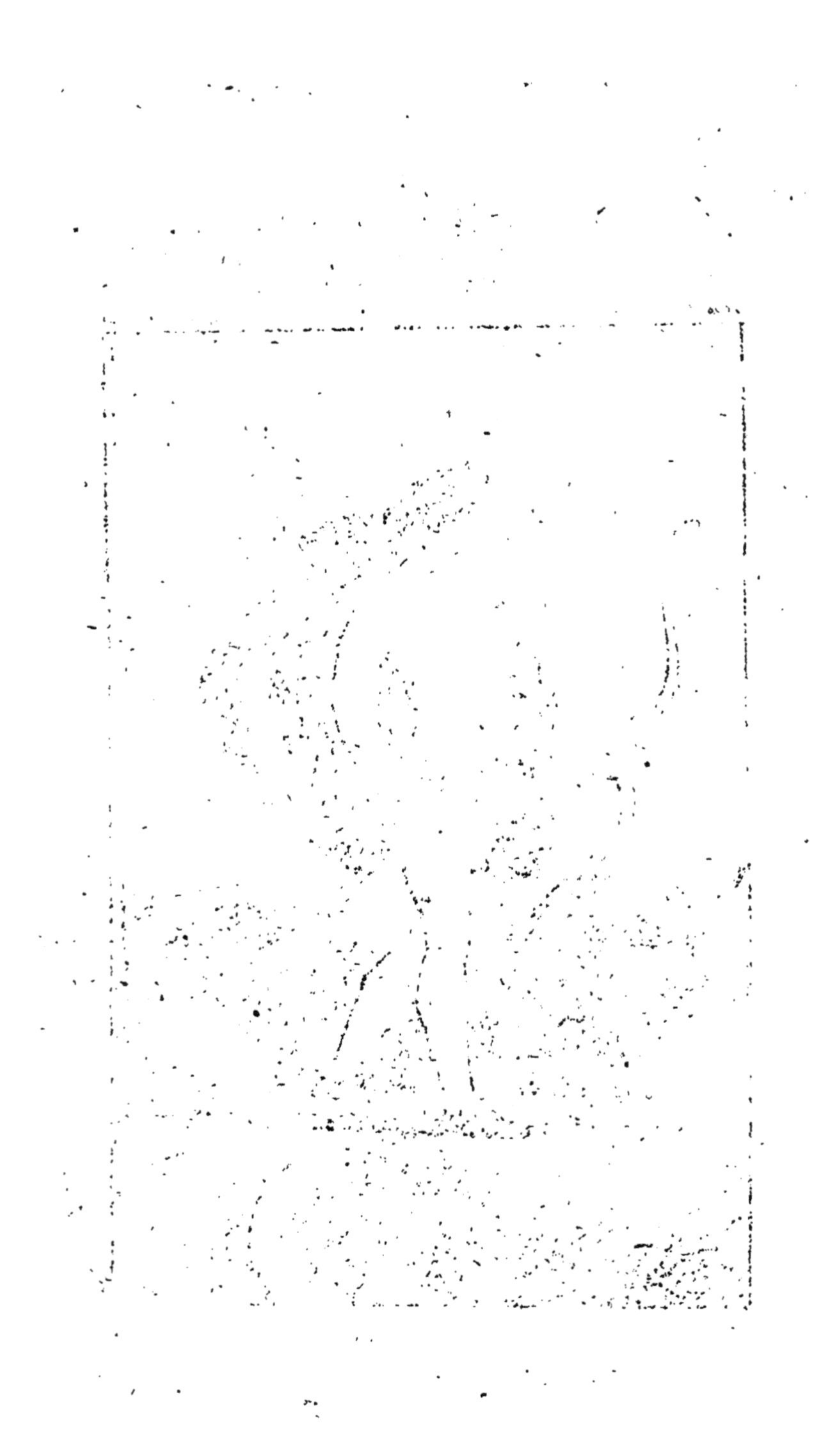

the poets assert, that the instrument which Apollo plays on is a harp with seven strings.

Besides, from the things sacrificed to Apollo, [c] it appears that he was the Sun: the first of these was the olive, the fruit of which cannot be nourished in places distant from it. 2. The laurel, [d] a tree always flourishing, never old, and conducing to divination; and therefore the poets are crowned with laurel. 3. Among animals, swans [e] were offered to him; because, as was observed before, they have from Apollo a faculty of divination; for they, foreseeing the happiness in death, die singing and pleased. 4. Griffins also, and crows, were sacred to him for the same reason; and the hawk, which has eyes as bright and piercing as the sun; the cock, which foretels his rising; and the grasshopper, a singing creature; hence [f] it was a custom among the Athenians to fasten golden grasshoppers to their hair, in honour of Apollo.

And especially, if [g] we derive the name of Latona, the mother of Apollo and Diana, from the Greek λανθάνω [*lanthano, to lie hid*] it will signify, that before the birth of Apollo and Diana, that is, before the production of the sun and the moon, all things lay involved in darkness; from which these two glorious luminaries afterward proceeded, as out of the womb of a mother.

But notwithstanding all this, several poetical fables have relation only to the Sun, and not to Apollo. And of those therefore it is necessary to treat apart.

QUESTIONS FOR EXAMINATION.

What were the chief properties of Apollo?

Why does Apollo's skill in music agree with the nature of the sun?

How is it inferred that he was the sun from the things sacrificed to him?

What is inferred from the name Latona, mother of Apollo and Diana?

[c] Theocr. in Herc. [d] Aerius. [e] Cic. Tuscul. 1. [f] Thucyd. Schol. Arist. [g] Vid. Lil. Gyr. 1. in Apoll.

CHAPTER III.

SECT. 1.—THE SUN. HIS GENEALOGY, NAMES, AND ACTIONS.

THIS glorious Sun, which illustrates all things with his light, is called Sol, as Cicero [h] says, either because he is the only star that is of that apparent magnitude; or because, when he rises, he puts out all the other stars, and only appears himself. Although the poets have said, that there were five Sols; yet, whatever they delivered concerning each of them severally, they commonly apply to one, who was the son of Hyperion, and nephew to Æther, begotten of an unknown mother.

The Persians call the sun [i] Mithra, accounting him the greatest of their gods, and worship him in a cave. His statue has the head of a lion, on which a turban, called *tiara*, is placed; it is clothed with Persian attire, and holds with both hands a mad bull by the horns. [k] Those that desired to become his priests, and understand his mysteries, did first undergo a great many hardships before they could attain to the honour of that employment. It was not lawful for the kings of Persia to drink immoderately, but upon that day in which the sacrifices were offered to Mithra [l].

The Egyptians called the sun [m] Horus; whence those parts, into which the sun divides the day, are called *horæ*, hours. They represented his power by a sceptre, on the top of which an eye was placed; by which they signified that the sun sees every thing, and that all things are seen by his means.

These [n] *horæ* were thought to be the daughters of

[h] Vel quia Solus ex omnibus sideribus tantus est; vel quia cum exortus est, obscuratis omnibus, Solus appareat. Cic. de Nat. Deor. 2. 3.

[i] Hesych. et Lactant. Gram. apud Lil. Gyr.

[k] Duris 7 Hist. ap. Athen.

[l] Greg Nazianz. Orat. 1. in Jul.

[m] Plut. et Osir.

[n] Hom. Il. & Odyss. 4. Plutarch. Boccat. l. 4. c. 4.

Sol and Chronis, who early in the morning prepare the chariot and the horses for their father, and open the gates of the day.

The most remarkable actions of Sol were as follow:

1. He slept with Venus in the island of Rhodes, at which time, [o]it is said that the heavens rained gold, and the earth clothed itself with roses and lilies; whence the island was called [p] Rhodes. 2. He had one son by Clymene, named Phaeton, and several daughters. 3. By Neæra, he had Pasiphae, and by Perce, Circe.

QUESTIONS FOR EXAMINATION.

What is Cicero's opinion with regard to Sol, and to whom does the name apply?

What is said of the Persians with regard to the sun?

What was necessary to be done by those who would become the priests of the sun?

What name did the Egyptians give to the sun, and how did they represent his power?

Who were the "horæ" and what was their business?

What remarkable circumstances are mentioned of Sol?

Rhodes having been mentioned, leads me to speak in

SECT. 2, OF THE SEVEN WONDERS OF THE WORLD.

The seven wonders of the world were:

1. The Colossus at Rhodes, [q]a statue of the sun, seventy cubits high, placed across the mouth of the harbour; a man could not grasp its thumb with both his arms. Its thighs were stretched out to such a distance, that a large ship under sail might easily pass into the port between them. It was twelve years making, and cost three hundred [r] talents. It stood fifty years, and at last was thrown down by an earthquake. And from this Coloss the people of Rhodes were named Colossenses; and now every statue of an unusual magnitude is called Colossus.

[o] Pindar in Olymp. [p] Ἀπὸ τοῦ ῥόδου ἀπὸ, à rosa. [q] Plin. 34. c. 17. [r] A Rhodian talent is worth 322*l*. 18*s*. 4*d*. English.

2. The temple of Diana, at Ephesus, a work of the greatest magnificence, which the ancients prodigiously admired. [s]Two hundred and twenty years were spent in finishing it, though all Asia was employed. It was supported by one hundred and twenty-seven pillars, sixty feet high, each of which was raised by as many kings. Of these pillars thirty-seven were engraven. The image of the goddess was made of ebony, as we learn from history.

3. The Mausoleum, or sepulchre of Mausolus, king of Caria, [t]built by his queen Artemisia, of the purest marble; and yet the workmanship of it was much more valuable than the marble. It was from north to south sixty-three feet long, almost four hundred and eleven feet in compass, and twenty-five cubits (that is, about thirty-five feet) high, surrounded with thirty-six columns, which were beautified in a wonderful manner. From this Mausoleum all other sumptuous sepulchres are called by the same name.

4. A statue of Jupiter, in the temple of the city [u]Olympia, carved with the greatest art by Phidias, out of ivory, and made of a prodigious size.

5. The walls of Babylon (the metropolis of Chaldea), [w]built by queen Semiramis; their circumference was sixty miles, and their breadth fifty feet, so that six chariots might conveniently pass upon them in a row.

6. The [x]Pyramids of Egypt; three of which, remarkable for their height, still remain. The first has a square basis, and is one hundred and forty-three feet long, and one thousand feet high: it is made of great stones, the least of which is thirty feet thick; and three hundred and sixty thousand men were employed in building it, for the space of twenty years. The other two, which are somewhat smaller, attract the admiration of all spectators. In these pyramids, it is reported, the bodies of the kings of Egypt lie interred.

[s] Plin. l. 7. c. 38. & l. 16. c. 40. [t] Plin. l. 36. c. 5. [u] Plin. l. 36. c. 3. [w] Plin. l. 6. c. 26. [x] Plin. l. 36. c. 13. Belo, l. 2. c. 32.

7. The palace of [y]Cyrus, king of the Medes, made by Menon, with no less prodigality than art; for he cemented the stones with gold.

QUESTIONS FOR EXAMINATION.

What is the first of the seven wonders of the world; how is it described, and what name did the inhabitants of Rhodes derive from it?

Describe the second of the wonders of the world.

Which was the third, and what technical term owes its origin to it?

Which was the fourth?

Describe the fifth.

Give some account of the sixth.

Which was the seventh?

SECT. 3.—THE CHILDREN OF THE SUN.

The most celebrated of Sol's children was Phaeton, who gave the poets an excellent opportunity of showing their ingenuity by the following action. Epaphus, one of the sons of Jupiter, quarrelled with Phaeton, and said, that though he called himself the son of Apollo, he was not; and that his mother Clymene invented this pretence only to cover her adultery. This slander so provoked Phaeton, that by his mother's advice, he went to the royal palace of the Sun, to bring thence some indubitable marks of his nativity. The Sun received him kindly, and owned him as his son; and, to take away all occasion of doubting hereafter, he gave him liberty to ask any thing, swearing by the Stygian lake, an oath which none of the gods dare violate, that he would not deny him. Phaeton then desired leave to govern his father's chariot for one day. This was the occasion of great grief to his father, [z]who endeavoured to persuade

[y] Calepin. V. Miraculum.

[z] ——"Temeraria dixit
Vox mea facta tua est. Utinam promissa liceret
Non dare. Confiteor, solum hoc tibi, nate, negarem.

him not to persist in his project, which no mortal was capable of executing. [a] Phaeton, however, pressed him to keep his promise, and perform what he had sworn by the river Styx. The father was forced to comply with his son's rashness: he directed him how to guide the horses, and especially advised him to observe the middle path. Phaeton was transported with joy, [b] mounted the chariot, and, taking the reins, began to drive the horses; which, finding him unable to govern them, ran away, and set on fire both the heaven and the earth. Jupiter, to put an end to the conflagration, struck him out of the chariot with thunder, and cast him headlong into the river Po. His sisters, Phaethusa, Lampetia, and Lampethusa, lamenting his death incessantly upon the banks of that river, were turned, by the pity of the gods, into poplars, from that time weeping amber instead of tears.

Dissuadere licet. Non est tua tuta voluntas;
Magna petis, Phaeton, et quæ non viribus istis
Munera conveniunt, nec tam puerilibus annis
Sors tua mortalis: non est mortale, quod optas." Ov. Met. 2.
'Twas this alone I could refuse a son,
Else by 's own wish and my rash oath undone.
Thou to thy ruin my rash vow dost wrest:
O! would I could break promise. Thy request,
Poor hapless youth, forego; retract it now,
Recal thy wish, and I can keep my vow:
Think, Phaeton, think o'er thy wild desires,
That work more years and greater strength requires:
Confine thy thoughts to thy own humble fate;
What thou would'st have, becomes no mortal state.

[a] ——— "Dictis tamen ille repugnat,
Propositumque premit, flagratque cupidine currûs."
In vain to move his son the father aim'd;
He, with ambition's hotter fire inflamed,
His sire's irrevocable promise claim'd.

[b] "Occupat ille levem juvenile corpore currum,
Statque super, manibusque datas contingere habenas
Gaudet, et invito grates agit inde parenti."
Now Phaeton, by lofty hopes possess'd,
The burning seat with youthful vigour press'd;
With nimble hands the heavy reins he weigh'd,
And thanks unpleasing to his father paid.

[c] Circe, the most skilful of all sorceresses, poisoned her husband, a king of the Sarmatians; for which she was banished by her subjects, and, flying into Italy, fixed her seat on the promontory Circæum, where she fell in love with Glaucus, a sea-god, who at the same time loved Scylla: Circe turned her into a sea-monster, by poisoning the water in which she used to wash. She entertained Ulysses, who was driven thither by the violence of storms, with great civility; and restored his companions, whom, according to her usual custom, she had changed into hogs, bears, wolves, and the like beasts, unto their former shapes.

[d] Pasiphae was the wife of Minos, king of Crete. She fell in love with a bull, and obtained her desire by the assistance of Dædalus; she brought forth a Minotaur, one part of which was like a man, the other like a bull. [e] Now the occasion of the fable, they say, was this: Pasiphae loved a man whose name was Taurus, and had twins by him in Dædalus' house; one of whom was very like her husband Minos, and the other like its father. But the Minotaur was shut up in a labyrinth, which Dædalus made by the order of king Minos. This labyrinth was a place diversified with very many windings and turnings, and cross-paths running into one another;—see *Theseus*. [f] Dædalus was an excellent artificer of Athens, and, as it is said, invented the ax, the saw, the plummet, the auger, and glue; he also first contrived masts and yards for ships; besides, he carved statues so admirably, that they not only seemed alive, but would never stand still in one place; nay, would fly away unless they were chained. This Dædalus, together with Icarus his son, was shut up by Minos in the labyrinth which he had made, because he had assisted the amours of Pasiphae; and finding no way to escape, he made wings for himself and his son, with wax and the feathers of birds: fastening these wings to their

[c] Ovid. Met. 14. [d] Ovid. Met. 1. [e] Serv. ap. Boccat. l. 4.
[f] Ovid. Met. 8. Pausan. in Attic.

shoulders, Dædalus flew out of Crete into Sicily, but Icarus in his flight, neglecting his father's advice, observed not his due course, and out of juvenile wantonness, flew higher than he ought; upon which the wax was melted by the sun, the wings broke in pieces, and he fell into the sea, which is since, [g] according to Ovid, named the Icarian sea, from him.

To these children of the Sun, we may add his niece and his nephew Byblis and Caunus. Byblis was in love with Caunus, and followed him so long to no purpose, that at last, being quite oppressed with sorrow and labour, she sat down under a tree, and shed such a quantity of tears, [h] that she was converted into a fountain.

QUESTIONS FOR EXAMINATION.

What is said of Phaeton, one of the children of the Sun?
Repeat Ovid's description of Sol's speech to his son.
What happened to Phaeton?
Who were his sisters, and what occurred to them?
Who was Circe, and what is related of her?
Who was Pasiphae, and how is the fable of the Minotaur explained?
Who was Dædalus, and what circumstances are related of him?
Who were the niece and nephew of Sol?
Repeat the lines from Ovid and Byblis.

[g] "Icarus Icariis nomina fecit aquis." Trist. 1.
Icarian seas from Icarus were called.

[h] "Sic lachrymis consumpta suis Phœbeia Byblis
Vertitur in fontem, qui nunc quoque vallibus imis
Nomen habet dominæ, nigraque sub illice manat." Ov. Met. 8.

Thus the Phœbeian Byblis, spent in tears,
Becomes a living fountain, which yet bears
Her name, and, under a black holm that grows
In those rank valleys, plentifully flows.

CHAPTER IV.

SECT. 1.—MERCURY. HIS IMAGE, BIRTH, QUALITIES, AND OFFICES.

MERCURY is represented [i] with a cheerful countenance and lively eyes; having wings fixed to his hat and his shoes, and a rod in his hand, which is winged, and bound about by two serpents. His face is partly black and dark, and partly clear and bright; because sometimes he converses with the celestial, and sometimes with the infernal gods. He wears winged shoes, which are called Talaria, and wings are also fastened to his hat, which is called Petasus, because, since he is the messenger of the gods, he ought not only to run but to fly.

His wings are emblematical of the wings which language gives to the thoughts of men. His character, as the swift messenger of the gods, is thus referred to by Homer:—

> —— The god who mounts the winged winds
> Fast to his feet the golden pinions binds,
> That high through fields of air his flight sustain,
> O'er the wide earth, and o'er the boundless main;
> He grasps the wand that causes sleep to fly,
> Or in soft slumbers seals the wakeful eye;
> Then shoots from heaven to high Pieria's steep,
> And stoops incumbent on the rolling deep.
>
> Odyssey.

[k] His parents were Jupiter, and Maia the daughter of Atlas; and for that reason they used to offer sacrifices to him in the month of May. They say that Juno suckled him, and once when he sucked the milk very greedily, his mouth being full, it ran out of it upon the heavens, and made that white stream which they call "[l] the Milky-way."

[i] Galen ap Nat. Com. l. 5. [k] Hesiod. in Theog. Hor. Carm. 1.
[l] Via lactea, quam Græci vocant Galaxiam, ἀπο τοῦ γάλακτος, à lacte. Macrob. et Suidas.

He had many offices. 1. [m]The first and principal was to carry the commands of Jupiter; whence he is commonly called "the Messenger of the gods." 2. He swept the room where the gods supped, and made the beds; and underwent many other the like servile employments: hence he was styled [n]Camillus or Casmillus, that is, an inferior servant of the gods; for anciently [o]all boys and girls under age were called Camilli and [p]Camillæ: and the same name was afterward given to the young men and maids, who [q]attended the priests at their sacrifices: though the people of Bœotia, [r]instead of Camillus, say Cadmillus; perhaps from the Arabic word *chadan*, to serve; or from the Phœnician word *chadmel*, god's servant, or *minister sacer*. 3. [s]He attended upon dying persons to unloose their souls from the chains of the body, and carry them to hell: he also revived, and placed in new bodies, those souls which had completed their full time in the Elysian fields. Almost all which things Virgil comprises in seven [t]verses.

His remarkable qualities were these. 1. He was the inventor of letters, and excelled in eloquence, so that the

[m] Lucian. dial. Maiæ et Mercurii.
[n] Stat. Tullian. 2. de vocab. rerum. [o] Serv. in Æn. 12.
[p] Pacuv. in Medea. Dion. Halicarn. l. 2. Macrob. Saturn. 3.
[q] Bochart. Geogr. l. 1. c. 2. [r] Soph. in Œdip. [s] Hom. Odyss. 24.
[t] "Dixerat. Ille patris magni parere parabat
Imperio, et primum pedibus talaria nectit
Aurea, quæ sublimem alis sive æquora supra,
Seu terram, rapido pariter cum flamine portant.
Tum virgam capit; hac animas ille evocat Orco
Pallentes, alias sub tristia Tartara mittit;
Dat somnos, adimitque, et lumina morte resignat." Æn. 4.
Hermes obeys; with golden pinions binds
His flying feet, and mounts the western winds:
And, whether o'er the seas or earth he flies,
With rapid force they bear him down the skies.
But first he grasps, within his awful hand,
The mark of sov'reign power, his magic wand:
With this he draws the souls from hollow graves;
With this he drives them down the Stygian waves;
With this he seals in sleep the wakeful sight,
And eyes, though clos'd in death, restores to light.

Greeks called him Hermes, from his [u]skill in interpreting or explaining; and therefore he is accounted the [w]god of the rhetoricians and orators.

2. He is reported to have been the inventor of contracts, weights, and measures; to have first taught the arts of buying, selling, and trafficking; and to have received the name of Mercury [x]from his understanding of merchandise. Hence he is accounted the god of the *merchants*, and the god of *gain*; so that all unexpected gain and treasure, which comes of a sudden, is from him called ἑρμεῖον or ἑρμαῖον.

3. In the art of thieving he certainly excelled all the sharpers that ever were, or will [y]be; and is the prince and god of thieves. The very day in which he was born, he stole away some cattle from king Admetus' herd, although Apollo was keeper of them; who complained much of the theft, and bent his bow against him: but, in the mean time, Mercury stole even his arrows from him. While he was yet an infant, and entertained by Vulcan, he stole his tools from him. He took away by stealth Venus' girdle, while she embraced him; and Jupiter's sceptre: he designed to steal the thunder too, but he was afraid lest it should burn him.

4. He was mightily skilful in making peace; and for that reason was sometimes painted with chains of gold flowing from his mouth, with which he linked together the minds of those that heard him. And he not only pacified mortal men, but also the immortal gods of heaven and hell; for whenever they quarrelled among themselves, he composed their differences.

This pacificatory faculty of his is signified by the rod that he holds in his hand, which Apollo heretofore gave him, because he had given Apollo a harp.

[u] Ἀπὸ τȣ ἑρμηνεύειν, *i. e.* ab interpretando.
[w] Tertul. de Coronis. Festus. Fulgent.
[x] A mercibus, vel à mercium cura. Philostrat. in Soph. 3.
[y] Lucian. Dial. Apoll. et Vulc.

[z]This rod had a wonderful faculty of deciding all controversies. The virtue was first discovered by Mercury, who seeing two serpents fighting, as he travelled, he put his rod between them, and reconciled them presently; for they mutually embraced each other, and stuck to the rod, which is called Caduceus. [a]Hence all ambassadors sent to make peace are called Caduceatores: for, as wars were denounced by [b]Feciales, so they were ended by Caduceatores.

QUESTIONS FOR EXAMINATION.

How is Mercury represented?
Why does he wear wings, and what are they called?
Who were his parents?
What is said to be the origin of the Milky-way?
What are Mercury's principal offices?
Repeat the lines from Virgil.
What was the first remarkable quality belonging to Mercury?
What was the second?
What was the third?
What was the fourth?
What emblem of peace does he carry?
How was this virtue discovered?
What is the rod called, and what name is derived from it?

SECT. 2.—ACTIONS OF MERCURY;

Of which the following are the most remarkable: He had a son by his sister Venus, called [c]Herma-

[z] "Pacis et armorum, superis imisque Deorum,
Arbiter, alato qui pede carpit iter." Ovid. Fast. 5.
Thee, Wing-foot, all the gods, both high and low,
The arbiter of peace and war allow.
"Atlantas Tegææ Nepos, commune profundis
Et superis numen, qui fas per limen utrumque
Solus habes, geminoque facis compendia mundo."
Claud. de. Rap. Pros.
Fair Maia's son, whose power alone doth reach
High heaven's bright towers, and hell's dusky beach,
A common god to both, does both the worlds appease.

[a] Hom. in Hym. [b] Lexic. Lat. in hoc Verbo. [c] i. e. Mercurio-Venus, nam Ἑρμῆς est Mercurius, et Ἀφροδίτη Venus.

phroditus, who was a great hunter. In those woods where he frequently hunted, a nymph called Salmacis lived, who greatly admired and fell in love with him; for he was very beautiful, but a great woman-hater. She often tempted the young man, but was as often repulsed; yet she did not despair. She lay in ambush at a fountain where he usually came to bathe, and, when he was in the water, she also leaped in to him: but neither so could she overcome his extraordinary modesty. Therefore, it is said, she prayed to the gods above, that the bodies of both might become one, which was granted. Hermaphroditus was amazed when he saw this change of his body; and desired that, for his comfort, some other persons might be like him. He obtained his request; for [d]whoever washed himself in that fountain became a hermaphrodite, that is, had both sexes.

A herdsman, whose name was Battus, saw Mercury stealing Admetus' cows, from Apollo their keeper. When Mercury perceived that his theft was discovered, he went to Battus, and desired that he would say nothing, and gave him a delicate cow. Battus promised him secrecy. Mercury, to try his fidelity, came in another shape to him, and asked him about the cows; whether he saw them, or knew the place where the thief carried them? Battus denied it; but Mercury pressed him hard, and promised that he would give him both a bull and a cow, if he would discover it. With this promise he was overcome; upon which Mercury was enraged, and, laying aside his disguise, turned him into a stone called Index. This story Ovid describes in very elegant [e]verse.

[d] Ovid. Met. 4.

[e] "At Battus, postquam est merces geminata, sub illis
Montibus, inquit, erant: et erant sub montibus illis.
Risit Atlantiades, et me mihi, perfide, prodis;

The ancients used to set up statues where the roads crossed: these statues they call Indices, because, with an arm or finger held out, they showed the way to this or that place. The Romans placed some in public places and highways: as the Athenians did at their doors to drive away thieves; and they call these statues Hermæ, from Mercury, whose Greek name was Hermes: concerning which Hermæ it is to be observed,

1. That they have neither [f] hands nor feet; and hence Mercury was called Cyllenius, and by contraction [g] Cyllius, which words are derived from a Greek word signifying a man without hands and feet: and not from Cyllene, a mountain in Arcadia, on which he was educated.

2. A purse was usually hung to a statue of Mercury, [h] to signify that he was the god of gain and profit, and presided over merchandising; in which, because many times things are done by fraud and treachery, they gave him the name of Dolius.

3. The Romans used to join the statues of Mercury and Minerva together, and these images they called [i] Hermathenæ; and sacrificed to both deities upon the same altar. Those who had escaped any great danger, always offered sacrifices to Mercury: [k] they offered up a calf, and milk, and honey, and especially the tongues of the sacrifices, which, with a great deal of ceremony,

Me mihi prodis ait? perjuraque pectora vertit
In durum silicem, qui nunc quoque dicitur Index."
Battus, on the double proffer, tells him, there;
Beneath those hills, beneath those hills they were.
Then Hermes laughing loud, What, knave, I say,
Me to myself, myself to me betray?
Then to a touchstone turn'd his perjur'd breast,
Whose nature now is in that name express'd.

[f] Sunt Ἄποδες καὶ ἄχειρες, Herod. l. 1.

[g] Κυλλὸς, i. e. manuum et pedum expers. Lil. Gyr. [h] Macrob. Suid. apud Lil. [i] Cicero. [k] Pausan. in Attic. Ovid. Met. 4. Callistrat. Homer.

Pl. IV. p. 51.

MERCURY

Published by Wilkie & Robinson Paternoster Row

they cast into the fire, and then the sacrifice was finished. It is said that the Megarenses first used this ceremony.

QUESTIONS FOR EXAMINATION.

What is related of Mercury in connexion with Venus?
What is the story of Battus?
Repeat the lines from Ovid, and give a translation of them.
What were the ancient Indices?
What were the Hermæ?
Why was Mercury called Cyllenius?
Why was he called Dolius?
What were the Hermathenæ?
What were the sacrifices offered to Mercury, and why?

CHAPTER V.

SECT. I.—BACCHUS. HIS IMAGE, AND BIRTH.

BACCHUS, *the god of wine*, and *the captain and emperor of drunkards*, is represented with swoln cheeks, red face, and a body bloated and puffed up. He is crowned with ivy and vine-leaves; and has in his hand a *thyrsus*, instead of a sceptre, which is a javelin with an iron head, encircled by ivy or vine-leaves. [l] He is carried in a chariot, which is sometimes drawn by tigers and lions, and sometimes by lynxes and panthers: and, like a king, he has his guards, [m] who are a drunken band of satyrs, demons, nymphs that preside over the wine-presses, fairies of fountains, and priestesses. Silenus oftentimes comes after him, sitting on an ass that bends under his burden.

[l] Ovid. de Art. Am. Aristoph. Scholiast. in Plutum. Strabo, l. 26. Ovid. Met. 3. 4. [m] Cohors satyrorum, Cobalorum, Lenarum, Naiadum, atque Baccharum.

He is sometimes painted an old man, and sometimes a smooth and beardless boy; as [n] Ovid and [o] Tibullus describe him. I shall give you the reason of these things, and of his horns, mentioned also in [p] Ovid.

According to the poets, the birth of Bacchus was both wonderful and ridiculous.

They say, that when Jupiter was in love with Semele, it excited Juno's jealousy, who endeavoured to destroy her; and, in the shape of an old woman, visited Semele, wished her joy on her acquaintance with Jupiter, and advised her to oblige him, when he came, by an inviolable oath, to grant her a request: then, says she to Semele, ask him to come to you as he is wont to come to Juno; and he will come clothed in all his glory, and majesty, and honour. Semele was greatly pleased with this advice; and therefore, when Jupiter visited her next, she [q] begged a favour

[n] —— "Tibi inconsumpta juventa?
Tu puer æternus, tu formosissimus alto
Conspiceris cœlo, tibi, cum sine cornibus adstas,
Virgineum caput est."
—— Still dost thou enjoy
Unwasted youth? Eternally a boy
Thou'rt seen in heaven, whom all perfections grace:
And when unhorn'd, thou hast a virgin's face.

[o] "Solis æterna est Phœbo Bacchoque juventa."
Phœbus and Bacchus only have eternal youth.

[p] "Accedant capiti cornua, Bacchus eris."
Clap to thy head a pair of horns, and Bacchus thou shalt be.

[q] —— "Rogat illa Jovem sine nomine munus.
Cui Deus, Elige, ait; nullam patiere repulsam:
Quoque magis credas, Stygii quoque conscia sunto
Numina torrentis, timor et Deus ille Deorum.
Læta malo, nimiumque potens, perituraque amantis
Obsequio Semele: Qualem Saturnia, dixit,
Te solet amplecti, Veneris cum fœdus initis,
Da mihi te talem." Ovid. Met. 3.
—— She ask'd of Jove a gift unnam'd.
When thus the kind consenting god reply'd:
Speak but the choice, it shall not be deny'd;
And, to confirm thy faith, let Stygian gods,
And all the tenants of hell's dark abodes,

of him, but did not expressly name the favour. Jupiter bound himself in the most solemn oath to grant her request, let it be what it would. Semele, encouraged by her lover's kindness, and little foreseeing that what she desired would prove her ruin, begged of Jupiter to come to her embraces in the same manner that he caressed Juno. What Jupiter had so solemnly sworn to perform, he could not refuse: he accordingly put on all his terrors, arrayed himself with his greatest glory, and in the midst of thunder and lightning entered Semele's house. [r] Her mortal body could not stand the shock; so that she perished in the embraces of her lover; for the thunder struck her down and stupified her, and the lightning reduced her to ashes. So fatal are the rash desires of the ambitious! Bacchus, her son, not yet born, was preserved, taken from his mother, and sewed into Jupiter's [s] thigh, whence in fulness of time he was born, and [t] delivered into the hands of Mercury to be carried into Eubœa, to Macris, the daughter of Aristæus, [u] who immediately anointed his lips with honey, and

Witness my promise: these are oaths that bind,
And gods that keep ev'n Jove himself confin'd.
Transported with the sad decree, she feels
Ev'n mighty satisfaction in her ills;
And just about to perish by the grant,
And kind compliance of her fond gallant,
Says, Take Jove's vigour as you use Jove's name,
The same the strength, and sinewy force the same,
As when you mount the great Saturnia's bed,
And, lock'd in her embrace, diffusive glories shed.

[r] —— "Corpus mortale tumultus
Non tulit æthereos; donisque jugalibus arsit."
Nor could her mortal body bear the sight
Of glaring beams and strong celestial light;
But scorch'd all o'er, with Jove's embrace expir'd,
And mourn'd the gift so eagerly desir'd.

[s] —— "Genetricis ab alvo
Eripitur, patrioque tener (si credere dignum)
Insuitur femori, maternaque tempora complet."

[t] Eurip. Bacch. Nat. Com. l. 4. [u] Apol. Argon. 4.

brought him up with great care in a cave, to which there were two gates.

QUESTIONS FOR EXAMINATION.

How is Bacchus represented?
By what is his chariot drawn?
How is he painted?
Repeat the lines from Ovid
Give some account of Bacchus's birth?
What does Ovid say of Semele's request?
What was the consequence of that request?
What did Macris do for Bacchus at his birth?

SECT. 2.—NAMES OF BACCHUS.

Bacchus was so called from a [w] Greek word, which signifies "to revel;" and, for the same reason, the *wild women*, his companions, are called [x] Thyades and [y] Mænades, which words signify madness and folly. They were also called [z] *Mimallones*, that is, imitators or mimicks; because they imitated all Bacchus' actions.

[a] Biformis, because he was reckoned both a young and an old man, with a beard, and without a beard: or, because wine (of which Bacchus is the emblem) makes people sometimes cheerful and pleasant, sometimes peevish and morose.

He was named [b] Brisæus, either from the nymph his nurse; or from the use of the grapes and honey which he invented, for *brisa* signifies a bunch of pressed grapes; or else from the promontory Brisa, in the island of Lesbos, where he was worshipped.

[w] Ἀπὸ τοῦ βακχεύειν seu βακχεῖν, ab insaniendo. Eustath. apud Lil.
[x] Ἀπὸ τῆς θυάς à furore ac rabie. Virg. Æn. 4.
[y] A μαίνομαι, insanio, ferocio. [z] A μιμέομαι, imitor.
[a] Δίμορφος. Diod. apud Lil.
[b] Cornut. in Pers. Sat. 1.

[c] Bromius, from the crackling of fire, and noise of thunder, that was heard when his mother was killed in the embraces of Jupiter.

[d] Bimater, because he had two mothers: the first was Semele, and the other the thigh of Jupiter, into which he was received after he was saved from the fire.

He is called also by the Greeks [e] Bugenes, that is, born of an ox, and thence Tauriformis, or Tauriceps; and he is supposed to have horns, because he first ploughed with oxen, or because he was the son of Jupiter Ammon, who had the head of a ram.

[f] *Dæmon bonus*, the "good angel;" and in feasts, after the victuals were taken away, the last glass was drunk round to his honour.

[g] Dithyrambus, which signifies either that he was born twice, of Semele and of Jove; or the double gate, that the cave had, in which he was brought up: or [h] perhaps it means that drunkards cannot keep secrets; but whatever is in the head comes in the mouth, and bursts forth, as fast as it would out of two doors.

Dionysius or Dionysus, [i] from his father Jupiter, or from the nymphs called Nysæ, by whom he was nursed, as they say; or from a Greek [k] word, signifying "to prick," because he pricked his father's side with his horns, when he was born; or from Jupiter's lameness, who limped when Bacchus was in his thigh; or from an island among the Cyclades, called Dia, or [l] Naxos, which was dedicated to him when he married Ariadne; or lastly, from the city of Nysa, in which Bacchus reigned.

[c] Ἀπὸ τοῦ βρέμειν, ab incendii crepitu, tonitrusque sonitu. Ovid. Met. 4.
[d] Idem, ibid.
[e] Βουγενής, à bove genitus. Clemens Strom. Eus. l. 4. præp. Evang.
[f] Diodr. l. 5. Idem, l. 3.
[g] Ἀπὸ τοῦ δὶς εἰς θύραν ἀναβαίνειν, à bis in januam ingrediendo. Diodr. Orig. Euseb.
[h] Quasi per geminam portam, his proverbialiter de vino, facit τὸ στόμα δίθυρον.
[i] Ἀπὸ τοῦ Διός, à Jove, Phurnut. in fab.
[k] Ἀ νύσσω, pungo. Lucian. Dial.
[l] Νόσος, i. e. claudus, Nonn. l. 9.

[m] Evius, or Evous: for, in the war of the Giants, when Jupiter did not see Bacchus, he thought that he was killed, and cried out, "[n] Alas, son!" or, because when he found that Bacchus had overcome the Giants, by changing himself into a lion, he cried out again, "[o] Well done, son."

[p] Evan, from the acclamations of Bacchantes, who were therefore called Evantes.

Euchius, [q] because Bacchus fills his glass plentifully, even up to the brim.

[r] Eleleus and Eleus, from the acclamation wherewith they animated the soldiers before the fight, or encouraged them in the battle itself. The same acclamation was also used in celebrating the Orgia, which were sacrifices offered up to Bacchus.

[s] Iacchus was also one of his names, from the noise which men make when drunk: and this [t] title is given him by Claudian; from whose account of Bacchus, we may learn, that he was not always naked, but sometimes clothed with the skin of a tiger.

Lenæus; because [u] wine palliates and assuages the sorrows of men's minds; or from a Greek [w] word, which signifies the "vat" or "press," in which wine is made.

[x] Liber and Liber Pater, from *libero;* as in Greek they call him Ελευθεριος [*Eleutherios*] the "Deliverer;"

[m] Eheu υἱε! Eheu fili! Eurip. in Bacch. [n] Virg. Æn. 7.
[o] Εὖ υἱε. Euge fili! Cornut. in Pers. Acron in Horat.
[p] Virg. Æn. 6. Ovid. Met. 4. [q] Ab εὐχέω, bene ac large fundo. Nat. Com. l. 5. [r] Ab ἐλελεῦ, exclamatione bellica. Ovid. Met. 4. Æschyl. in Prometh.
[s] Ab ἰακχεύω, clamo, vociferor.

[t] —— "Lætusque simul procedit Iacchus
Crinali florens hedera: quem Parthica tigris
Velat, et auratos in nodum colligit ungues." Rap. Pros.
——— The jolly god comes in,
His hair with ivy twin'd, his clothes a tiger's skin,
Whose golden claws are clutch'd into a knot

[u] Quod leniat mentem vinum. [w] Ἀπὸ τοῦ ληνοῦ or ληνοῦ, i. e. torculari. Serv. in Geo 2. [x] Virg Ecl 7 Plut. in Probl. Pausan. in Attic.

for he is the symbol of liberty, and was worshipped in all free cities.

Lyæus and Lyceus signify the same with Liber: for wine [y] frees the mind from cares; and those who have drank plentifully, speak whatever comes in their minds, as [z] Ovid says below.

The sacrifices of Bacchus were celebrated in the night, therefore he is called [a] Nyctilius and Nysæus, because he was educated upon the mountain [b] Nysa.

Rectus, Ὀρθος [*Orthos*], because he taught a king of Athens to dilute his wine with water: thus men, who through much drinking staggered before, by mixing water with their wine, begin to go straight.

His mother Semele and his nurse were sometimes called Thyo: therefore from this they called him [c] Thyoneus.

Lastly, he was called [d] Triumphus; because, when in triumph the conquerors went into the capitol, the soldiers cried out, "*Io Triumphe!*"

QUESTIONS FOR EXAMINATION.

From what is the name Bacchus derived?

What are his companions called?

Why was Bacchus called Biformis?

Why, Briseus?

Why, Bromius?

Why, Bimater?

Why, Bugenes?

Why, Dithyrambus?

Why, Dionysius?

Why, Evius?

Why, Evan?

Why, Eleus?

Why, Iacchus?

[y] Ἀπὸ τοῦ λύειν, à solvendo

[z] "Cura fugit, multo diluiturque mero." Art. Am.
The plenteous bowl all care dispels

[a] Νυκτίλεω, nocte perficio. Phurnut. in Bacch. Ovid. Met. 4.

[b] Ovid. ib. [c] Hor. Carm. 1. [d] Θριαμβος, Var. de Ling. Lat.

Why, Liber?
Why, Nyctilius?
Why, Rectus?
Why, Triumphus?

SECT. 3.—ACTIONS OF BACCHUS.

Bacchus invented [e] so many things useful to mankind, either in finishing controversies, in building cities, in making laws, or obtaining victories, that he was declared a god by the joint suffrages of the whole world. What Bacchus could not himself do, his priestesses were able to accomplish: for by striking the earth with their *thyrsi*, they drew forth rivers of milk and honey, and wine, and wrought several other miracles, without the least labour. Yet these received their whole power from Bacchus.

1. He invented the [f] use of wine: and first taught the art of planting the vine from which it is made; as also the art of making honey, and tilling the earth. This [g] he did among the people of Egypt, who therefore honoured him as a god, and called him Osiris. The ass of Nauplia merits praise, because by gnawing vines he taught the art of pruning them.

2. He invented [h] commerce and merchandise, and found out navigation, when he was king of Phœnicia.

3. At the time when men wandered about unsettled, like beasts, [i] he reduced them into society: he taught them to worship the gods.

4. He subdued India, and many other nations, riding on an elephant: [k] he victoriously subdued Egypt, Syria, Phrygia, and all the east; where he erected pillars, as Hercules did in the west: he first invented triumphs and crowns for kings.

5. Bacchus was desirous to reward Midas the king of

[e] Diod. l. 5. Hist. et Oros. l. 2. Hor. Ep. 2. [f] Ovid. Fast. 3.
[g] Dion. de Situ Orbis. Vide Nat Com. [h] Idem, ibid.
[i] Ovid. Fast. Eurip. in Bacch. [k] Dion. de Situ Orbis.

Phrygia, because he had done him some service; and bid him ask what he would. Midas desired, that whatever he touched might become gold: [l] Bacchus was troubled that Midas asked a gift which might prove so destructive to himself; however, he granted his request, and gave him the power he desired. Immediately whatever Midas touched became gold, even his meat and drink; he then perceived that he had foolishly begged a destructive gift; and desired Bacchus to take his gift to himself again. Bacchus consented, and bid him bathe in the river Pactolus; Midas obeyed; and hence the sand of that river became gold, and the river was called Chrysorrhoos, or Auriflüus.

6. When he was yet a child, some Tyrrhenian mariners found him asleep; and carried him into a ship: Bacchus first stupified them, stopping the ship in such a manner that it was immoveable; afterward he caused vines to spring up the ship on a sudden, and ivy twining about the oars; and when the seamen were almost dead with the fright, he threw them headlong into the sea, and changed them into [m] dolphins.

QUESTIONS FOR EXAMINATION.

Why was Bacchus declared a god?
What were his priestesses able to perform?
What was the first invention attributed to him?
Why does the ass of Nauplia merit praise?
What were Bacchus' second and third inventions?
What did he do as a conqueror?
What was Midas' request?
What circumstance occurred when he was but a child?

[l] "Annuit optatis, nociturаque munera solvit
Liber; et indoluit, quod non meliora petisset." Ov. Met. 11.
To him his harmless wish Lyæus gives,
And at the weakness of his wish he grieves.
"Lætus habet gaudetque malo."
Glad he departs, and joys in 's misery.

[m] Ovid Met. 3.

SECT. 4.—THE SACRIFICES OF BACCHUS.

In sacrifices there are three things to be considered; *viz.* the creatures offered, the priests who offered them, and the sacrifices themselves, which are celebrated with peculiar ceremonies.

1. The [n] fir, the ivy, bindweed, the fig, and the vine, were consecrated to Bacchus. So also were the dragon and the pie, signifying the talkativeness of drunken people. The goat was slain in his sacrifices, because he is a creature destructive to the vines. The Egyptians sacrificed a swine to his honour before their doors.

2. The priests and priestesses of Bacchus were [o] the Satyrs, the Sileni, the Naiades, but especially the revelling women called Bacchæ, from Bacchus' name.

3. The sacrifices themselves were various, and celebrated with different ceremonies, according to the variety of places and nations. They were celebrated on stated days of the year, with the greatest regard to religion, as it was then professed.

Oscophoria [p] were the first sacrifices offered up to Bacchus: they were instituted by the Phœnicians, and when they were celebrated, the boys, carrying vine-leaves in their hands, went in ranks praying, from the temple of Bacchus, to the chapel of Pallas.

The [q] Trieterica were celebrated in the winter at night, by the Bacchæ, who went about armed, making a great noise, and pretending to foretel things to come. They were entitled Trieterica, because Bacchus returned from his Indian expedition after three years.

The [r] Epilenæa were games celebrated in the time of vintage, before the press for squeezing the grapes was invented. They contended with one another, in tread-

[n] Xenoph. in Sacerd. Plut. in Probl. Symp. Eurip. in Bacch. Herodot. Euterpe.

[o] Vide Nat. Com. l. 5.

[p] Pausan. in Attic.

[q] Ovid. Fast. et Met. 6.

[r] Scholiast. in Aristoph.

ing the grapes, who should soonest press out most *must*; and in the mean time they sung the praises of Bacchus, begging that the *must* might be sweet and good.

[s] Canephoria, among the ancient Athenians, were performed by marriageable virgins, who carried golden baskets filled with the first fruits of the year. [t] Nevertheless, some think that these sacrifices were instituted to the honour of Diana, and that they did not carry fruit in the basket, but presents wrought with their own hands, which they offered to this goddess, to testify that they were desirous to marry.

Apaturia were feasts celebrated in honour of Bacchus, setting forth how greatly men are [u] deceived by wine. These festivals were principally observed by the Athenians.

Ambrosia [w] were festivals observed in January, a month sacred to Bacchus; for which reason this month was called Lenæus or Lenæo, because the wine was brought into the city about that time. [x] But the Romans called these feasts Brumalia, Bruma, one of the names of Bacchus among them; and they celebrated them twice a year, in the months of February and August.

Ascolia, feasts so called from a Greek [y] word signifying a boracho, or leathern bottle; several of which were produced filled with air, or, as others say, with wine. [z] The Athenians were wont to leap upon them with one foot, so that they would sometimes fall down; however, they thought they did a great honour to Bacchus hereby, because they trampled upon the skins of the goat, which animal is the greatest enemy to the vines. But among the Romans, rewards were distributed to those who, by artificially leaping upon these leathern bottles, overcame the rest: then all of them together called aloud upon Bacchus confusedly, and in unpolished verse; and put-

[s] Demarat. in Certam: Dionys. [t] Doroth Sydon. apud Nat. Com.

[u] A decipiendo ab απατάω, fallo, dicta sunt απατουρια. Vide Nat. Com. in Bac. [w] Idem, ibid. [x] Cœl. Rhod. l. 18. c. 5.

[y] Ab ασκὸς, utris. Tzetses in Hesiod. [z] Menand. l. de Myster.

ting on masks, they carried his statue about their vine-yards, daubing their faces with the bark of trees and the dregs of wine: and returning to his altar, they presented him with their oblations in basons, and then burnt them. In the last place, they hung upon the highest trees little wooden or earthen images of Bacchus, which from the smallness of their mouths were called Oscilla: they intended that the places, where these small images were set up in the trees, should be as it were so many watch-towers, from which Bacchus might look after the vines, and see that they suffered no injuries. These festivals, and the images hung up when they were celebrated, are elegantly described by [a] Virgil, in the second book of his Georgics.

Lastly, the Bacchanalia, or Dionysia, or Orgia, were the feasts of [b] Bacchus, among the Romans, which at first were solemnized in February, at midday, by women only; but afterward they were performed in the most gross and scandalous manner by men and women together, and young boys and girls, till the [c] senate by an edict abrogated this festival, as Diagondus did at [d] Thebes. Pentheus, king of Thebes, attempted the

[a] ——— "Atque inter pocula læti
Mollibus in pratis unctos saliere per utres:
Nec non Ausonii, Trojâ gens missa coloni,
Versibus incomptis ludunt, risuque soluto,
Oraque corticibus sumunt horrenda cavatis:
Et te, Bacche, vocant per carmina læta, tibique
Oscilla ex altâ suspendunt mollia pinu.
Hinc omnis largo pubescit vinea fœtu," &c.
And glad with Bacchus, on the grassy soil,
Leap'd o'er the skins of goats besmear'd with oil.
Thus Roman youth, deriv'd from ruin'd Troy,
In rude Saturnian rhymes express their joy;
Deform'd with vizards cut from barks of trees,
With taunts and laughter loud their audience please:
In jolly hymns they praise the god of wine,
Whose earthen images adorn the pine,
And there are hung on high, in honour of the vine.
A madness so devout the vineyard fills, &c.

[b] Virg. Geo. 4. et Æn. 6. 7. [c] Liv. l. 9. Aug. de Civ. Dei, 6
[d] De Leg. l. 2. c. 11.

same thing, but the Bacchæ barbarously killed him; whence came the story, that his mother and sisters tore him in pieces, fancying he was a boar. [e]There is a story, that Alcithoe, the daughter of Ninyas, and her sisters, despising the sacrifices of Bacchus, staid at home spinning while the Orgia were celebrating, and on that account were changed into bats. [f]And it is said that Lycurgus, who attempted many times to hinder these Bacchanalia in vain, cut off his own legs, because he had rooted up the vines to the dishonour of Bacchus.

QUESTIONS FOR EXAMINATION.

What are the three things to be considered in regard to sacrifices?

What things were consecrated to Bacchus?

Who were the priests and priestesses of Bacchus?

Were the sacrifices all of one kind?

Which were the first sacrifices; by whom were they instituted, and how were they celebrated?

What were the Epilenæa?

Who performed the Canephoria?

What were the Apaturia?

What were the Ambrosia?

What were the Ascolia, and how were they celebrated?

What were the Oscilla?

Repeat the lines of Virgil on this subject.

What were the Bacchanalia?

SECT. 5.—THE HISTORICAL SENSE OF THE FABLE. BACCHUS AN EMBLEM EITHER OF NIMROD OR MOSES.

Some writers say, that [g]Bacchus is the same with Nimrod: the reasons of this opinion are, 1. The similitude of the words Bacchus and Barchus, which signifies the Son of Chus, that is, Nimrod. 2. They think the name of Nimrod may allude to the Hebrew word *namur*, or the Chaldee, *namer*, a tiger; and ac-

[e] Ovid. Met. 4. [f] Apud Nat. Com. [g] Bochart. in Phaleg.

cordingly [h] the chariot of Bacchus was drawn by tigers, and himself clothed with the skin of a tiger. 3. Bacchus is sometimes called [i] Nebrodes, which is the very same as Nimrodus. 4. Moses styles Nimrod "a great hunter," and we find that Bacchus is styled [k] Zagreus, which in Greek signifies the same thing. Nimrod presided over the vines, since he was [l] the first king of Babylon, where were the most excellent wines, as the ancients often say.

Others think that [m] Bacchus is Moses; because many things in the fable of the one seemed derived from the history of the other. For, first, some feign that he was born in Egypt, and presently shut up in an ark, and thrown upon the waters, as Moses was. 2. The surname of [n] Bimater, which belongs to Bacchus, may be ascribed to Moses, who, beside one mother by nature, had another by adoption, king Pharaoh's daughter. 3. They were both beautiful men, brought up in Arabia, good soldiers, and had women in their armies. 4. Orpheus directly styles Bacchus [o] a lawgiver, and calls him [p] Moses, and further attributes to him [q] the two tables of the law. 5. Bacchus was called [r] Bicornis; and accordingly the face of Moses appeared double-horned, when he came down from the mountain, where he had spoken to God; the rays of glory that darted from his brow, resembling the sprouting out of horns. 6. As snakes were sacrificed, and a dog given to Bacchus, as a companion; so Moses had his companion Caleb, which in Hebrew signifies "a dog." 7. As the Bacchæ brought water from a rock, by striking it with their *thyrsi*, and the country wherever they came flowed with wine, milk, and honey; so the land of Canaan, into which Moses conducted the Israelites, not

[h] Anthol. l. 1. c. 38. Ep 1. [i] Νηβρώδης. [k] Ζαγρεύς; i. e. robustus venator. [l] Ex Athenæo. [m] Vossius apud Bochart. in suo Canaan. et Huet. in Demonstr. Evangel. [n] Διμήτωρ. [o] Θεσμοφόρον. [p] Μώσην. [q] Δίπλακα θεσμὸν, Exod. xxxiv. 29. [r] Eurip. in Bacch.

Pl. V. p. 68.

H. Moses del. et sculp.

BACCHUS

only flowed with milk and honey, but with wine also; [s] as appears from that large bunch of grapes which two men carried between them upon a staff. 8. Bacchus [t] dried up the rivers Orontes and Hydaspes, by striking them with his *thyrsus*, and passed through them, as Moses passed through the Red Sea. 9. It is said also, [u] that a little ivy-stick, thrown down by one of the Bacchæ upon the ground, crept like a dragon, and twisted itself about an oak. And, 10 That [w] the Indians once were all covered with darkness, while those Bacchæ enjoyed a perfect day.

From this you may collect, that the ancient inventors of fables have borrowed many things from the Holy Scriptures, to patch up their conceits. Thus [x] Homer says, that Bacchus wrestled with Pallene, to whom he yielded; which fable is taken from the history of the angel wrestling with Jacob. [y] In like manner Pausanias reports, that the Greeks at Troy found an ark that was sacred to Bacchus; which when Euripidus had opened, and viewed the statue of Bacchus laid therein, he was presently struck with madness: the ground of which fable is in the second book of Kings, where the Sacred History relates that the Bethshemites were destroyed by God, because they looked with too much curiosity into the ark of the covenant.

Wine and its effects are understood in this fable of Bacchus. He was educated by the Naiades, nymphs of the rivers and fountains; whence men may learn to dilute their wine with water.

Bacchus is naked, he cannot conceal any thing. [z] Wine always speaks truth, it opens all the secrets of the mind.

The poet says [a] Bacchus has horns.

[s] Numbers xiii. 24. [t] Nonn. in Dionys l. 23 et 35. 25. 45.
[u] Apud eundem. [w] Nonnus Vos. ap. Bochart. in Can.
[x] Iliad, 48. [y] Pausan in Achaic.
[z] In vino veritas. Erasm. in Adag.

[a] "Accedant capiti cornua, Bacchus eris." Ov. Ep. Saph.
But put on horns, and Bacchus thou shalt be.

[b] Wine makes [c] even the meanest people bold, insolent, and fierce, exercising their fury and rage against others, as a mad ox gores with its horns.

He is crowned with ivy; because that plant, being always green and flourishing, by its natural coldness assuages the heat occasioned by too much wine.

QUESTIONS FOR EXAMINATION.

In what respects do Bacchus and Nimrod resemble each other?
In what respects is Bacchus like Moses?
What does the fable of Bacchus teach?

CHAPTER VI.

SECT. I.—MARS. HIS IMAGE AND DESCENT.

MARS is fierce and sour in his aspect; terror is everywhere in his looks, as well as in his dress; he sits in a chariot drawn by a pair of horses, which are driven by a distracted woman; he is covered with armour, and brandishes a spear in his right hand, as though he breathed fire and death, and threatened every body with ruin and destruction.

Mars, the god of war, who is often seen on horseback, in a formidable manner, with a whip and a spear together. The dog was consecrated to him, for his vigilance in the pursuit of his prey; the wolf, for his rapaciousness; the raven, because he diligently follows armies when they march, and watches for the carcases

[b] "Cura fugit, multo diluiturque mero."
Full bowls expel all grief, dissolve all care.
[c] "Tunc veniunt risus, tunc pauper cornua sumit."
By wine and mirth the beggar grows a king.

of the slain; and the cock, for his watchfulness, whereby he prevents all surprise. But that you may understand every thing in the picture, observe that the creatures which draw the chariot are not horses, but Fear and Terror. Sometimes Discord goes before them in tattered garments, and Clamour and Anger go behind. Yet some say, that Fear and Terror are servants to Mars; and accordingly, he is not more [d] awful and imperious in his commands, than they are [e] ready and exact in their obedience.

Bellona is the [f] goddess of war, and the companion of Mars; or, as others say, his sister or wife. She prepares for him his chariot and horses when he goes to fight. It is plain that she is called Bellona from *bellum*. She is otherwise called Duellona from *duellum*, or from the Greek word βελονη [*belone*], a "needle," whereof she is said to be the inventress. Her priests, the Bellonarii, sacrificed to her in their own blood; they [g] hold in each hand naked swords, with which they cut their shoulders, and wildly run up and down like men mad and possessed: upon which [h] people thought, that (after the sacrifice was ended) they were able to foretel future

[d] "Fer galeam, Bellona, mihi, nexusque rotarum
Tende, Pavor; Fræna rapidos, Formido, jugales."

Claud. in Ruf.

My helmet let Bellona bring; Terror my traces fit;
And, panic Fear, do thou the rapid driver sit.

[e] —— "Sævit medio in certamine Mavors,
Cælatus ferro, tristesque ex æthere Diræ,
Et scissa gaudens vadit Discordia palla,
Quam cum sanguineo sequitur Bellona flagello."

Virg. Æn. 8.

Mars in the middle of the shining shield
Is grav'd, and strides along the liquid field.
The Diræ come from heaven with quick descent,
And Discord, dy'd in blood, with garments rent,
Divides the press: her steps Bellona treads,
And shakes her iron rod above their heads.

[f] Silius. l. 4. Strat. Theb. l. 7. [g] Sectis humeris et utraque manu districtos gladios exerentes, currunt, efferuntur, insaniunt. Lactan. l. 1. c. 12

[h] Juven. Sat. 4. Lucan. l. 1. Eutrop.

events. Claudian introduces Bellona combing snakes; and another [i] poet describes her shaking a burning torch, with her hair hanging loose, stained and clotted with blood, and running through the midst of the ranks of the army, uttering horrid shrieks and dreadful groans. And in Homer we have a description of a battle in which Mars, Minerva, and Discord are engaged:

> Loud clamours rose from various nations round;
> Mix'd was the murmur, and confus'd the sound.
> Each host now joins, and each a god inspires;
> These Mars incites, and those Minerva fires.
> Pale Flight around, and dreadful Terror reign;
> And Discord, raging, bathes the purple plain.
> Discord, dire sister of the slaught'ring pow'r,
> Small at her birth, but rising ev'ry hour;
> While scarce the skies her horrid head can bound:
> She stalks on earth, and shakes the world around;
> The nations bleed where'er her steps she turns;
> The groan still deepens, and the combat burns. Iliad.

Before the temple of this goddess there stood a pillar called Bellica, [k] over which the herald threw a spear, when he proclaimed war.

Mars is said to be the son of Jupiter and Juno, though, according to Ovid's story, he is the child of Juno [l] only.

He married [m] Nerio or Nerione, which word in the Sabian language signifies "[n] valour and strength," and from her the Claudian family derived the name of Nero.

[i] "Ipsa faciem quatiens, et flavam sanguine multo
Sparsa comam, medias acies Bellona pererrat.
Stridet Tartarea nigro sub pectore Diva
Lethiferum murmur." Sil. l. 5.

Her torch Bellona waving through the air,
Sprinkles with clotted gore her flaming hair,
And through both armies up and down doth flee;
While from her horrid breast Tisiphone
A dreadful murmur sends.

[k] Alex. ab Alexandro l. 8. [l] Hom. Iliad. 5. Hesiod. in Theog. [m] Vide de la Cerda in Virg. Æn. l. 8.

[n] Virtutem et robur significat.

QUESTIONS FOR EXAMINATION.

How is Mars represented?
How is his chariot drawn and driven?
What animals are consecrated to Mars?
Repeat the lines in Virgil.
Who is Bellona?
Who are the Bellonarii?
How is Bellona represented by Claudian?
Repeat the lines.
Who was Mars?
Whom did he marry?

SECT. 2.—NAMES AND ACTIONS OF MARS.

The name [o] Mars sets forth the power and influence he has in war, where he presides over the soldiers; and his other name, [p] Mavors, shows that all great exploits are executed and brought about through his means.

The Greeks call him [q] Αρης [*Ares*], either from the destruction and slaughter which he causes; or from the [r] silence which is kept in war, where actions, not words, are necessary. But from whatever words this name is derived, it is certain that those famous names Areopagus and Areopagita are derived from Αρης. The Areopagus, that is, the "hill" or "mountain" of Mars, was a place at Athens, in which Mars, being accused of murder and incest, was forced to defend himself in a trial before twelve gods, and was acquitted by six voices; from which time, that place became a court wherein were tried capital causes, and the things belonging to religion. [s] The Aeropagitæ were the judges, whose integrity and credit was so great, that no person could be admitted

[o] Quod maribus in bello præsit.
[p] Quòd magna vertat. Var. de Ling. Lat.
[q] Ἀπὸ τοῦ αἴρειν tollere, vel ἀναιρεῖν interficere, Cic. de Nat. Deor. 5. Phurnut. [r] Ab ἀ non et ἐρῶ loquor, ὅτι ἐν τῷ πολέμῳ οὐ λόγων ἀλλ' ἔργων χρεία, quòd in bello necessaria non sint verba sed facta. Suidas. Pausan. in Attici. [s] Budæus in Pandect. l. ult. de len.

E

into their society, unless he delivered in public an account of his past life, and was found in every part thereof blameless. And, that the lawyers who pleaded might not blind the eyes of the judges by their charms of eloquence, they were obliged to plead their causes without any ornaments of speech; if they did otherwise, they were immediately commanded to be silent. And, lest they should be moved to compassion by seeing the miserable condition of the prisoners, they gave sentence in the dark, without lights; not by words, but in paper; hence, when a man speaks little or nothing, they used proverbially to say of him, that [t] "He is as silent as one of the judges in the Areopagus."

His name Gradivus comes from his stateliness in [u] marching; or from his vigour in [w] brandishing his spear.

He is called Quirinus, from [x] *Curis* or *Quiris*, signifying a spear; whence comes *securis* or *semicuris*, a piece of a spear. And this name was afterward attributed to Romulus, because he was esteemed the son of Mars; from whom the Romans were called Quirites. [y] Gradivus is the name of Mars when he rages; and Quirinus, when he is quiet. And accordingly there were two temples at Rome dedicated to him; one within the city, which was dedicated to Mars Quirinus, the keeper of the city's peace; the other without the city, near the gate, to Mars Gradivus, the warrior, and the defender of the city against all outward enemies.

The ancient Latins applied to him the title of [z] Salisubsulus, or "dancer," from *salio*, because his temper is very inconstant and uncertain, inclining sometimes to this side, and sometimes to that, in wars: whence we say, [a] that the issue of battle is uncertain, and the chance dubious. But we must not think that Mars

[t] Areopagitâ taciturnior. Cic. ad Attic. l. 1. [u] A gradiendo.
[w] Απο τοῦ κραδαινειν, ab hastæ vibratione. [x] Serv. in Æn. 1.
[y] Idem, ibid. [z] Pacuv. in Nonn.
[a] Mars belli communis est, Cic. l. 6, ep. 4.

was the only god of war; [b] for Bellona, Victoria, Sol, Luna, and Pluto, used to be reckoned in the number of martial deities. It was usual with the Lacedæmonians to shackle the feet of the image of Mars, that he should not fly from them: and among the Romans, the priests Salii were instituted to look after the sacrifices of Mars, and go about the city dancing with their shields.

The poets relate only one action of this terrible god: this is the adultery between him and Venus, from which [c] Hermione, a tutelar deity, was [d] born. Sol was the first that discovered it, and he immediately acquainted Vulcan, Venus' husband, with his wife's treachery. Vulcan instantly made a net of iron, whose links were so small and slender, that it was invisible; and spread it over the bed of Venus. By this the lovers were caught, and Vulcan called all the gods to witness the sight: after they had been long exposed to the jest of the company, Vulcan, at the request of Neptune, unloosed their chains, and gave them their liberty. But Alectryon, Mars' favourite, suffered punishment, because when he was appointed to watch, he fell asleep, and so gave Sol an opportunity to slip into the chamber; therefore Mars changed him into a [e] cock, which to this day is so mindful of his old fault, that he constantly gives notice of the approach of the sun, by his crowing.

QUESTIONS FOR EXAMINATION.

What does the name of Mars import?

What do the Greeks call him?

What names are derived from Αρης?

Who were the Areopagitæ?

[b] Serv. in Æn. 11. [c] Plut. in Pelopida.

[d] "Fabula narratur, toto notissima cœlo.
Mulciberis capti Marsque Venusque dolis.
The tale is told through heaven far and wide,
How Mars and Venus were by Vulcan ty'd."

[e] Græcè ἀλεκτρυών, gallus.

From what does Mars derive his name Gradivus?
Why is he called Quirinus?
On what account has he the title of Salisubsulus?
Was Mars the only god of war?
What action is related of Mars?
Who discovered Venus's treachery, and what was done in consequence?
What happened to Alectryon?

SECT. 3.—THE STORY OF TEREUS; AND THE SACRIFICES OF MARS.

Tereus, the son of Mars, by the nymph Bistonis, married [f] Progne the daughter of Pandion, king of Athens, when he himself was king of Thrace. This Progne had a sister called Philomela, a virgin in modesty and beauty inferior to none. She lived with her father at Athens. Progne, being desirous to see her sister, asked Tereus to fetch Philomela to her, with which he complied. Tereus fell desperately in love with Philomela; and, as they travelled together, because she refused to comply with his desires, he overpowered her, cut out her tongue, and threw her into a gaol; and returning afterwards to his wife, pretended that Philomela died in her journey; and that his story might appear true, he shed many tears and put on mourning. But [g] injuries sharpen the wit, and a desire of revenge makes people cunning: for Philomela, though she was dumb, found out a way to tell her sister the villany of Tereus. She described the violence offered her in embroidery, and sent the work folded up to her sister. Progne no sooner viewed it, but she was so transported with passion, that she could [h] not speak, her thoughts

[f] Ovid. Met. 6.

[g] ———— "Grande doloris
Ingenium est, miserisque venit solertia rebus."
Desire of vengeance makes th' invention quick,
When, miserable, help with craft we seek.

[h] "Et (mirum potuisse) silet; dolor ora repressit,
Verbaque quærenti satis indignantia linguæ

being wholly taken up in contriving how she should avenge the affront. First, then, she hastened to her sister, and brought her home without Tereus' knowledge. While she was thus meditating revenge, her young son Itys came embracing his mother; but she carried him aside into the remote parts of the house, and slew him while [i] he hung about her neck, and called her mother. When she had killed him, she cut him into pieces, and dressed the flesh, and gave it Tereus for supper, who [k] fed heartily on it. After supper he sent for his son Itys: [l] Progne told him what she had done, and Philomela showed him his son's head. Tereus, incensed with rage, rushed on them both with his drawn sword; but they fled away, and fear added wings to their flight: so that Progne became a swallow, and Philomela a nightingale. Tereus was also changed into a hoopoe [*upupa*], which is one of the filthiest of all birds. The gods out of pity changed Itys into a pheasant.

To Mars [m] were sacrificed the wolf for his fierceness; the horse for his usefulness in war; the wood-

Defuerant, nec flere vacat: sed fasque nefasque
Confusura ruit, pœnæque in imagine toto est."
She held her peace; 'twas strange; grief struck her mute;
No language could with such a passion suit;
Nor had she time to weep: right, wrong, were mixt
In her fell thoughts, her soul on vengeance fixt.

[i] "Et mater, mater, clamantem et colla petentem
Ense ferit."
——— He, mother, mother, cries,
And on her clings, while by her sword he dies.

[k] "Vescitur, inque suam sua viscera congerit alvum."
——————————— does eat,
And his own flesh and blood does make his meat.

[l] "Intus habes quod poscis, ait. Circumspicit ille,
Atque ubi sit, quærit: quærenti, iterumque vocanti.
Prosiluit, Ityosque caput Philomela cruentum
Misit in ora patris."
Thou hast, said she, within thee thy desire.
He looks about, asks where. And while again
He asks and calls, all bloody with the slain,
Forth, like a fury, Philomela flew,
And at his face the head of Itys threw.

[m] Virg. Æn. 9.

pecker and the vulture for their ravenousness; the cock for his vigilance, which is a prime virtue among soldiers; and grass, because it grows in towns laid desolate by war.

Among the ancient rites belonging to Mars, the most memorable is the following: [n] Whoever undertook the conduct of any war, went into the vestry of the temple of Mars; and first shook the Ancilla, a holy shield, afterwards the spear of the image of Mars, and said, "Mars, watch."

QUESTIONS FOR EXAMINATION.

Who was Tereus, and whom did he marry?

Give some account of the story of Philomela. [The pupil might shut the book, and write the story from memory, in his own words.]

Into what were Progne, Philomela, Tereus, and Itys metamorphosed?

What were the sacrifices offered to Mars, and on what account?

What rite did the ancient warriors perform before they went out to battle?

Repeat in Latin the speech of Progne to Tereus.

CHAPTER VII.

SECT. 1.—THE CELESTIAL GODDESS, JUNO. HER IMAGE AND DESCENT.

We have viewed the five celestial gods; let us now look upon the goddesses that follow them in order. First observe Juno, riding in a [o] golden chariot, drawn by peacocks, holding a sceptre in her hand, and wearing a crown beset with roses and lilies.

[n] Qui belli alicujus susceperat curam, sacrarium Martis ingressus, primò Ancilia commovebat, post hastam simulacri ipsius; dicens, Mars, Vigila. Servius.

[o] Ovid. Met. 2. Apuleius, l. 10.

Juno's chariot is finely represented by Homer; and Hebe is mentioned as her attendant:—

At her command rush forth the steeds divine;
Rich with immortal gold their trappings shine.
Bright Hebe waits: by Hebe, ever young,
The whirling wheels are to the chariot hung.
On the bright axle turns the bidden wheel
Of sounding brass; the polish'd axle, steel:
Eight brazen spokes in radiant order flame;
Such as the heav'ns produce: and round the gold
Two brazen rings of work divine were roll'd.
The bossy naves, of solid silver, shone;
Braces of gold suspend the moving throne;
The car, behind, an arching figure bore;
The bending concave form'd an arch before;
Silver the beam, th' extended yoke was gold,
And golden reins th' immortal coursers hold. Homer.

Juno is the queen of the gods, and both the [p] sister and wife of Jupiter. Her father was [q] Saturn, and her mother Ops; she was born in the island Samos, and there lived till she was married.

She seems very august and majestical. How beautiful is that face, how comely are all her limbs! how well does a sceptre become those hands, and a crown that head! how much beauty is there in her smiles! how much gracefulness in her breast! Her carriage is stately, her dress elegant and fine. She is full of majesty, and worthy of the greatest admiration.

Her servant is Iris, [r] the daughter of Thaumas and Electra, and sister to the Harpies. She is Juno's messenger, as Mercury is Jupiter's; though Jupiter and the other gods, the Furies, nay sometimes men, have sent her on messages. Because of her swiftness she is painted with wings, and she sometimes rides on a rainbow, as [s] Ovid says.

[p] ——— "Jovisque
Et soror et conjux." Virg. Æn. 1.

[q] Apollon. Argon. 1.

[r] Virg. Æn. 9. Nonn. 20. Idem 31. Hom. Iliad, 23.

[s] "Effugit, et remeat per quos modo venerat arcus." Met. 2.
On the same bow she went she soon returns.

It is her office to unloose the souls of women from the chains of the body, as Mercury unlooses those of men. We have an example of this in Dido, who laid violent hands on herself; for, when she was almost dead, Juno sent Iris to loose her soul from her body, as [t] Virgil describes at large in the fourth book of his Æneid.

But in this Iris differs from Mercury; for he is sent both from heaven and hell, but she is sent from heaven [u] only. He oftentimes was employed in messages of peace, whence he was called the [w] peacemaker; but Iris was always sent to promote strife and dissension, as if she were the goddess of discord: and therefore some think that her [x] name was given her from the contention which she perpetually creates; though others say, she was called [y] Iris, because she delivers her messages by speech, and not in writing.

[t] "Tum Juno omnipotens longum miserata dolorem,
Difficilesque obitus, Irim demisit Olympo,
Quæ luctantem animum nexosque resolveret artus.
Ergo Iris croceis per cœlum roscida pennis,
Mille trahens varios adverso Sole colores,
Devolat, et supra caput astitit: hunc ego Diti
Sacrum jussa fero, teque isto corpore solvo.
Sic ait, et dextra crinem secat: omnis et unà
Dilapsus calor, atque in ventos vita recessit."
Then Juno, grieving that she should sustain
A death so ling'ring, and so full of pain,
Sent Iris down to free her from the strife
Of lab'ring nature, and dissolve her life.
Downward the various goddess took her flight,
And drew a thousand colours from the light;
Then stood about the dying lover's head,
And said, I thus devote thee to the dead:
This off'ring to th' infernal gods I bear.
Thus, while she spoke, she cut the fatal hair:
The struggling soul was loos'd, and life dissolv'd in air.

[u] Hesiod in Theog. [w] Εἰρηνοποιός, pacificator. Vid. Serv. in Æn. 4. [x] Ἶρις quasi Ἔρις Contentio, Servius.
[y] Παρὰ τὸ εἴρειν, à loquendo.

QUESTIONS FOR EXAMINATION.

How is Juno represented?
Repeat Homer's description of her chariot.
Who is Juno, and what relation does she bear to Jupiter and Saturn?
How is she represented with regard to her figure?
Who is Iris, and for what purposes was she employed?
How is she painted?
Give the line from Ovid.
What office does Iris bear with respect to the souls of women?
Repeat the description of her office in Latin: and also the translation.
In what does Iris differ from Mercury?
How is her name supposed to be derived?

SECT. 2.—THE CHILDREN, AND DISPOSITION OF JUNO.

Vulcan, Mars, and Hebe, were the children of Juno by Jupiter. [z] Although some say that Hebe had no other parent than Juno. Hebe, on account of her extraordinary beauty, was, by Jupiter, made goddess of youth, and held the office of cupbearer of Jupiter. But by an unlucky fall she offended the king of the gods, who turned her out from her office, and put Ganymede in her stead.

Juno's worst fault was jealousy, of which the following are instances Jupiter loved Io, the daughter of Inachus; and lived with her. When Juno observed that Jupiter was absent from heaven, she suspected that the pursuit of his amours was the cause of his absence. Therefore she immediately flew down to the earth after him, and luckily found the place where Jupiter and Io were entertaining themselves in private. As soon as Jupiter perceived her coming, fearful of a chiding, he turned the young lady into a white cow. Juno, seeing the cow, asked who she was, and what was

[z] Pausan. in Corinth.

her origin? Jupiter said, she was born on a sudden out of the earth. The cunning goddess, suspecting the matter, desired to have the cow, which Jupiter could not refuse, lest he should increase her suspicion. So Juno, taking the cow, [a] gave it Argus to keep: this Argus had a hundred eyes, two of which in their turns slept, while the others watched. Thus was Io under constant confinement; nor was the perpetual vigilance of her keeper the only misfortune; for she was fed with nothing but insipid leaves and bitter herbs. This hardship Jupiter could not endure, therefore he sent Mercury to Argus, to set Io free. Mercury, under the disguise of a shepherd, came to Argus, and with the music of his pipe lulled him asleep, and then cut off his head. Juno was grieved at Argus' death, and to make him some amends, she turned him into a peacock, and [b] scattered his hundred eyes about the tail of the bird. Nor did her rage against Io cease, for she committed her to the Furies to be tormented. Despair and anguish made her flee into Egypt, where she begged of Jupiter to restore her to her former shape. Her request being

[a] "Servandam tradidit Argo,
Centum luminibus cinctum caput Argos habebat;
Inde suis vicibus capiebant bina quietem;
Cetera servabant, atque in statione manebant.
Constiterat quocunque loco, spectabat ad Io;
Ante oculos Io, quamvis aversus, habebat." Ov. Met. 1.
The goddess then to Argus straight convey'd
Her gift, and him the watchful keeper made.
Argus' head a hundred eyes possest,
And only two at once declin'd to rest:
The others watch'd, and, in a constant round,
Refreshments in alternate courses found.
Where'er he turn'd he always Io view'd;
Io he saw, though she behind him stood.

[b] —— "Centumque oculos nox occupat una
Excipit hos, volucrisque suæ Saturnia pennis
Collocat, et gemmis caudam stellantibus implet."
There Argus lies; and all that wond'rous light,
Which gave his hundred eyes their useful sight,
Lies buried now in one eternal night.
But Juno, that she might his eyes retain,
Soon fix'd them in her gaudy peacock's train.

granted, she thenceforth took the name of Isis, the goddess of the Egyptians, and was worshipped with divine honour.

Juno gave another evidence of her jealousy. [c] For, when her anger against Jupiter was so violent, that nothing could pacify her, king Cithæron [d] advised Jupiter to declare that he intended to take another wife. The contrivance pleased him, wherefore he takes an oaken image, dressed very beautifully, and puts it into a chariot; and declares publicly, that he was about to marry Platæa, the daughter of Æsopus. The report came to Juno's ears, who immediately fell furiously upon the image, and tore its clothes, till she discovered the jest; and laughing very heartily, she was reconciled to her husband. She was afterward called Citheronia, from king Cithæron, the adviser of the trick. The rest of her names follow.

QUESTIONS FOR EXAMINATION.

Who were Juno's children?

What was Hebe's office, how did she lose it, and who succeeded her in it?

What was Juno's great fault?

With whom was Jupiter enamoured?

Into what was Io metamorphosed by Jupiter, and what account did he give of the matter to his wife?

What did Juno do with Io in her new form?

Repeat the lines from Ovid descriptive of the fact.

How did Jupiter contrive to liberate Io?

What became of the eyes of Argus after his death?

Repeat the lines from Ovid.

What became of Io?

To what was Jupiter advised by Cithæron, and what was the result?

[c] Doroth. de Nat. Fabulæ. [d] Plut. in Arist.

SECT. 3.—NAMES OF JUNO.

Juno was called Argiva, from the [e] Argivi, among whom the sacrifices called Ἡραια were celebrated to her honour; in which a hecatomb, that is, one hundred oxen, were sacrificed to her. They made her image of gold and ivory, holding a pomegranate in one hand, and a sceptre in the other; upon the top of which stood a cuckow, because Jupiter changed himself into that bird, when he fell in love with her.

Bunea, from [f] Bunæus the son of Mercury, who built a temple to this goddess at Corinth.

Colenaaris, from the old word [g] *calo*, to call; for she was called upon by the priests, upon the first days of every month; which days are called Calendæ.

Caprotina, [h] or the nones of July, that is, on the seventh day, maid-servants celebrated her festival, together with several free-women, and offered sacrifice to Juno under a wild fig-tree (*caprificus*) in memory of the extraordinary virtue, which enabled the maid-servants to preserve the honour of the Roman name. For after the city was taken, the enemy, determined to oppress the Romans, sent a herald to them, saying, if they desired to save the remainder of their city from ruin, they must send them their wives and daughters. The senate was distracted at the thought. A maid-servant, named Philotis or Tutela, took with her several other maid-servants, some dressed like mistresses of families, and some like virgins, and went over to the enemy. Livy, the dictator, disposed them about the camp; they incited the men to drink much, because it was a festival: the wine made the soldiers sleep soundly; and a sign being given from a wild fig-tree, the Romans came and slew them all. These maid-servants were made

[e] Doroth. l. 2. Met. et Pausan. [f] Pausan. in Corinth.
[g] Macrob. in Sat. [h] Plutarch. et Ovid. Art. Am. Var. de Ling. Lat.

free, and portions out of the public treasury were given them: the day was afterwards called Nonæ Caprotinæ, from the wild fig-tree, whence they had the sign: and they ordered an anniversary sacrifice to Juno Caprotina to be celebrated under a wild fig-tree, the juice of which was mixed with the sacrifices in memory of the action.

Curis or Curitis, from her spear, [i] called Curis in the language of the old Sabines. The matrons were understood to be under her guardianship; whence, says [k] Plutarch, the spear is sacred to her, and many of her statues lean upon spears, and she herself is called Quiritis and Curitis. Hence springs the custom, that the bride combs her hair with a [l] spear found sticking in the body of a gladiator, and taken out of him when dead, which spear was called Hasta Celibaris.

Cingula, [m] from the girdle which the bride wore when she was led to her marriage; for this girdle was unloosed with Juno's good leave, who was thought the patroness of marriage.

Dominduca and Interduca, [n] from bringing home the bride to her husband's house.

Egeria, [o] because she promoted, as they believed, the facility of the birth.

Februalis, Februata, Februa, or Februla, [p] because they sacrificed to her in the month of February. [q] Her festival was celebrated on the same day with Pan's feasts, when the Luperci, the priests of Pan, the god of shepherds, running naked through the city, and [r] striking the women with Juno's cloak (that is, with the skin of a goat) [s] purified them; and they thought that this ceremony caused to the women fruitfulness and easy labours. All sorts of purgation in any sacrifices were

[i] Festus. [k] In Ramulo.

[l] Crinis nubentium comebatur hasta celiberi, quæ scilicet in corpore gladiatoris stetisset abjecti occisique. Festus, Arnob. contra Gentes.

[m] A cingulo. Martin de Nupt.

[n] A ducenda uxore in domum mariti. Aug. de Civ. Dei. 7.

[o] Quòd eam partui egerendo opitulari crederent. Festus.

[p] Ex Sext. Pomp [q] Cum Lupercalibus. [r] Ovid. Fast. 2.

[s] Februabant, id est, purgabant; Cic. 2 Phil.

called Februa. The animals sacrificed to Juno [t] were a white cow, a swine, and a sheep: the goose and the peacock were also sacred to her.

Fluonia, [v] because she assisted women in other cases.

Hoplosmia, that is, [u] "armed completely:" she was worshipped at Elis; and hence Jupiter is called Hoplosmius.

[w] Juga, because she is the goddess of marriages. [x] A street in Rome, where her altar stood, was hence called Jugarius: and anciently people used to enter into the yoke of marriage at that altar. She is also, by some, called Socigena, because [y] she assists in the coupling the bride and bridegroom.

Lacinia, from the temple Lacinium, built and dedicated to her by [z] Lacinius.

Lucina, and Lucilia, either from [a] the grove, in which she had a temple; or from the light of this world, into which infants are brought by her. [b] Ovid comprises both these significations in a distich.

Moneta, [c] either because she gives wholesome counsel to those who consult her; or because she was believed to be the goddess of money.

[d] Nuptialis; and when they sacrificed to her under this name, [e] they took the gall out of the victim, and cast it behind the altar; to signify that there ought to be no gall or anger between those who are married.

Opigena, [f] because she gives help to women in labour.

[t] Virg. Æn. 4. Idem 8.

[v] Ovid ibid. Quòd fluoribus menstruis adest.

[u] Lil Gyr.

[w] Et Græce Ζυγία, à jugo aut conjugo Serv. in Æn. 4.

[x] Festus.

[y] Quòd nubentes associet.

[z] Strabo, l. 6. Liv l. 24.

[a] A luco vel luce. Var. de Ling. Lat.

[b] "Gratia Lucina, dedit hæc tibi nomina lucus.
Vel quia principium tu, dea, lucis habes." Fast. 2.

Lucina, hail, so nam'd from thy own grove,
Or from the light thou giv'st us from above.

[c] Vel quod reddat monita salutaria, vel quod sit Dea monetæ, id est, pecuniæ. Liv. l. 7. Suid. Ovid. Epist. Parid.

[d] Græce Γαμηλία.

[e] Euseb. de Præp. Evang. 3. Plut. in Sympos.

[f] Opem in partu laborantibus fert. Lil Gyr.

Parthenos the virgin; or [g] Parthenia, virginity; and she was so called, as [h] we are told, from this circumstance: there was a fountain among the Argivi, called Canathus, where Juno, washing herself every year, was thought to recover her youth and beauty.

Perfecta, that is, perfect: for [i] marriage was esteemed the perfection of human life.

She was called [k] Pronuba: marriages were not lawful, unless Juno was first called upon.

Regina, queen; which title she gives herself, as we read in [l] Virgil.

Sospita, [m] because all the women were supposed to be under her safeguard, every one of which had a Juno, as every man had his Genius.

Unxia was another of her names; [n] because the posts of the door were anointed, where a new-married couple lived; whence the wife was called [o] Uxor.

QUESTIONS FOR EXAMINATION.

Why was Juno called Argiva?

How did the Argivi represent her?

Why was she called Bunea and Colenaaris?

Give in writing the reasons for her name Caprotina.

How did she obtain the name Curis and Curitis?

What custom arose from this?

Why was she named Cingula?

On what account was she named Dominduca and Interduca?

Why was she called Februalis?

What animals were sacrificed to her?

Why was she named Hoplosmia?

[g] Pindar. in Hymn Olymp. [h] Pausan. in Corinth.

[i] Jul. Pollux. l. 3. Apud Græcos eodem sensu Juno vocabatur τελεία, et conjugium ipsum τέλειον, quòd vitam humanam reddat perfectam. Vide Scholiast. Pindar. Od. 9. Veme.

[k] Sen. in Medea.

[l] "Ast ego, quæ divûm incedo regina, Jovisque
Et soror et conjux." Æn. 1.
But I who walk in awful state above,
The queen of heav'n, sister and wife of Jove.

[m] A sospitando. Cic. de Nat. Deor. [n] Ab unguendo. Lil. Cyr.

[o] Quasi Unxor, ab ungendis postibus.

On what account was she named Juga and Socigena?

Why is she called Lacinia and Lucina?

Why has she the name Moneta?

What circumstance took place when they sacrificed to Juno under the name of Nuptialis?

Why was she called Parthenos, and why Perfecta?

What title does she give herself in Virgil?

Why is she called Sospita and Unxia?

CHAPTER VIII.

SECT. I. —MINERVA, OR PALLAS. HER IMAGE AND BIRTH.

MINERVA derives her name, as some think, [p] from the threats of her stern and fierce look.

It may be asked why she is clothed with armour, rather than with women's clothes. [q] What means the headpiece of gold, and the crest that glitters so? To what purpose has she a golden breastplate, and a lance in her right hand, and a terrible shield in her left? On her shield is a grisly head beset with snakes: and the cock and the owl are painted on it.

Minerva is armed, rather than dressed in women's clothes, because she is [r] the president and inventress of war. The cock stands by her, because he is a fighting bird, and is often painted sitting on her headpiece. The head, which seems so formidable with snakes, she not only carries on her shield, but sometimes also in the midst of her breast; it is the head of Medusa, one of the Gorgons, of which [s] Virgil gives a beautiful description.

p Minerva dicitur à minis. q Apollon. 90.

r Virg. Æn 11. Cic. de Nat Deor.

s "Ægidaque horriferam, turbatæ Palladis arma
Certatim squamis serpentum auroque polibant;
Connexosque angues, ipsamque in pectore Divæ
Gorgona, desecto vertentem lumina collo." Æn. 8.

The basilisk also is sacred to her, to denote the great sagacity of her mind, and the dreadful effects of her courage, she being the goddess both of wisdom and of war; for the eye of the basilisk is not only piercing enough to discover the smallest object, but it is able to strike dead whatsoever creature it looks on. She wears an olive crown, because it is the [t] emblem of peace; and war is only made that peace may follow. Though there is another reason, too, why she wears the olive: for she first taught mankind the use of that tree. When Cecrops built a new city, Neptune and Minerva contended about its name; and it was resolved, that whichsoever of the two deities found out the most useful creature to man, should give their name to the city. Neptune brought a horse; and Minerva caused an olive to spring out of the earth, which was judged a more useful creature for man than the horse: therefore Minerva named the city, and called it Athenæ, after her own name, in Greek Ἀθηνα.

The most celebrated of the statues of Phidias, after that of Jupiter Olympius, was the statue of Minerva in her temple at Athens; it was thirty-nine feet high.

History mentions five [u] Minervas. We shall speak of that only which was born of Jupiter, and to whom the rest are referred. The account given of her birth is this: when Jupiter saw that his wife Juno was barren, he through grief struck his forehead, and after three months brought forth Minerva; whence she was called [w] Tritonia. Vulcan [x] striking his head with the blow of a

> The rest refresh the scaly snakes that fold
> The shield of Pallas, and renew their gold:
> Full on the crest the Gorgon's head they place,
> With eyes that roll in death, and with distorted face.

[t] Plut. in Themistoc. Herod. in Terosich.

[u] Cic. de Nat Deor.

[w] Quasi Τριτόμηνις vel Τριτομηνίς tertio mense nata, Athena, apud Gyr.

[x] Lucian. in Dial. Deor.

hatchet, was amazed to see [y] an armed *virago* leap out of the brain of her father, instead of a tender infant. Others give a different account of it.

They say besides, [z] that it rained gold in the island of Rhodes, when Minerva was born; an observation made by [a] Claudian also.

QUESTIONS FOR EXAMINATION.

From what does Minerva derive her name?

How is she represented, and what are the figures represented on the shield?

Why is she armed, and what does the cock signify?

Repeat Virgil's description of the shield.

Why is the basilisk sacred to Minerva?

Why does she wear an olive crown?

How did Athens derive its name?

Which is the most celebrated statue of Minerva?

What was the origin of Minerva?

What happened at Rhodes when Minerva was born?

SECT. 2.—NAMES OF MINERVA.

Minerva is so called from [b] diminishing. And it is very true, that she, being the goddess of war, diminishes the numbers of men, and deprives families of their head, and cities of their members. [c] But the name may be derived from threatenings, because her looks threaten the beholders with violence, and strike them with terror. Or, perhaps, she has her name from the

[y] ——"De capitis fertur sine matre paterni
Vertice, cum clypeo prosiluisse suo."
Out of her father's skull, as they report,
Without a mother, all in arms leap'd forth.

[z] Hesiod. in Theog. Strabo, l. 14

[a] "Auratos Rhodiis imbres, nascente Minerva,
Induxisse Jovem ferunt."
At Pallas' birth, great Jupiter, we're told,
Bestrew'd the Rhodians with a show'r of gold.

[b] Quod minuit vel minuitur. Cic. de Nat. Deor.

[c] Vel à minis, quòd vim minetur, Cornif. ap. Gyr.

good [d] admonition she gives; because she is the goddess of wisdom. She is commonly thought to be wisdom itself; hence, when men pretend to teach those that are wiser than themselves, it is proverbially said, [e] "That sow teaches Minerva." And from this name of Minerva come *minerval*, or [f] *minervale*, signifying the salary that is given by the scholars to their masters.

The Greeks call her Athena, because she never sucked the breast of a mother or [g] nurse; for she was born out of her father's head, in full strength, and was therefore called [h] motherless. Plato says she had this name from her skill [i] in divine affairs. Others think she was so named, [k] because she is never enslaved, but enjoys the most perfect liberty: and indeed wisdom and philosophy give their votaries the most perfect freedom, as the Stoics well observe, who say, [l] The philosopher is the only free-man.

She is called Pallas, from a giant of the same name, whom she slew; or from the lake Pallas, where she was first seen by men; or lastly, which is more probable, from [m] brandishing her spear in war.

She had many other names; but we shall only mention two or three, after we have given some account of the Palladium.

The Palladium was an image of Pallas, preserved in the castle of the city of Troy; for while the castle and temple of Minerva were building, they say this image fell from heaven into it, before it was covered with a roof. This raised every-body's admiration; and when the oracle of Apollo was consulted, he answered, "That the city should be safe so long as that image

[d] Vel à monendo. Festus.

[e] Sus Minervam, σῦς Ἀθηνᾶν, Cic. 9. Epist. 18.

[f] Græcè διδακτρὸν

[g] Ἀθηνη quasi Ἀθηλη ab ἀ non et θηλαζειν mammam sugere.

[h] Ἀμήτρος καὶ ἀμητωρ, matre carens. Pollux. Phurnut.

[i] Ἀθηνᾶ, quasi θειογνόν, vel Ἠθηνόν, hoc est, quæ divina cognoscit. Plato in Cratylo.

[k] Ab ἀ not et θήσεσθαι servire.

[l] Liber nemo est nisi sapiens. Tollius in Paradox.

[m] Ἀπὸ τοῦ πάλλειν τὸ δόρυ, à vibrandâ hastâ. Serv. in Æn. 1.

remained within it." Therefore when the Grecians besieged Troy, they found [n] that it was impossible to take the city, unless the Palladium was taken out of it. This business was left to Ulysses and Diomedes, who undertook to creep into the city through the common sewers, and bring away the fatal image. When they had performed the task, Troy was taken without difficulty. [o] Some say it was not lawful for any person to remove the Palladium, or even to look upon it. Others add, that it was made of wood, so that it was a wonder how it could move the eyes and shake the spear. Others, on the contrary, report, that it was made of the bones of Pelops, and sold to the Trojans by the Scythians. They add, that Æneas recovered it, after it had been taken by the Greeks, from Diomedes, and carried it with him into [p] Italy, where it was laid up in the temple of Vesta as a pledge of the stability of the Roman empire, as it had been before a token of the security of Troy. And lastly, others write, that there were two Palladia; one of which Diomedes took, and the other Æneas carried with him.

Parthenos, *i. e.* virgin, was another of Minerva's names: whence [q] the temple at Athens, where she was most religiously worshipped, was called Parthenon. For Minerva, like Vesta and Diana, was a perpetual virgin; and such a lover of chastity, that she deprived Tiresias of his sight, because he saw her bathing in the fountain of Helicon: [r] but Tiresias' mother, by her humble petitions, obtained, that, since her son had lost the eyes of his body, the sight of his mind might be brighter and clearer, by having the gift of prophecy. [s] Ovid, indeed, assigns a different cause of his blindness. There is another illustrious instance of the chastity of Minerva: [t] when Neptune had enjoyed the beautiful Medusa (whose

[n] Ovid. Fast. 5.
[o] Herodian. l. 1. Plut. in Paral. Serv. in Æn. 2. Clem. in Protrep. [p] Dion. Hal. l. Antiq.
[q] Hom. in Hymn. ad Venerem. [r] Hom. Odyss. 10.
[s] Lib. Metam. [t] Nat. Com. l. 7. c. 18.

hair was gold) in the temple of Minerva, the goddess changed into snakes that hair which had tempted him; and decreed, that those who looked upon her thereafter, should be turned into stone.

Her name Tritonia was taken from the lake [u] Triton, where she was educated; as we also may learn from [w] Lucan, who mentions the love which Pallas bears to this lake; or from τριτω, or τριτων [*triton*] a word which in the old Bœotian and Æolick language signifies a head, because she was born from Jupiter's head. Yet, before we leave the lake Triton, let me tell you the ceremonies that were performed upon the banks of it in honour of Minerva. [x] A great concourse of people out of the neighbouring towns assembled to see the following performance: all the virgins came in companies, armed with clubs and stones, and on a sign being given, they assaulted each other; she who was first killed was not esteemed a virgin, and therefore her body was disgracefully thrown into the lake; but she who received the most and the deepest wounds, and did not desist, was carried home in triumph in a chariot, in the midst of the acclamations and praises of the whole company.

Ἐργατις [y] [*Ergatis*], *operaria*, "workwoman," was her name among the Samians, her worshippers; because she invented divers arts, especially the art of spinning, as we learn from the [z] poets: thus [a] the distaff is

[u] Pausan. in Bœot. l. 9.

[w] "Hanc et Pallas amat, patrio quod vertice nata
Terrarum primam Lybien (nam proxima cœlo est,
Ut probat ipse calor) tetigit, stagnique quietâ
Vultus vidit aquâ, posuitque in margine plantas,
Et se delectâ, Tritonida dixit, ab unda."
This Pallas loves, born of the brain of Jove,
Who first on Lybia trod (the heat doth prove
This land next heav'n): she standing by the side,
Her face within the quiet water spy'd,
And gave herself from the lov'd pool a name,
Tritonia.

[x] Herodot. in Melp. [y] Ex. Hesych. Isidor. l. 10.

[z] Ovid Met. 6. Virg. Æn. 7. Theocrit. Ecl. 34.

[a] "Non illa colo calathisque Minervæ
Fœmineas assueta manus."
To Pallas' arts her hands were never train'd.

ascribed to her, and sometimes she is called [b] Minerva, from her name, because she was the inventress of it. Although Minerva so much excelled all others in spinning, yet Arachne, a young lady of Lydia, very skilful at spinning, challenged her in this art; but it proved her ruin; for the goddess tore her work, and struck her forehead with a [c] spoke of the wheel. This disgrace drove her into despair, so that she hanged herself; but Pallas, out of compassion, brought her again to life, and turned her into a spider, [d] which continues still employed in spinning. The art of building, especially of castles, was Minerva's invention; and therefore she was believed to preside over them.

She is called Musica; because, says Pliny, [e] the dragons or serpents on her shield, which instead of hair encompassed the Gorgon's head, did ring and resound, if the strings of a harp near them were touched. But it is more likely that she was so named, because she invented the pipe; upon which, when she played by the river-side, and saw in the water how much her face was swelled and deformed by blowing it, she was moved with indignation, and threw it aside, saying, [f] The sweetness of the music is too dear, if purchased with so much loss.

[b] "Cui tolerare colo vitam tenuique Minerva." Virg. Æn. 8.
By th' spinsters trade she gets her livelihood.

[c] —— "Frontem percussit Arachnes;
Non tulit infælix, laqueoque animosa ligavit
Guttura, pendentem Pallas miserata levavit:
Atque ita, Vive quidem, pende tamen, improba dixit." Ov. Met. 6.

Arachne thrice upon the forehead smote;
Whose great heart brooks it not: about her throat
A rope she ties: remorseful Pallas staid
Her falling weight:—Live, wretch; yet hang, she said.

[d] —— "Et antiquas exercet aranea telas."
And now, a spider turn'd, she still spins on.

[e] Dicta est musica, quòd dracones in ejus Gorgone ad ictus citharæ tinnitu resonabant. Nat. Hist. l. 34. c. 8.

[f] —— "I procul hinc, non est mihi tibia tanti,
Ut vidit vultus Pallas in amne suos."
Away, thou art not so much worth, she cry'd,
Dear pipe; when she her face i' th' stream espy'd.

[g] Glaucopis was another of her names; because her eyes, like the eyes of an owl, were grey or sky-coloured, that is, of a green colour mixed with white.

She was also called Pylotis, from a [h] Greek word, signifying a "gate:" for, as the image of Mars was set up in the suburbs, so her effigy or picture was placed on the city gates, or doors of houses; by which they signified, that we ought to use our weapons abroad, to keep the enemy from entering our towns; but in the town we must use the assistance of Minerva, not of Mars; that is, the state ought to be governed at home by prudence, counsel, and law.

QUESTIONS FOR EXAMINATION.

What are the reasons given for the name Minerva?

What proverb has her great wisdom furnished, and what does the term Minervale signify?

Why is she called Athena?

Why is she named Pallas?

Give some account in writing of the Palladium.

Why was she called Parthenos?

What is the history of Tiresias?

What is related of Neptune and Medusa?

Why was Minerva named Tritonia?

Repeat the lines from Ovid.

What ceremony was performed on the banks of the lake Triton?

Why is Minerva called Ergatis?

What is the story of Arachne?

Repeat the lines from Ovid.

Who invented building, and particularly castles?

Why is Minerva called Musica?

Why is she named Glaucopis?

Why is she called Pylotis?

What inference is drawn from this circumstance?

[g] Γλαυκῶπις, habens oculos glaucos et cæsios, quales habet γλαυξ, noctua. Pausan. in Attic. Phurnut. Æschyl. in Eumenid.

[h] Απὸ τῆς πύλης, à porta.

SECT. 3.—THE SIGNIFICATION OF THE FABLE.

By this story of Minerva [i] the poets intended to represent wisdom; that is, true and skilful knowledge, joined with discreet and prudent manners. They hereby signified also the understanding of the noblest arts, and the accomplishments of the mind; likewise the virtues, and especially chastity: for,

1. Minerva is said to be born out of Jupiter's brain; because the wit and ingenuity of man did not invent the useful sciences, which for the good of men were derived from the brain of Jupiter; that is, from the inexhausted fountain of the Divine Wisdom, whence not only the arts and sciences, but the blessings of wisdom and virtue also proceed.

2. Pallas was born armed; [k] because, a wise man's soul being fortified with wisdom and virtue, is invincible: he is prepared and armed against fortune; in dangers [l] he is intrepid, in crosses unbroken, in calamities impregnable. Thus though the image of Jupiter perspires in bad weather, yet as Jupiter himself is dry and unconcerned, so a wise man's mind is hardened against the assaults that fortune can make upon his body.

3. She invented and exercised the art of spinning: and hence other young women may learn, if they would preserve their chastity, never to indulge idleness, but to employ themselves continually in some sort of work; after the example of [m] Lucretia.

4. As the spindle and the distaff were the invention of Minerva, so they are the arms of every virtuous woman. For which reason those instruments were formerly carried before the bride when she was brought to her husband's house; and somewhere it is a custom,

[i] Cic. de Offic. [k] Cic. in Paradoxis.

[l] Quemadmodum enim non colliquescit Jupiter dum simulacrum ejûs liquefit; sic sapientis animus ad quoslibet adversæ fortunæ casus obdurescit. Seneca. [m] Livy, l. I.

H. Moses del. et sculp.

MINERVA

Publish'd by Wilkie & Robinson, Paternoster Row May 1, 1810.

at the funeral of women, to throw the distaff and spindle into the grave with them.

5. An owl, a bird seeing in the dark, was sacred to Minerva, and painted upon her images, which is the representation of a wise man, who, scattering and dispelling the clouds of ignorance and error, is clear-sighted where others are stark blind.

QUESTIONS FOR EXAMINATION.

What do the poets represent by the story of Minerva?

Why is Minerva said to have originated from Jupiter's brain?

Why was she said to be born armed?

What lesson should Minerva teach as the inventress of spinning?

Why were the spindle and distaff carried before the bride, when she went to her husband's house?

What does the owl represent as sacred to Minerva?

CHAPTER IX.

SECT. 1.—VENUS. HER IMAGE. HER DESCENT.

TURN your eyes now to a sweet object, and view that goddess in whose countenance the graces sit playing, and discover all their charms. You see a pleasantness, a mirth, and joy in every part of her face. Observe with what becoming pride she holds up her head and views herself, where she finds nothing but joys and soft delights. She is clothed with a [n] purple mantle glittering with diamonds. By her side stand two Cupids, and round her are three Graces, and after follows the lovely beautiful Adonis, who holds up the goddess' train. The chariot in which she rides is made of ivory, finely carved, and beautifully painted and gilded. It is drawn by

[n] Philostrat. in Imag. Ovid. Met. 10 et 15. Apul. l. 6. Hor. Od. 3.

swans and doves, or swallows, as Venus directs, when she pleases to ride.

Venus, whom in more honourable terms men style the "goddess of the Graces," the author of elegance, beauty, neatness, delight, and cheerfulness, is in reality the mistress, president, and patron of all manner of licentiousness; and it should seem, by the worship which was formerly paid to her, that men used at that period to erect altars to, and deify, their vices; that they hallowed the greatest impieties with frankincense, and thought to ascend into heaven by the steps of their iniquities.

You will sometimes see her painted like a young virgin rising from the sea, and riding in a shell: at other times like a woman holding the shell in her hand, her head being crowned with roses. [o] Sometimes her picture has a silver looking-glass in one hand, and on the feet are golden sandals and buckles. In the pictures of the Sicyonians, she holds a poppy in one hand, and an apple in the other. They consecrated to her the thighs of all sacrifices except swine, because a boar killed Adonis her gallant. [p] At Elis she was painted treading on a tortoise; showing, thereby, that young women ought not to ramble abroad; and that married women ought to keep silence, love their home, and govern their family. [q] She wore a girdle or belt, called Cestus; in which all kinds of pleasures were folded, and which was supposed to excite irresistible affection. Some give her arrows; and make Python Suada, the goddess of eloquence, her companion.

We learn from several authors, [r] that there were four Venuses, born of different parents: but this Venus of whom we speak was the most eminent, and had the beauties as well as the disgraces of the others commonly ascribed to her. [s] She sprang from the froth of the sea.

[o] Philostrat. in Imag. Pausan. in Corinth.
[p] Plut. in præc. connub. et lib. de Isid. et Osir
[q] Hom. Iliad. 14. 26. Eurip. in Medea. Ex. Phurn.
[r] Cic. de Nat. Deor. [s] Hesiod. in Theog.

[t] She was by the Greeks called Aphrodite; some persons think she was so named from the madness with which lovers abound. [v] As soon as she was born, she was laid, like a pearl, in a shell instead of a cradle; and was driven by Zephyrus upon the island Cythera, where the Horæ, or hours, received, educated, accomplished, and adorned her; and, when she came of age, carried her into heaven, and presented her to the gods, all of whom, being taken with her beauty, desired to marry her: but she was at length betrothed to Vulcan, and married to him.

QUESTIONS FOR EXAMINATION.

How is Venus described?

By whom is she attended?

How is her chariot drawn?

What different descriptions are given of her?

What may be inferred from the worship paid to Venus?

How is she painted?

What was consecrated to her?

How is she painted at Elis, and what does that denote?

What was she called by the Greeks?

What happened to her as soon as she was born?

By whom was she educated, and who did she marry?

SECT. 2.—NAMES OF VENUS.

She is called Venus, says Cicero, [u] because all things are subject to the laws of love, or are produced and begotten by love. Or else, as [w] others say, her name is given her because she is eminently beautiful; for she is the goddess of beauty. Or lastly, she is so called, because she [x] was a stranger or foreigner to the Romans; for she was first worshipped by the Egyptians, and

[t] Ex ἀφρὸς spuma; vel, ut alii dicunt, ἀπὸ τῦ ἀφραίνειν, insanire. Ex. Euripid. et Phurnut. [v] Hom. in Hymn. ad Venerem.

[u] A veniendo, quòd ad omnes res veniat, vel quòd per eam omnia proveniant ac propignantur.

[w] Venus quasi venusta. Pausan. in Attic.

[x] Venus à veniendo, quasi adventitia, sic Græcorum Doctrina adventitia et transmarina vocabatur. Cic. de Offic.

from the Egyptians she was translated to the Greeks, and from them to the Romans. Let us now proceed to her other names.

Amica, Εταιρα [*Hetaira*] was a name given her by the Athenians; [y] because she joins lovers together; and this Greek word is used both in good and bad senses.

Armata; because, [z] when the Spartan women sallied out of their town, besieged by the Messenians, and beat them, a temple was dedicated to Venus Armata.

Apaturia, that is [a] "the deceiver;" for nothing is more deceitful than love, which flatters our eyes, and pleases us, like roses in their finest colours, but at the same time leaves a thorn in the heart.

She was called by the Romans, [b] Barbata; because, when the Roman women were so troubled with a disease that caused their hair to fall off, they prayed to Venus, and their hair grew again; upon which they made an image of Venus with a comb, and gave it a beard, that she might have the signs of both sexes.

Cypris, Cypria, and Cyprogenia, because she was worshipped in the island of Cyprus: Cytheris and Cytherea; from the island of [c] Cythera, whither she was first carried in a sea-shell.

There was a temple at Rome dedicated to Venus Calva; [d] because, when the Gauls possessed that city, ropes for the engines were made with the women's hair.

Erycina, from the mountain [e] Eryx in the island of Sicily; upon which Æneas built a splendid and famous temple to her honour, because she was his mother. [f] Horace makes mention of her under this name.

[y] Εταιρα id est, socia, quod amicos et amicas jungeret. Festus ex Apol. et Hesych.

[z] Pausan. in Lucan. et in Attic. Lucian. de Dea Syr. Strabo, l. 11.

[a] Ab ἀπατάω, fallo.

[b] Serv. Macrob. Suidas et alii.

[c] Festus.

[d] Lactant. l. 1. Divin. Institut.

[e] Plin. 1, 15. Polyb. l. 1. Serv. in Æn. 1.

[f] "Sive tu mavis, Erycina ridens,
Quam jocus circum volat et Cupido." Hor. l. 1. Od. 2.

[g] She is properly called Ridens, and Homer calls her [h] a lover of laughing: for she is said [i] to be born laughing, and thence called the "goddess of mirth."

Hortensis, because she looks after the production of seed and plants in gardens. And Festus tells us, that the word Venus is by Nævius put for herbs, as Ceres is for bread, and Neptunus for fish.

[k] Idalia and Acidalia, from the mountain Idalus, in the island Cyprus, and the fountain Acidalius, in Bœotia.

Marina, because she was born of the sea, to which [l] Ausonius refers his poem.

She is called [m] Aphroditis and Anadyomne, that is, emerging out of the waters, as Apelles painted her; and Pontia, from Pontus. Hence came the custom, that those who had escaped any danger by water, used to sacrifice to Venus. Hence also the mariners observed those solemnities called Aphrodisia, which Plutarch describes in a treatise against Epicurus.

Melanis, or Melænis, [n] that is, dark and concealed; whence the Egyptians worshipped a Venus, called [o] Scoteia, a goddess to be admired in the night.

[p] Migonitis signifies her power in the management of love. Therefore Paris dedicated the first temple to [q] Venus Migonitis; and [r] Virgil uses a like expression.

[g] Suidas Phurnut. [h] Φιλομμειδής, *i. e.* amans risus. Iliad, 2[illegible].
[i] Hesiod. [k] Virg. Æn. 1. et Serv. Horat. sæpe.

[l] "Orta salo, suscepta solo, patre edita Cælo."
Heav'n gave her life, the sea a cradle gave,
And earth's wide regions her with joy receive.

[m] Plin. 35. c. 10. Alex. ab Alex. 2. Clitipho et Leucippe.

[n] Nigra et tenebrosa, à μιλὰς, niger, quod omne amoris opus amat tenebras. Paus. in Arcad

[o] Σκοτεία καὶ νυκτὶ θαυμαστή, Dea admiranda à noctu et tenebris. Eurip. in Hippol. [p] A μίγνυμι, *i. e.* misceo. Pausan. in Lacon. [q] Veneri Migonitidi.

[r] —— "Quem Rhea sacerdos
Furtivo partu, sub luminis edidit auras,
Mixta Deo mulier." Æn 7.
—— Him priestess Rhea bore
Into the lightsome world; so stol'n by joy,
Mixt with a deity, she brought a boy.

Paphia, from the city Paphos in the island of Cyprus, where they sacrificed flowers and frankincense to her. And this is mentioned by [s] Virgil. This image had not a human shape: but as [t] Tacitus says, "It was from the top to the bottom of an orbicular figure, a little broad beneath; the circumference was small and sharpening toward the top like a sugar-loaf." [u] Lucan observes, that it was usual to worship other gods in confused shapeless figures. [w] Tertullian says, "Even Pallas the Athenian goddess, and Ceres the goddess of corn, without any certain effigies but mere rugged stakes, and shapeless pieces of wood, are things that are bought and sold." And [x] Arnobius adds, "the Arabians worshipped a stone, without form or shape of a deity."

Her name [y] Verticordia signifies the power of love to change hearts, and to ease the minds of men from all cares that perplex them. [z] Ovid mentions this power, and for the same reason Venus is called in the Greek [a] Epistrophia.

[s] "Ipsa paphum sublimis adit, sedesque revisit
Læta suas, ubi templum illi, centumque Sabæo
Thure calent aræ, sertisque recentibus halant." Æn. 1.
This part perform'd, the goddess flies sublime
To visit Paphos and her native clime;
Where garlands, ever green and ever fair,
With vows are offer'd, and with solemn pray'r:
A hundred altars in her temple smoke,
A thousand bleeding hearts her pow'r invoke.

[t] Erat continuus orbis, latiore initio, tenuem in ambitum, metæ modo exurgens; et ratio in obscuro. Lib. 3.

[u] "Simulacraque mœsta Deorum
Arte carent, cæcisque extant informia truncis."
All artless, plain, mishapen trunks they are;
Their moss and mouldiness procures a fear.

[w] Et Pallas Attica et Ceres farrea sine effigie rudi palo, et informi ligno prostant. Tertul. in Apol.

[x] Arabes informem coluerunt lapidem. Arnob. contra Gentes.

[y] Quasi corda vertens

[z] "Templa jubet fieri Veneri, quibus ordine factis,
Inde Venus verso nomina corde tenet." Fast 4.
Temples are rais'd to Venus, whence the name,
From changing minds, of Verticordia came

[a] Επιστροφία, quòd vertat homines. Pausan. in Attic.

QUESTIONS FOR EXAMINATION.

How does Cicero account for the name of Venus?

How do others account for it?

Why is she called Amica and Armata?

Why was she called Apaturia and Barbata?

Why was she denominated Cypris and Cytheris?

Why was a temple dedicated to Venus Calva at Rome?

Why was she called Erycina and Ridens?

Why was she denominated Hortensis, Idalia, and Acidalia?

How did she derive her names Marina and Aphroditis?

Why is she called Melænis, and why Migonitis?

Why is she called Paphia and Verticordia?

SECT. 3.—ACTIONS OF VENUS.

She, inspired by impure desire, [b] is said to have committed wickedness with her father Nycteus; for which she was changed into an owl, the dismal bird of the night, which, [c] conscious of her guilt, never appears in the daytime, but seeks to conceal her shame, and cover it by darkness, being driven from the society of all birds.

By similar depravity she was the mother of Adonis, which proved her ruin, [d] for she was turned into a tree, which always, as it were, bewails its impurity, and sends forth drops like tears.

Pygmalion, a statuary, considering the great inconveniences of marriage, had resolved to live single; but

[b] —— "Patrium temerâsse cubile." Ovid. Met. 2.
—— To have defiled her father's bed.

[c] ———— "Conscia culpæ
Conspectum lucemque fugit; tenebrisque pudorem
Celat, et à cunctis expellitur aëre toto."
Still conscious of her shame avoids the light,
And strives to shroud her guilty head in night,
Expell'd the winged choir.

[d] "Quæ quanquam amisit veteres cum corpore sensus,
Flet tamen, et tepidæ manant ex arbore guttæ." Ov. Met. 10.
Though sense with shape she lost, still weeping, she
Sheds bitter tears, which trickle from her tree.

afterward making a most elegant and artificial image of Venus, he fell so much in love with his own workmanship that he begged of Venus to turn it into a woman, and enliven the ivory. His wishes were granted, and of her he had Paphos, from whom the island [e] Paphos had its name.

Pyramus and Thisbe were both inhabitants of the city of Babylon; equal in beauty, age, conditions, and fortune. They began to love each other from their cradles. Their houses were contiguous, so that their love arose from their neighbourhood, grew greater by their mutual play, and was perfected by their singular beauty. This love increased with their years, and when they were marriageable, they begged their parents' consent; which was refused; because of some former quarrels between the two families. And, that the children might not attempt any thing against their parents' will, they were not permitted to see each other. There was a partition-wall between both houses, in which wall there was a small chink, never discovered by any of the servants. This crevice [f] the lovers found, and met here: their words and their sighs went through, but kisses could not pass; which, when they parted, they [g] printed on each side of the wall. By some contrivance they met and agreed upon an interview under the shade of a large mulberry tree, which stood close to a fountain. When night came on, Thisbe deceives her keepers, and

[e] —— "De quo tenet insula nomen." Ov. Met. 10.
From whom the island does its name receive.

[f] "(Quid non sentit amor?) primi sensistis amantes,
Et voci fecistis iter, tutæque per illud
Murmure blanditiæ minimo transire solebant."
Ovid. Met 4.

This, for so many ages undescry'd,
(What cannot love find out?) the lovers spy'd;
By which their whisp'ring voices softly trade,
And passion's am'rous ambassies convey'd.

[g] ———— "Partique dedere
Oscula quisque sua, non pervenientia contra."
———— Their kisses greet
The senseless stones with lips that cannot meet.

escapes first, and flies into the wood; for love gave her wings. When she got to the appointed place, [h] a lioness, fresh from the slaughter of some cattle, came to drink at the fountain. Thisbe was so frightened that she ran into a cave, and in the flight her veil fell from her head; the lioness, returning from the fountain, found the veil, and tore it with her jaws smeared with blood. Pyramus comes next, and sees the print of a wild beast's foot, and finds the veil of Thisbe bloody and torn. He, imagining that she was killed and devoured by the beast, grew distracted, and hastened to the appointed tree: but not finding Thisbe, he threw himself upon his sword, and died. Thisbe in the mean time, recovered from her fright, came to the [i] mulberry tree; where she saw Pyramus in the struggles of death: she [k] embraced her

[h] ———— "Venit ecce recenti
Cæde leæna boum spumantes oblita rictus,
Depositura sitim vicini fontis in unda."
When, lo! a lioness, with blood besmear'd,
Approaching to the well known spring appear'd.

[i] ———— "Tremebunda videt pulsare cruentum
Membra solum."
———— In great surprise
Blood-reeking earth and trembling limbs she spies.

[k] "Sed postquam remorata suos cognovit amores;
Percuit indignos claro pangore lacertos:
Et laniata cornas; amplexaque corpus amatum,
Vulnera sublevit lacrymis; fletumque cruori
Miscuit: et gelidis in vultibus oscula figens,
Pyrame, clamavit, quis te mihi casus ademit?
Pyrame, responde. Tua te, charissima, Thisbe
Nominat. Exaudi: vultusque attolle jacentes.
Ad nomen Thisbes oculos in morte gravatos
Pyramus erexi, visâque recondidit illâ."
But when a nearer view confirm'd her fear,
That 'twas her Pyramus lay welt'ring there;
She kiss'd his lips, and, when she found them cold,
No longer could from wild complaints withhold.
What strange mischance, what envious destiny
Divorces my dear Pyramus from me?
Thy Thisbe calls—O, Pyramus, reply!
Can Pyramus be deaf to Thisbe's cry?
When Thisbe's name the dying lover heard,
His half-clos'd eyes for one last look he rear'd;
Which, having snatch'd the blessing of that sight,
Resign'd themselves to everlasting night.

F 5

dying lover, mingled her tears with his blood, and folding her arms about him, called upon him to answer her, but he was speechless, and looking up expired. Thisbe, distracted with grief, tore her cheeks, beat her breasts, rent her hair, and shed a deluge of tears upon his cold face; nor did she cease to mourn, till she perceived her veil, bloody and torn, in Pyramus' hand. She then understood the occasion of his death, and drew the sword from the body of her lover, plunged it into her own, and falling accidentally on him, gave him a cold kiss, and breathed her last breath into his bosom. The tree, warmed with the blood of the slain lovers, became sensible of their misfortune, and mourned. Its berries, which were before white, became first red with grief, and blushed for the death of Pyramus; when Thisbe also died, the berries then became black and dark, as if they had put on mourning. Such were the fatal effects of love.

In the next place hear the story of Atalanta and Hippomenes. She was the daughter of king Schæneus, or Cæneus. It was doubted whether her beauty or swiftness in running were greater. When she consulted the oracle, whether she would marry or not, this answer was given, "That marriage would be fatal to her." Upon which the virgin hid herself in the woods, and lived in places remote from the conversation of men. But the more she avoided them, the more eagerly they courted her; for her disdain inflamed their desires, and her pride raised their adoration. At last, when she saw she could not otherwise deliver herself from the importunity of her lovers, she made this agreement with them: "You court me in vain; he who overcomes me in running shall be my husband; but they who are beaten by me shall suffer death; I will be the victor's prize, but the vanquished's punishment. If these terms please, go with me into the field." They all agreed to these [1] con-

[1] Venit ad hanc legem temeraria turba procorum."

Ov. Met. 10.

All her mad wooers take the terms proposed.

ditions; they strove to outrun her; but they were all beaten, and put to death according to the agreement; suffering the loss of their lives for the fault of their feet. Yet the example of these lovers did not deter Hippomenes from undertaking the race, who entertained hopes of winning the victory, because Venus had given him three golden apples, gathered in the gardens of the Hesperides; and also told him how to use them. Hippomenes briskly set out and began the race; and when he saw that Atalanta overtook him, he threw down a golden apple; the beauty of it enticed her, so that she [m] went out of her way, followed the apple, and took it up. Afterward he threw down another, which she pursued also to obtain; and again a third; so that while Atalanta was busied in gathering them up, Hippomenes reached the goal, and took the lady as the prize of his victory. But, forgetful of the gratitude and respect due to Venus, he met with a signal punishment. Himself and Atalanta were turned into a lion and a lioness.

Another proof of the fatal effects of love is the case of Paris and Helena. Paris was the son of Priamus king of Troy, by Hecuba. His mother, when she was pregnant, dreamed that she brought forth a burning torch: and asking the oracle for an interpretation, was answered, "That it portended the burning of Troy," and that the fire should be kindled by her son. Therefore, as soon as the child was born, by the command of Priamus, he was exposed upon the mountain Ida: where the shepherds brought him up privately, educated him, and called him Paris. When he was grown to man's estate, he gave such tokens of singular prudence and equity in deciding controversies, that on a great difference which arose among the goddesses, they referred it to his judgment to be determined. The god-

[m] "Declinat cursus, aurumque volubile tollit."
She, greedy of the shining fruit, steps back
To catch the rolling gold.

dess [n] Discordia was the occasion of this contention: for, because all the gods and goddesses, except herself, were invited to the marriage of Peleus, she was angry, and resolved to revenge the disgrace; therefore, when they all met and set down at the table, she came in privately, and threw down upon the table an apple of gold, on which was this inscription, "[o] Let the fairest take it" Hence arose a quarrel among the goddesses; for every one thought herself the most beautiful. But at last, all the others yielded to the three superior goddesses, Juno, Pallas, and Venus; who disputed so eagerly, that Jupiter himself was not able to bring them to agreement. He resolved therefore to leave the final determination of it to the judgment of Paris; so that she should have the apple to whom Paris should adjudge it. The goddesses consent, and call for Paris, who was then feeding sheep upon a mountain. They tell him their business, and court his favour with great promises: Juno promised to reward him with power; Pallas with wisdom; and Venus promised him the most beautiful woman in the world. He pronounced Venus the fairest, and assigned to her the apple of gold. Venus did not break her promise to Paris; for in a little time Paris was owned to be king Priam's son, and sailed into Greece with a great fleet, under the colour of an embassy, to fetch away Helena, the most beautiful virgin in the world, who was betrothed to Menelaus, king of Sparta, and lived in his house. When he came, Menelaus was from home, and, in his absence, Paris carried away Helena to Troy. Menelaus demanded her, but Paris refused to send her back; and this occasioned that fatal war between the Grecians and Trojans, in which Troy, the metropolis of all Asia, was taken and burnt, in the year of the world 2871. There were killed eight hundred sixty-eight thousand of the Grecians; among whom Achilles, one of their generals,

[n] Dion. Chrysost. Orat. 20. Philostrat. in Icon.

[o] Pulchrior accipiat, vel, Detur pulchriori.

lost his life by the treachery of Paris himself. There were slain six hundred seventy-six thousand of the Trojans, from the beginning of the war to the taking of the city, among whom Paris himself was killed by Pyrrhus or Philoctetes; and his brother Hector, [p] the pillar of his country, was killed by Achilles. When the city was taken and burnt, king Priamus, the father of Paris and Hector, at once lost all his children, his queen Hecuba, his kingdom, and his life. Helena, after Paris was killed, married his brother Deiphobus: yet she at length betrayed the castle to the Grecians, and admitted Menelaus into her chamber to kill Deiphobus; by which, it is said, she was reconciled to the favour of Menelaus again These things, however, belong rather to history than to fable.

QUESTIONS FOR EXAMINATION.

Why was Nictimene changed into an owl?
What happened to Pygmalion?
Can you give in short the story of Pyramus and Thisbe?
Repeat the Latin lines.
"Sed postquam remorata," &c.
Give the story of Atalanta and Hippomenes
Give an abridged account of the fates of Paris and Helena.

SECT. 4 —THE COMPANIONS OF VENUS; VIZ. HYMENÆUS, THE CUPIDS, THE GRACES, ADONIS.

The first of Venus' companions was the god Hymenæus. He presided over marriage, and was the protector of young unmarried women. [q] He was the son of Bacchus and Venus Urania, born in Attica, where he used to rescue virgins carried away by thieves, and restore them to their parents. He was of a very fair complexion; crowned with the *amaracus* or sweet marjoram, and sometimes with roses; in one hand he carried a torch, in the other a veil of flame colour, to

[p] Patriæ columen. [q] Philostrat. in Icon.

represent the blushes of a virgin. Newly married women offered sacrifices to him, as they did also to the goddess Concordia.

Cupid was the next of Venus' companions. He is called the god of love, and many different parents are ascribed to him, because there were many Cupids. Plato [r] says, he was born of Penia, the goddess of poverty, by Poros, the son of Counsel and Plenty. [s] Hesiod relates, that he was born of Chaos and Terra. Sappho derives him from Venus and Cœlum. Alcæus says he was the son of Lite and Zephyrus. Simonides attributed him to Mars and Venus; and Alcmæon, to Zephyrus and Flora. But whatever parents Cupid had, this is plain, he always accompanies Venus, either as a son or as a [t] servant.

The poets speak of two Cupids. One of which is an ingenious [u] youth, the son of Venus and Jupiter, a celestial deity; the other the son of Erebus and Nox (*Hell* and *Night*), a vulgar god, whose companions are drunkenness, sorrow, enmity, contention, and such kind of plagues. One of these Cupids is called Eros, and the other Anteros; both of them are boys, and naked, and winged, and blind, and armed with a bow and arrows and a torch. [w] They have two darts of different natures; a golden dart, which procures love, and a leaden dart, which causes hatred. [x] Anteros is also the god who avenges slighted love.

Although this be the youngest of all the celestial gods, yet his power is so great, that he is esteemed the strongest, for he subdues them all. Without his assistance his mother Venus is weak, and can do nothing, as she herself [y] confesses in Virgil.

He is naked, because the lover has nothing of his

[r] Plato in Sympos.

[s] Vide Nat. Com. et Li'. Gyr. [t] Cic. de Nat. Deor.

[u] Plato in Phædro. [w] Plat. apud Stobæam.

[x] Scholiast. in Theocr. 10. Idyll. Pausan. in Bœot. Plut. in Sympos.

[y] "Nate, meæ vires, mea magna potentia, solus." Æn. 4.
Thou art my strength, O son, and power alone.

own, but deprives himself of all that he has, for his mistress' sake.

Cupid is a boy, because he is void of judgment. His chariot is drawn by lions, for the rage and fierceness of no creature is greater than the extravagance and madness of violent love. He is blind, because a lover does not see the faults of his beloved object, nor consider in his mind the mischief proceeding from that passion He is winged, because nothing flies swifter than love, for he who loves to-day may hate to-morrow. Lastly, he is armed with arrows, because he strikes afar off.

The Grace scalled [z] Charites were three sisters, the daughters of Jupiter and Eurynome, or Eunomia, as Orpheus says; or rather, as others say, the daughters of Bacchus and Venus. The first was called [a] Aglaia, from her cheerfulness, her beauty, or her worth; because kindnesses ought to be performed freely and generously. The second, [b] Thalia, from her perpetual verdure; because kindness ought never to die, but to remain fresh always in the receiver's memory. The third, [c] Euphrosyne, from her cheerfulness; because we ought to be free and cheerful, as well in doing as in receiving a kindness.

These sisters were painted naked, or in transparent and loose garments, young and merry, with hands joined. One was turned from the beholder, as if she was going from him; the other two turned their faces, as if they were coming to him; by which we understand, that when one kindness is done, thanks are twice due; once when received; and again when it is repaid. The Graces are naked, because kindnesses ought to be done in sincerity and candour, and without disguise. They are young, because the memory of kindnesses received ought never to grow old. They are virgins,

[z] Χαριτες dictæ ἀπὸ τῆς χαρᾶς, i. e. à gaudio. [a] Ἀγλαΐα, id est, splendor, honestas, vel dignitas. [b] Θαλία (nam Θαλεία est Musæ nomen) id est, viriditas et concinnitas à Θαλλω vireo. [c] Ευφροσυνη, id est, lætitia et urbanitas. Vide Hesiod. in Theog.

because kindnesses ought to be pure, without expectation of requital. Their hands are joined, because [d] one good turn requires another; there ought to be a perpetual intercourse of kindness and assistance among friends.

Adonis was the son of Cinyras, king of Cyprus, and Myrrha. As he was very handsome, Venus took great delight in him, and loved his company. When he hunted, a boar gored him with his tusks, and killed him. Venus bewailed his death with much sorrow and concern, and changed his blood, which was shed on the ground, into the flower *anemone*, which ever since has retained the colour of blood. While she flew to assist him, being led by his dying voice, a thorn ran into her foot, and the blood that came thence fell on the rose, which before was white, but hereby made red.

Venus besought of, and obtained from Jupiter, that he should return to life for six months in every year; so that Adonis revives and dies in incessant succession. In Greece, Phœnicia, and some other countries, festivals were appointed expressive of this circumstance: the solemnity continued several days; the first part being spent in lamentations for his loss, and the second in joy for his restoration.

QUESTIONS FOR EXAMINATION.

Who was Hymenæus, and of whom was he the protector?

Whose son was he, and how was he represented?

Who was Cupid, and whose son was he said to be?

How many Cupids do the poets describe, and how are they represented?

What is his character with regard to power?

Why is he represented naked?

How is his chariot drawn?

Why is he represented blind, winged, and armed with arrows?

Who were the Graces, and what were their names?

How are they represented in paintings?

[d] Χάρις χάριν τίκτει, i. e gratia gratiam parit-in Adag.

Pl. IX. p. 112.

VENUS

Publish'd by Wilkie & Robinson, Paternoster Row, May 1, 1810.

Why are they said to be ever young, naked, and with their hands joined?

Who was Adonis? What was the cause and consequence of his death?

CHAPTER X.

LATONA.

LATONA [e] was the daughter of Phœbe, by Cæus the Titan. So great was her beauty, that Jupiter fell in love with her, which excited the jealousy of Juno, who caused her to be cast out of heaven to the earth; not contented with this, she obliged Terra, by an oath, not to give her a habitation, and besides [f] she set the serpent Python upon her, to persecute her wherever she went. Juno, however, was disappointed, for the island Delos received Latona, where, under a palm or an olive tree, she brought forth Diana; who, as soon as she was born, nursed and took care of her brother Apollo.

Her reception at Delos, notwithstanding the oath of Terra, is thus accounted for. This island formerly floated in the sea, and [g] they say that at the time it was hidden under the waters, when Terra took her oath, but that it emerged afterwards by the order of Neptune, and became fixed and immoveable for Latona's use, from which time it was called [h] Delos, because it was visible like other places.

The island Delos emerged for Latona's use, because it was sister to Latona. Some say, that her name was formerly Asteria, whom Jupiter loved and courted, but she was converted into an island: others report, that she was [i] converted into a quail, and flew into this island,

[e] Apollod. l. 1. Ovid. Met. 6. [f] Orph. in Hymn.
[g] Lucian in Dial Iridis et Neptuni. [h] Δῆλος, id est, conspicua et manifesta. [i] Ovid. Met. 15.

which was therefore, among other names, called [k] Ortygia. Niobe's pride, and the barbarity of the countrymen of Lycia, increase the fame of this goddess.

Niobe was the daughter of Tantalus, and the wife of Amphion, king of Thebes. [l] She was so enriched with all the gifts of nature and fortune, and her happiness so great, that she could not bear it: being puffed up with pride, and full of self conceit, she began to despise Latona, and to esteem herself the greater, saying: "Is any happiness to be compared to mine, who am out of the reach of fortune? She may rob me of much wealth, but she cannot injure me, since she must leave me still very [m] rich. Does any one's wealth exceed mine? Is any one's beauty like mine? Have I not seven most beautiful daughters, and as many ingenious and handsome sons? and have I not therefore reason to be [n] proud?" In this manner she boasted of her happiness, and despised others: but her pride, in a short time, deprived her of all the happiness which she had possessed, and reduced her from the height of good fortune to the lowest degree of misery. For when Latona saw herself despised, and her sacrifices disturbed by Niobe, she appointed Apollo and Diana to punish the injury that was offered to their mother. Immediately they went, with their quivers well

[k] Ἀπὸ τῆς ὄρτυγος, à coturnice. [l] Ovid. Met. 6.

[m] "Major sum quàm cui possit Fortuna nocere;
Multaque ut eripiat, multo mihi plura relinquet."
Ov. Met. 6.

My state's too great for Fortune to bereave;
Though much she lavish, she much more must leave.

[n] "In quamcumque domus adverti lumina partem,
Immensæ spectantur opes. Accedat eodem
Digna Deâ facies. Huc natas adjice septem,
Et totidem juvenes; et mox generosque nurusque:
Quærite nunc, habeat quam nostra superbia causam?"
Throughout my court, behold in every place
Infinite riches! add to this a face
Worthy a goddess. Then, to crown my joys,
Seven beauteous daughters, and as many boys:
All these by marriage to be multiply'd.
Behold! have we not reason for our pride?

filled with arrows, to Niobe's house; where first they killed the sons, then the daughters, and next the father, in the sight of Niobe, who by that means [o] was stupified with grief, till at length she was turned into marble, which, because of this misfortune, is said to shed many tears to this day.

The rustics of the country of Lycia, in Asia, did also experience the anger of Latona with their ruin; for when she wandered in the fields, the heat of the weather and the toil of her journey brought such a drought upon her, that she almost fainted for thirst. At last discovering a spring in the bottom of the valley, she ran to it with great joy, and fell on her knees [p] to drink the cool waters; but the neighbouring clowns hindered her, and bid her depart. She earnestly begged leave, and they denied it: she did not desire, [q] she said, to injure the stream by washing herself in it, but only to quench

[o] ——— "Orba resedit.
Exanimes inter natos, natasque, virumque,
Diriguitque malis."
She by her husband, sons, and daughters sits
A childless widow, waxing stiff with woes.

[p] —— "Gelidos potura liquores."
To quench her thirst with the refreshing stream.

[q] "Quid prohibetis aquas? usus communis aquarum:
Nec solem proprium natura, nec aëra fecit,
Nec tenues undas. Ad publica munera veni.
Quæ tamen ut detis supplex peto. Non ego nostros
Abluere hic artus, lassataque membra parabam.
Sed relevare sitim. Caret os humore loquentis,
Et fauces arent, vixque est via vocis in illis.
Haustus aquæ mihi nectar erit: vitamque fatebor
Accepisse simul."
——— Why hinder you, said she,
The use of water that to all is free?
Nor sun, air, nor nature, did water frame
Peculiar; a public gift I claim:
Yet humbly I entreat it, not to drench
My weary limbs, but killing thirst to quench.
My tongue wants moisture, and my jaws are dry;
Scarce is there way for speech. For drink I die.
Water to me were nectar. If I live,
'Tis by your favour.———

her thirst. They regarded not her entreaties, [r] but with threats endeavoured to drive her away This great inhumanity moved the indignation of Latona, who cursed them, and said, [s] "May you always live in this water." Immediately they were turned into frogs, and leaped into the muddy waters, where they ever after lived.

QUESTIONS FOR EXAMINATION.

Who was Latona, and what was the consequence of Jupiter's affection for her?

Where was Diana born, and how was she employed immediately after her birth?

How is Latona's reception at Delos accounted for?

What is said of her transmigrations into an island and quail?

Who was Niobe, and what is said of her pride and self-sufficiency?

Repeat the lines from Ovid.—

"In quamcunque domus," &c.

What was Latona's conduct towards Niobe?

Into what was Niobe changed?

What happened to the rustics of Lycia, and why were they so punished?

Repeat the lines—

"Quid prohibetis aqua," &c.

Repeat the lines—

"Quem non blanda Deæ."

[r] "Quem non blanda Deæ potuissent verba movere?
Hi tamen orantem perstant prohibere; minasque,
Ni procul abscedat, conviciaque insuper addunt
Nec satis est: ipsos etiam pedibusque, manuque
Turbavere lacus; imoque è gurgite mollem
Huc illuc limum saltu movere maligno"
With whom would not such gentle words prevail?
But they, persisting to prohibit, rail;
The place with threats command her to forsake;
Then, with their hands and feet, disturb the lake;
And, leaping with malicious motions, move
The troubled mud; which, rising, floats above

[s] "Æternum stagno, dixit, vivatis in isto;
Eveniunt optata Deæ."

CHAPTER XI.

AURORA.

AURORA, the daughter of Terra and Titan, the sister of the Sun and the Moon, and the mother of the Stars and the Winds, is a goddess drawn in a chariot of gold by white horses; her countenance shines like gold; her fingers are red like roses: so [t] Homer describes Aurora. The [u] Greeks call Aurora by another name, and [w] some say that she was the daughter of Hyperion and Thia, or of Pallas, from whom the poets also called her Pallantias. [x] She by force carried two beautiful young men, *viz.* Cephalus and Tithonus, into heaven.

Cephalus married Procris, the daughter of the king of Athens. When Aurora could, by no persuasion, move him to violate his marriage-vow, she carried him into heaven; but even there she could not shake his constancy; therefore she sent him again to his wife Procris, disguised in the habit of a merchant. After this she gave him an arrow, that never missed the mark, which she had received from Minoe. When Cephalus had this arrow, he spent his whole time in hunting and pursuing wild beasts. [y] Procris, suspecting the constancy of her husband, concealed herself in a bush, to discover the truth; but when she moved carelessly in the bush, her husband thinking some wild beast was there, drew his bow, and shot his wife to the heart.

Tithonus was the son of Laomedon, and brother of Priamus: [z] Aurora, for his singular beauty, carried him

[t] Hymn. in Vener.

[u] Græcè dicitur 'Ηώς et 'Εώς unde Eous et Heous. Latinis nominatur Aurora, quasi Aurea. Est enim, ut inquit Orpheus in Hymnis, 'Αγγελία Θεῦ Τιτᾶνος, id est, Solis Nuncia.

[w] Hesiod. in Theogon.

[x] Ovid Met. 7. Pausan. in Lacon.

[y] Ovid. Met. 7.

[z] Horatius, L 2. Carm.

up to heaven, and married him; and, instead of a portion, obtained from the Fates immortality for him. She had Memnon by him, but she forgot to ask the Fates to grant him perpetual youth, so that he became so old and decrepid, that, like an infant, he was rocked to sleep in a cradle. Hereupon he grew weary of life, and wishing for death, asked Aurora to grant him power to die. She said that it was not in her power to grant it; but that she would do what she could; [a] and therefore turned her husband into a grasshopper, which they say moults when it is old, and grows young again.

Memnon went to Troy, to assist the king Priam, where, in a duel with Achilles, he was killed; [b] and in the place where he fell, a fountain arose, which every year, on the same day on which he died, sends forth blood instead of water. But as his body lay upon the funeral pile to be burnt, it was changed into a bird by his mother Aurora's intercession; and many other birds of the same kind flew out of the pile with him, which, from his name, were called Aves Memnoniæ: these, dividing themselves into two troops, and furiously fighting with their beaks and claws, with their own blood appeased the ghost of Memnon, from whom they sprung.

There was a statue of this Memnon, made of black marble, and set up in the temple of Serapis at Thebes, in Egypt, of which they relate an incredible story: for it is [c] said, that the mouth of this statue, when first touched by the rays of the rising sun, sent forth a sweet and harmonious sound, as though it rejoiced when its mother Aurora came; but at the setting of the sun, it sent forth a low melancholy tone, as lamenting her departure.

[a] Ovid. Met. 13. [b] Ib. ibid. [c] Lucian. in Philo. Tzetzes Chil. 6.

QUESTIONS FOR EXAMINATION.

Who was Aurora, how was her chariot drawn, and how is she described by Homer?

Who did she carry to heaven?

What is said of Cephalus, and what became of his wife Procris?

Who was Tithon, and what is related of him?

Into what was he changed, and why?

What became of Memnon, and what is said to have happened where he was killed?

Into what was his dead body changed?

Where was his statue erected, and what is reported of it?

PART II.

OF THE TERRESTRIAL DEITIES.

CHAPTER I.

SECT. I.—SATURN. HIS IMAGE, FAMILY, AND ACTIONS.

LOOK upon the wall on the right hand. On that wall, which is the second part of the *Pantheon*, as well as of our discourse, you see the terrestrial deities divided into two sorts; for some of them inhabit both the cities and the fields indifferently, and are called in general "[a] the terrestrial goddesses:" but the others live only in the countries and the woods, and are properly called "[b] the gods of the woods." We will begin with the first.

Of the terrestrial gods, which are so called, because their habitation is in the earth, the most celebrated are Saturn, Janus, Vulcan, Æolus, and Momus. The terrestrial goddesses are Vesta, Cybele, Ceres, the Muses, and Themis: they are equal in number to the celestial gods and goddesses.

We will begin with the eldest, Saturn, who is represented as a decrepid old [c] man, with a long beard and hoary head. His shoulders are bowed like an arch, his jaws hollow and thin, his cheeks sunk; his nose is flat, his

[a] Dii terrestres urbes et campos promiscuè incolunt.
[b] Dii autem sylvestres rure tantum et in sylvis degunt.
[c] Virg. Æn. 7.

forehead full of furrows, and his chin turned up; [d] his right hand holds a rusty scythe, and his left a child, which he is about to devour. He is the son of Terra, or Vesta, and Cœlum, [e] Cœlus, or Cœlius, [f] who was the son of Æther and Dies, and the most ancient of all the gods. This Cœlum married his own daughter Vesta, by whom he had many children. The most eminent of them was Saturn, whose brothers were the Cyclops, Oceanus, Titan, the hundred-handed [g] giants, and divers others; his sisters were Ceres, Tethys, and Ops, or Rhea, whom he afterward married. The sisters persuaded their mother Vesta to exclude Titan, or Titanus, the eldest son, and to appoint Saturn heir of his father's kingdom. When Titan saw the fixed resolution of his mother and sisters, he would not strive against the stream, but voluntarily quitted his right, and transferred it to Saturn, under condition that he should not bring up any male children, so that after Saturn's death, the kingdom might return to the children of Titan.

His wife Ops, perceiving that her husband devoured all her male children, when she brought forth the twins, Jupiter and Juno, she only sent Juno to him, and sent Jupiter to be nursed in Mount Ida, by the priestesses of Cybele, who were called Curetes, or Corybantes. It was their custom to beat drums and cymbals while the sacrifices were offered up, and the noise of them hindered Saturn from hearing the cries of Jupiter. By the same trick she also saved Neptune and Pluto from her devouring husband.

Titan, when he saw himself cheated, and the agreement broken, to revenge the injury, raised forces, and brought them against Saturn, and making both him and Rhea prisoners, he bound them, and shut them together in hell, [h] where they lay till Jupiter, a few years after, overcame the Titans, and set his father and mother again at liberty. After this Saturn strove to take away

[d] Martian. apud Lil. Gyr. [e] Græcè dicitur Οὐρανός. [f] Nonn. l. 21. Dionys. Lact. Placid. in Thebaid. l. 6. [g] Centimani.
[h] In Tartaro.

his life; [i] because he heard by an oracle that he should be driven out of his kingdom by a son, as in reality he was afterward: for Jupiter deposed him from the throne, and expelled him the kingdom, because he had conspired to take away his life. [k] Beside this, when he found Saturn almost drunk with mead, he bound and maimed him, as Saturn had also maimed his father Cœlum before with his sickle.

Saturn having thus lost his kingdom went into Italy, [l] which was anciently called Saturnia. He lived there with king Janus; and that part of Italy, in which he lay hidden, was afterward called Latium, and the people Latini; as [m] Ovid observes. King Janus made Saturn partner of his kingdom; upon which [n] Saturn reduced the people to civil society, and joined them to each other, as it were, in *chains of brass*, that is, by the *brass money* which he invented; and therefore, on one side of the money was stamped a ship, [o] because Saturn came thither in a ship; and on the other side was stamped a Janus Bifrons. But although the money was *brass*, [p] yet this was the *golden age* in which Saturn lived, when, as [q] the poets, who magnify the happiness of that age, would persuade us, the earth without the labour of ploughing and sowing brought forth its fruits, and all things were common to all. [r] Virgil hath given an

[i] Enn. in Eumero. [k] Stat. Theb. 8. Claud. de Rap. Pros. 1.
[l] Virg. Æn. 8. Cyprian. de Idolorum Vanitate.

[m] "Inde diu Genti mansit Saturnia nomen:
Dicta fuit Latium terra, latente Deo." Fast. 1.
The name Saturnia thence this land did bear,
And Latium too, because he shelter'd here.

[n] Diodor. l. 5. Biblioth.

[o] "At bona posteritas puppim signavit in ære,
Hospitis adventum testificata Dei." Fast. 3.
A ship by th' following age was stampt on coin,
To show they once a god did entertain.

[p] Virg. Geo. 1. [q] Vide Tibull. Hesiod. Pherecrat. Trog. ap. Justin. l. 41. Martial. 12. ep. 73.

[r] "Primus ad æthereo venit Saturnus Olympo,
Arma Jovis fugiens, et regnis exul ademptis.
Is genus indocile, ac dispersum montibus altis,
Composuit, legesque dedit. Latiumque vocari

elegant description of this happy age in the eighth book of his Æneid. [s] Ovid likewise describes it; and [t] Virgil again in another place.

QUESTIONS FOR EXAMINATION.

How are the terrestrial deities divided, and why?

Which are the most celebrated of the celestial deities?

How is Saturn described?

Whose son was he, and who were his brothers and sisters?

What was the conduct of his sisters to him?

How did Titan act, and for what did he stipulate?

By what means did Jupiter escape, and who besides were saved in the like manner?

Who were the Corybantes; and what was their custom in offering sacrifices?

How did Titan avenge himself upon Saturn?

Who released Saturn, and how did he requite the exertions of Jupiter in his behalf?

How did Jupiter act afterwards?

What is the origin of the name Latini?

Repeat the two Latin and English lines.

What did he perform at Latium?

How is the age in which Saturn flourished described by the poets?

Repeat the lines from Virgil—

"Primus ad æthereo venit," &c.

Maluit, his quoniam latuisset tutus in oris:
Aureaque, ut perhibent, illo sub rege fuêre
Sæcula, sic placida populos in pace regebat."
Then Saturn came, who fled the pow'rs of Jove,
Robb'd of his realms, and banish'd from above:
The men dispers'd on hills to town he brought,
The laws ordain'd, and civil customs taught,
And Latium call'd the land, where safe he lay
From his unduteous son, and his usurping sway.
With his wild empire, peace and plenty came;
And hence the Golden Times deriv'd their name.

[s] "Signabat nullo limite fossor humum." Amor. 3.
The delver made nor bound nor balk.

[t] "Nec signare quidem aut partire limite campum
Fas erat." Geo. 1.
No fences parted fields, no marks, nor bounds
Distinguish'd acres of contiguous grounds.

SECT. 2.—NAMES OF SATURN. SACRIFICES, &c.

Many derive the name Saturnus [u] from sowing, because he first taught the art of sowing and tilling the ground in Italy; and therefore he was esteemed the god of husbandry, and called Stercutius by the Romans, because he first fattened the earth with dung: he is accordingly painted with a sickle, with which the meadows are mowed and the corn is cut down. This sickle was thrown into Sicily, and there fell within a city then called Trepanum, and since Trepano, from [w] that circumstance; though others affirm, that this city had its name [x] from that sickle which Ceres had from Vulcan, and gave the Titans when she taught them to mow. But others say, the town had its name because it was crooked and hollow, like a sickle. Indeed Sicily is so fruitful in corn and pasture, that the poets justly imagined that the sickle was invented there.

Saturnus is derived from that [y] fulness which is the effect of his bounty when he fills the people with provisions; as his wife was called [z] Ops, because "she helps the hungry." Others affirm, that he is called Saturn, [a] because he is *satisfied with the years* that he devours; for Saturn and Time are the same.

Men were sacrificed to Saturn, because he was delighted, as they thought, with human blood: therefore the gladiators were placed under his protection, and fought at his feasts. [b] The Romans esteemed him an infernal god, as Plutarch says, because the planet Saturn is malignant and hurtful. Those who sacrificed to him had their heads bare, and his priests wore scarlet gar-

[u] Saturnus dictus est à Satu, sicút à Portu Portunus, et à Neptu Neptunus. Festus. Serv. in Æn. 7. Lips. Sat. 3. [w] Falx, enim Græcè dicitur δρέπανον, Apollod. Argon. 4. [x] Ovid. Fast. 3. [y] A saturando, quasi saturet populos annonâ.

[z] Quòd esurientibus opem ferat. [a] Quòd ipse saturetur annis quos ipse devorat. Cic. de Nat. Deor. 2.

[b] Macrob. 1. Saturnal. c. 10. Tertull. de Testimon. et de Pallio.

ments. On his altar were placed wax tapers lighted, because by Saturn men were brought from the darkness of error to the light of truth.

The feasts [c] Saturnalia, in the Greek language Κρόνια [*Cronia*] were instituted either by Tullus, king of the Romans, or, if we believe Livy, by Sempronius and Minutius, the consuls. [d] Till the time of Julius Cæsar they were finished in one day, *viz.* on the 19th of December; after this they began to celebrate them for three days; and then, during four or five, by the order of Caligula: and some write, that they have lasted seven days. Hence they called these days [e] the first, the second, the third, &c. festivals of Saturn: and when these days were added to the feast, the first day of celebrating it was the seventeenth of December.

Upon [f] these festival days, 1. The senate did not sit. 2. The schools kept holyday. 3. Presents were sent among friends. 4. It was unlawful to proclaim war, or execute offenders. 5. Servants were allowed to be jocose and merry toward their masters; as we learn from [g] Ausonius. 6. Nay, the masters waited on their servants, who sat at table, in memory of that liberty which all enjoyed in ancient times in Saturn's reign, when there was no servitude. 7. Contrary to the custom, [h] they washed them as soon as they arose, as if they were about sitting down to table. 8. And lastly, [i] they put on a certain festival garment, called *synthesis*, like a cloak, of purple or scarlet colour, and this gentlemen only wore.

[c] Dion. Halicarn. l. 2. [d] Lips. Sat. 1. Dio. l. 59 et 60. Suet. in Calig. Cic. ad Attic. 13. ep. 50. [e] Prima, secunda, tertia, Saturnalia. [f] Martial 7. ep. 27. Plin. 8. ep. 7. Mart. passim. Dio. l. 58. Athen. 14. Senec. Ep.

[g] "Aurea nunc revocet Saturni festa December;
Nunc tibi cum domino ludere, verna, licet." Ecl. de Men.
December now brings Saturn's merry feasts,
When masters bear their sportive servants' jests.

[h] Tertul. ap. Lips. [i] Petron. Arbiter.

QUESTIONS FOR EXAMINATION.

How is the name of Saturn derived, and why is he esteemed the god of husbandry?

Why is he often painted with a sickle in his hand?

How do others derive the name as an assistant of the poor?

Why were gladiators put under his protection?

How was he esteemed by the Romans?

How were his sacrifices made?

When were the Saturnalia instituted, and how long did they last in each year?

What peculiarities were observed during these feasts?

SECT. 3.—THE HISTORICAL SENSE OF THE FABLE. BY SATURN IS MEANT NOAH.

Although it is generally said, that [k] Saturn was Nimrod, the founder of the empire of Babylon, yet I am more inclined to believe the opinion of [l] Bochartus, who maintains that Saturn and Noah were the same. The reasons which he brings are these:

1. In the time of Noah [m] the whole earth spake one language: and the ancient mythologists say, that the beasts understood this language. And it is said [n] that in Saturn's age there was but one language, which was common to men and brutes.

2. Noah is called in the Hebrew language [o] *a man of the earth*, that is, a husbandman, according to the usual phrase of Scripture, which calls a soldier [p] *a man of war*; a strong man [q] *a man of arms*; a murderer [r] *a man of blood*; an orator [s] *a man of words*; and a shepherd, [t] *a man of cattle*. Now Saturn is justly called *a man of the earth*, because he married Tellus, whose other names were Rhea and Ops.

3. As Noah was the first planter of vineyards, so the

[k] Berosus, l. 3.

[l] Bochart. in suo Phaleg. l. 1. c. 1.

[m] Genesis, xi. 1.

[n] Plato in Politicis.

[o] Vir terræ, Genesis, ix. 20.

[p] Josh. v. 4.

[q] Job, xxii. 8.

[r] 2 Sam. xvi. 17.

[s] Exod. iv.

[t] Gen. xlvi. 32.

[v] art of cultivating vines and fields is attributed to Saturn's invention.

4. As Noah was once overcome with wine, because perhaps he never experienced the strength of it before; [w] so the Saturnalians did frequently drink excessively, because Saturn protected drunken men.

5. As Noah cursed his son Ham, because he saw his father's nakedness with delight; [x] so Saturn made a law that whoever saw the gods naked should be punished.

6. Plato says "[y] that Saturn and his wife Rhea, and those with them, were born of Oceanus and Thetis:" and thus Noah, and all that were him, were in a manner new born out of the waters of the deluge, by the help of the ark. And if a ship was stamped upon the ancient coins, [z] because Saturn came into Italy in a ship; surely this honour belonged rather to Noah, who in a ship preserved the race of mankind from utter destruction.

7. Did Noah foretel the coming of the flood? So did Saturn foretel, "[a] that there should be great quantities of rain, and an ark built, in which men, and birds, and creeping things should all sail together."

Saturn is said to have devoured all his sons, except Jupiter, Neptune, and Pluto. So Noah may be said to have condemned all men, [b] because he foretold that they would be destroyed in the flood. For in the Scripture phrase, the prophets are said to "do the things which they foretel shall be done hereafter." But

[v] Aurel. Victor. de Origine Gentis Romanæ.

[w] Macrob. Sat. I. c. 6. Lucian. in Ep. Sat. [x] Callimachus in Hymn. [y] Κρόνος καὶ 'Ρέα ὅσοι μετὰ τούτων, &c. id est, Saturnus et Rhea et qui cum illustuêre ex Oceano et Thetide nati perhibentur. Plato in Timæo. [z] Plutarch. in Ῥωμαϊκοῖς.

[a] Κρόνος προσημαίνειν ἔσεσθαι πλῆθος ὄμβρων, &c. id est, Saturnus prænunciat magnam imbrium vim futuram, et fabricandam esse arcam, et in ea cum volucribus, reptilibus, atque jumentis esse navigandum. Alex. Polyhistor. apud Cyril. contra Julian. l. 1.

[b] Hebrews, xi. 7.

as Saturn had three sons left to him not devoured; so Noah had three, Shem, Cham or Ham, and Japhet, who were not destroyed in the flood.

Furthermore, these reasons may persuade us that Noah's son Cham is Jupiter: 1. His Hebrew name Ham is by many called Cham, from which the Egyptians had the name Ἀμȣν [*Amoun*] and the Africans had Ammon or Hammon. 2. Cham was the youngest son of Noah, as Jupiter was of Saturn. 3 Jupiter is feigned to be [c] lord of the heavens; thus Cham had Africa, which country is esteemed nearer the heavens than other countries, because it has the planets vertical.

Japhet is the same with Neptune; [d] for as Neptune had the command of the sea, so the islands and peninsulas fell chiefly to Japhet's lot.

Shem is supposed to be the Pluto of the ancients, which is thus accounted for: he was so holy, and so great an enemy to idolatry, that the idolators hated him while he lived, and endeavoured to blacken his memory when he died, by sending him to the Stygian darkness, and putting into his hand the sceptre of hell.

The Greek [e] words signifying Saturn and Time differ only in one letter, from which it is plain, that by Saturn, Time may be meant. And on this account [f] Saturn is painted devouring his children, and throwing them up again; as Time devours and consumes all things that it has produced, which at length revive and are renewed. Or days, months, and years, are the children of Time, which he constantly devours and produces anew.

Lastly, as Saturn has his scythe, so has Time too,

[c] Callimach. Hymn. ad Jovem. Lucan. 2. 9.

[d] Lactan. de falsa Relig l. 1. c. 1.

[e] Κρόνος Saturnus, Χρονο, Tempus.

[f] Cic. de Nat. Deor. Orph. in Hymn. ad Saturn. Æschyl. in Eumen.

with which he mows down all things; neither can the hardest adamant withstand the edge thereof.

QUESTIONS FOR EXAMINATION.

With what Scripture character has Saturn been identified?

What is the first reason for supposing Saturn and Noah to be the same persons?

What is the second?

What is the third?

What is the fourth?

What is the fifth?

What is the sixth?

What is the seventh?

What is the eighth?

What are the reasons for supposing Noah's son Cham to be Jupiter?

With which of the Scripture characters is Neptune compared?

How is it accounted for that Shem and Pluto are the same personages?

Point out the arguments to prove that Saturn and Time are the same.

CHAPTER II.

SECT. 1.—JANUS. HIS IMAGE, NAMES, AND ACTIONS.

JANUS is the [g] two faced god; holding a key in his right hand, and a rod in his left. Beneath his feet you see twelve altars; some [h] say he was the son of Cœlus and Hecate; and that his name was given to him [i] from a word signifying to go or pass through. [k] Whence it is, that thoroughfares are called, in the plural number,

[g] Bifrons Deus, Ovid.

[h] Arnob. cont. Gentes.

[i] Janus quasi Eanus *ab eundo*.

[k] Unde fit, ut transitiones perviæ Jani (plurali numero) foresque in limis profanarum ædium Januæ dicerentur. Cic. de Nat. Deor.

jani; and the gates before the door of private houses, *januæ.* A place at Rome was called Jani, in which [l] were three images of Janus: and there usurers and creditors met always to pay and receive money. This place is mentioned both by [m] Tully and [n] Horace.

As he is painted with two faces, so he is called by Virgil [o] Bifrons, and by Ovid [p] Biceps; because so great was his prudence, that he saw both the things past, and those which were future. Or because by Janus the world was thought to be meant, viewing with its two faces the two principal quarters, the east and west: he is also described [q] with four faces, from the four quarters of the world; because he governs them by his counsel and authority. Or because, as he is lord of the day, with his two faces he observes both the morning and the evening; as [r] Horace says.

When Romulus, king of the Romans, made a league with Tatius, king of the Sabines, they set up an image of Janus Bifrons, intending hereby to represent [s] both nations between which the peace was concluded. Numa afterward built a temple, which had double doors, and dedicated it to the same Janus. When Falisci, a city of Hetruria, was taken, [t] there was an image of Janus found with four faces; upon which the temple of Janus

[l] Acron. in Horat. l. 2. sat. 8.

[m] Viri optimi ad medium Janum sedentes. Cic. de Offic. 2. Dempster. in Paralip.

[n] Imus et summus Janus. Horat. l. 1. ep. 1. [o] Virg. Æn. 12.

[p] " Jane Biceps anni tacitè labentis imago,
Solus de superis, qui tua terga vides."
Thou, Double-pate, the sliding year dost show,
The only god that thine own back canst view.

[q] Quadrifons.

[r] " Matutine pater, seu Jane, libentior audis,
Unde homines operum primos vitæque labores
Instituunt."
Old Janus, if you please, grave two-faced father,
Or else bright god o' th' morning, choose you whether,
Who dat'st the lives and toils of mortal men.

[s] Effecerunt simulacrum Jane Bifronti quasi ad imaginem duorum populorum. Serv. in Æn. 12. [t] Captis Faliscis inventum est simulacrum Jani Quadrifrontis. Serv. in Æn. 7.

had four gates. But of that temple we shall speak by-and-by..

He was called [u] Claviger, "turnkey" or "club-bearer," from the rod and key in his hands. He held the rod, because he was the [x] guardian of the ways; and the key, for these reasons:

1. He was the inventor of locks, doors, and gates, which are called *januæ*, after his name: and himself is called [y] Janitor, because doors were under his protection.

2. He is the Janitor of the year, and of all the months; the first of which takes the name of January from him. To Juno belong the calends of the months, and she committed them to his care, therefore he is called by some Junonius, and [z] Martial takes notice, that the government of the year was committed to him; for which reason [a] twelve altars were dedicated to him, according to the number of the months; as there were also twelve small chapels in his temple. [b] The consuls at Rome were inaugurated in the temple of Janus, who were from this said [c] to open the year. Upon the calends of January (and as Macrobius says on the calends of March) a new laurel was hung upon the statue of Janus, and the old laurel was taken away; to which custom [d] Ovid refers.

Pliny thought this custom was occasioned because Janus rules over the year; "[e] The statue," says he, "of

[u] Ovid. Fast. 1. [x] Rector viarum. Lil. Gyr.

[y] Græcè Θυραῖος.

[z] "Annorum, nitidique sator pulcherrime mundi.
l. 10. ep. 28.

Gay founder of the world, and of our years.

[a] Var. lib. Human. Sidon. Apollin. Carm. 7. 1. Sat. c. 12.

[b] Sidon. ibid. [c] Aperire annum. Vide Lexicogr.

[d] "Laurea Flaminibus, quæ toto perstitit anno,
Tollitur, et frondes sunt in honore novæ." Fast. 3.
The laurel, that the former year did grace,
T' a fresh and verdant garland yields his place.

[e] Quòd Janus Geminus à Numâ rege dicatus digitis ita figuratis ut trecentorum quinquaginta quinque (sexaginta quinque *alii legunt*)

Janus, which was dedicated by Numa, had its fingers so composed, as to signify the number of three hundred and sixty-five days; to show that Janus was a god, by his knowledge in the year, and time, and ages." [f] He had not these figures described on his hand, but had a peculiar way of numbering them, by bending, stretching, or mixing his fingers, of which numeration many are the opinions of authors.

3. He holds a key in his hand, because he is, as it were, the [g] door through which the prayers of mankind have access to the gods: for, in all sacrifices, prayers were first offered up to Janus. And Janus himself gives the same reason, as we find in [h] Ovid, why, before men sacrificed to any of the other gods, they first offered sacrifice to him. But Festus says, because men thought that all things took their being from Janus, therefore they first made their supplications to him as to a common father. For though the name [i] *father* is given to all the gods, yet Janus was particularly called by this name.

He first built temples and altars, [k] and instituted religious rites; and [l] for that reason, among others, in all sacrifices they begin their rites by offering bread, corn, and

dierum notâ, per significationem anni, temporis, et ævi, se Deum in dicaret. Plinius. Vide etiam Athen. l. 34. c. 7. et Lil. Gyr.

[f] Tiraq. Lil. Gyr. Apuleii 2. Apol. &c.

[g] Arnob. contra Gentes.

[h] —— "Cur quamvis aliorum numina placem,
Jane, tibi primum thura merumque fero?
Ut possis aditum per me, qui limina servo,
Ad quoscunque voles inquit, habere deos." Fast. 1.
Why is't that though I other gods adore,
I first must Janus' deity implore?—
Because I hold the door, by which access
Is had to any god you would address.

[i] Quòd fuerit omnium primus à quo rerum omnium factum putabant initium: Ideo et supplicabant velut parenti. Festus, l. 3. in verbo *Chaos*.

[k] Virg. Æn. 8. Juv. Sat. 6. Serv. in Geo. 2.

[l] Propterea que in omni sacrificio perpetua ei præfatio præminitur, farque illi et vinum prælibatur. Fab. Pict. l. 1. de Ant. Lat.

wine to Janus, before any thing is offered to any other deity. Frankincense was never offered to him, though Ovid mentions it in the verses adjoined, which therefore he inserts either by poetical license, or only in respect to the sacrifices which were in use in his time. For [m] Pliny asserts that they did not sacrifice with frankincense in the times of the Trojans. Neither does Homer in the least mention frankincense in any place where he speaks concerning sacrifices. He was also called Patulcius and Clusius, or Patulacius and Clausius; from [n] opening and shutting; for in the time of war Janus' temple was open, but shut in the time of peace. This temple was founded by Romulus and Tatius. Numa ordained that it should be opened when the Romans waged war, but shut when they enjoyed peace.

Ovid mentions both these latter names of Janus in a [o] distich; and Virgil describes the [p] manner and occasion of opening his temple, and also the [q] consequences of

[m] Illacis Temporibus Thure non supplicatum. Plin. l. 13. c. 1. Vide Dempst. in Paralip. [n] A patendo vel patefaciendo et claudendo. Serv. in Æn. 1. Claud. de Hon. 6. Cons.

[o] "Nomina ridebis, modo namque Patulcius idem,
Et modò sacrificio Clusius ore vocor."
The priest this moment me Patulcius calls, and then
Next moment me he Clusius names again.

[p] "Sunt geminæ belli portæ sic nomine dicunt,
Religione sacræ et sævi formidine martis.
Centum ærei claudunt vectes æternaque ferri
Robora; nec custos absistit limine Janus.
Has ubi certa sedet patribus sententia pugnæ,
Ipse Quirinali trabea cictuque Gabino
Insignis, reserat stridentia limina consul." Æn. 7.
Two gates of steel (the name of Mars they bear,
And still are worshipp'd with religious fear)
Before his temple stand: the dire abode
And the fear'd issues of the furious god
Are fenc'd with brazen bolts; without the gates
The weary guardian Janus doubtly waits.
Then when the sacred senate votes the wars,
The Roman consul their decree declares,
And in his robes the sounding gates unbars.

[q] "Aspera tum positis mitescent sæcula bellis:
Cana fides, et Vesta, Remo cum fratre Quirinus

shutting it again. It is remarkable, that within the space of seven hundred years, this temple of Janus was shut only [r] thrice: once by Numa; the secoud time by the consuls Marcus Attilius and Titus Manlius, after the Carthaginian war; and lastly, by Augustus, after the victory at Actium.

In this story of [s] Janus, we may behold the representation of a very prudent person; whose wisdom consists "[t] in the remembrance of things past, and in the foresight of things to come." The prudent man ought therefore to have, as it were, two faces; that, according to his natural sagacity of mind and ripeness of judgment, observing both things past and future, he may be able to discern the causes, beginnings, and progress of all events and things.

QUESTIONS FOR EXAMINATION.

Who was Janus, and from what is his name derived?

Who mentions the place called the Jani at Rome, and for what was it used?

What is he named by Virgil and Ovid, and why?

What happened in the reigns of Romulus and Numa?

Why was he called Claviger?

> Jura dabunt: diræ ferro et compagibus arctis
> Claudentur belli portæ; Furor impius intus,
> Sæva sedens super arma, et centum vinctus ahenis
> Post tergum nodis, fremit horridus ore cruento."
> Then dire debate and impious war shall cease,
> And the stern age be soften'd into peace:
> Then banish'd faith shall once again return,
> And vestal fires in hallow'd temples burn:
> And Remus with Quirinus shall sustain
> The righteous laws, and fraud and force restrain.
> Janus himself before his fane shall wait,
> And keep the dreadful issues of his gate,
> With bolts and iron bars. Within remains
> Imprison'd Fury, bound in brazen chains;
> High on a trophy rais'd of useless arms
> He sits, and threats the world with vain alarms.

[r] Liv. l. 2. Oros. l. 5. cap. 12. Dio. l. 51. [s] Munst. 2. Cosm. 9. Fab. Pict. [t] In præteritorum memorie et providentia futurorem. Cic. de Senect.

H. Moses del. et sculp.

JANUS

Publish'd by Wilkie & Robinson, Paternoster Row, May 1. 1810.

Why was he named Janitor?
Which month is said to be named after him?
Why is he called Junonius?
Why were the Roman consuls said to open the year?
To what custom does Ovid refer?
Repeat the lines in Latin and English.
What does Pliny say on this subject?
Why does he hold a key in his hand?
Repeat the lines from Ovid.
What is the opinion of Festus?
What did Janus do?
What sacrifices were offered to him?
Why was he called Patulcius and Clusius?
By whom was the temple of Janus founded?
Repeat the lines of Virgil in Latin and English:—
[2] "Sunt geminæ belli portæ," &c.
Give Virgil's description of the consequences of shutting the temple.
In how long was it only thrice shut?
What does the story of Janus teach?

CHAPTER III.

VULCAN. HIS SERVANTS AND SONS.

VULCAN is both a smith and a god, and had a shop in the island Lemnos, where he exercised his trade, and where, though he was a god himself, he made Jupiter's thunder and the arms of the other gods. [1] He was born of Jupiter and Juno; some say of Juno only; and being contemptible for his deformity, was cast down from heaven into the island Lemnos, whence he is called Lemnius; he broke his leg with the fall, and if the Lemnians had not caught him when he fell, he had certainly broke his neck: he has ever since

[1] Phurnut. de Nat. Deor. Hesiod. Lucian. de Sacrific. Virg. Æn. 6.

been lame. [v] In requital of their kindness, he fixed his seat among them, and set up the craft of a smith; teaching them the manifold uses of fire and iron; and from softening and polishing iron, [u] he received the name Mulciber, or Mulcifer. He was the god of fire, the inventor and patron of the art of fabricating arms and all kinds of utensils from the metals. His most celebrated works are the famous palace of the sun; the armour of Achilles and Æneas; the beautiful necklace of Hermione, and the crown of Ariadne. According to Homer, the shield of Achilles was enamelled with metals of various colours, and contained twelve historical designs, with groups of figures of great beauty: the seats which Vulcan constructed for the gods were so contrived, that they came self-moved from the sides of the apartment to the place where each god seated himself at the table, when a council was to be held. He is described by Homer in the midst of his works:

——————— the silver-footed dame
Reach'd the Vulcanian dome, eternal frame!
High-eminent, amid the works divine,
Where heaven's far beaming brazen mansions shine.
There the lame architect the goddess found,
Obscure in smoke, his forges flaming round;
While, bath'd in sweat, from fire to fire he flew,
And, puffing loud, the roaring bellows blew.
Then from his anvil the lame artist rose;
Wide with distorted legs oblique he goes,
And stills the bellows, and, in order laid,
Locks in their chests the instruments of trade.
Then with a sponge the sooty workman drest
His brawny arms imbrown'd, and hairy breast:
With his huge sceptre grac'd, and red attire,
Came halting forth the sov'reign of the fire. Homer.

He obtained in marriage the most beautiful goddess Venus; and not long after, when he caught her and Mars

[v] Ὑιὸν ἔχεις τὸν Ἔρωτα, γυναῖκα δὲ τὴν Ἀφροδίτην,
Οὐκ ἀδίκως χαλκεῦ τὸν πόδα χωλὸν ἔχεις.
Cupid is Vulcan's son, Venus his wife,
No wonder then he goes lame all his life.

[u] A mulcendo ferro. Vide Lucan l. 1.

committing adultery, he linked them together with chains, and exposed them to the laughter of all the gods. He desired to marry Minerva, and Jupiter consented, if he could overcome her modesty. For when Vulcan made arms for the gods, Jupiter gave him leave to choose out of the goddesses a wife, and he chose Minerva; but he admonished Minerva at the same time to refuse him, as she successfully did.

At Rome were celebrated the Vulcania, [w] feasts in honour of Vulcan; at which they threw animals into the fire to be burnt to death. The Athenians instituted other feasts to his honour, called Chalsea. A temple besides was dedicated to him upon the mountain [x] Ætna, from which he is sometimes named Ætnæus. This temple was guarded by dogs, [y] whose sense of smelling was so exquisite, that they could discern whether the persons that came thither were chaste and religious, or whether they were wicked; they used to meet, and flatter and follow the good, esteeming them the acquaintance and friends of Vulcan their master.

It is feigned, that the first woman was fashioned by the hammer of Vulcan, and that every god gave her some present, whence she was called Pandora. Pallas gave her wisdom, Apollo the art of music, Mercury the art of eloquence, Venus gave her beauty, and the rest of the gods gave her other accomplishments. [z] They say also, that when Prometheus stole fire from heaven, to animate the man which he had made, Jupiter was incensed, and sent Pandora to Prometheus with a sealed box, but Prometheus would not receive it. He sent her with the same box again to the wife of Epimetheus, the brother of Prometheus; and she, out of a curiosity natural to her sex, opened it, which as soon as she had done, all sorts of diseases and evils, with which it was filled, flew among mankind, and have infested them

[w] Ita dictus ἀπο τῆς ἐρίδος καί χθονὸ; ex contentione et terra. Vide Virg. Geo 3.

[x] Var. ap. Lil

[y] Pollux, l. 7. apud Lil. Gyr.

[z] Pausan. in At.

ever since. And nothing was left in the bottom of the box but Hope.

Vulcan's servants were called [a] Cyclops, because they had but one eye, which was in the middle of their foreheads, of a circular figure: Neptune and Amphitrite were their parents. The [b] names of three of them were Brontes, Steropes, and Pyracmon: besides these there were many more, all of whom exercised the [c] art of smithery under Vulcan, as we are taught by Virgil.

Cacus, so called [d] from his wickedness, tormented all Latium with his fires and robberies; living like a beast in a dismal cave. He stole Hercules' oxen, and dragged them backward by their tails into his cave, that the track of their feet might not discover this repository of his thefts. But Hercules passing by, heard the lowing of the oxen in the cave, broke open the doors, and seizing the villain, [e] put him to death. [f] His cave was so dark,

[a] A κύκλος circulus, et ὤψ oculus.

[b] "Ferrum exercebant vasto Cyclopes in antro,
Brontesque, Steropesque, et nudus membra Pyracmon." Æn. 8.

On their eternal anvils here he found
The brethren beating, and the blows go round.

[c] "Alii ventosis follibus auras
Accipiunt redduntque: alii stridentia tingunt
Æra lacu: gemit impositis incudibus antrum.
Illi inter sese multa vi brachia tollunt
In numerum, versantque tenaci forcipe ferrum." Ibid.

One stirs the fire, and one the bellows blows.
The hissing steel is in the smithy drown'd;
The grot with beaten anvils groans around:
By turns their arms advance, in equal time,
By turns their hands descend, and hammers chime;
They turn the glowing mass with crooked tongs:
The fiery work proceeds with rustic songs.

[d] 'Απὸ τοῦ κακοῦ, à malo.

[e] "Hic Cacum in tenebris incendia vana vomentem
Corripit, in nodum complexus; et anget inhærens
Elisos oculos, et siccum sanguine guttur." Ibid.

The monster spewing fruitless flames he found;
He squeez'd his throat, he wreath'd his neck around,
And in a knot his crippled members bound:
Then from the sockets tore his burning eyes;
Roll'd on a heap the breathless robber lies.

[f] "Hic spelunca fuit vasto submota recessu,
Semihominis Caci facies quam dira tenebat

Pl. XIII. p. 138.

VULCAN.

Published by Wilkie & Robinson Paternoster Row May 1.1810.

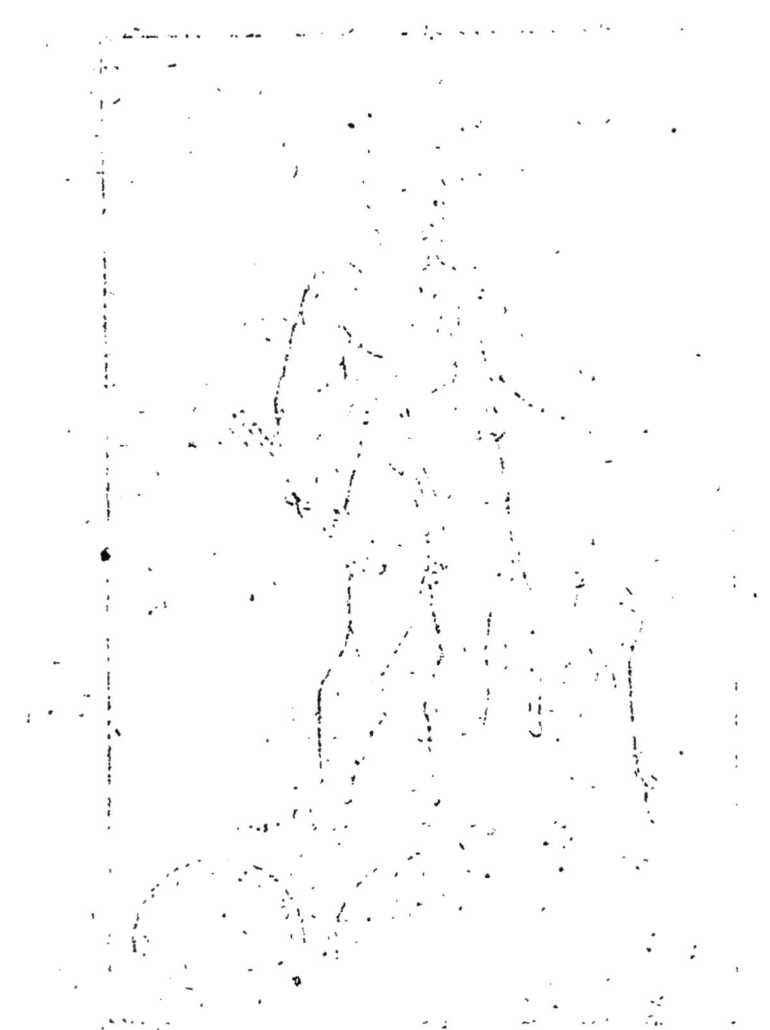

that it admitted not the least ray of light; the floor of it was red with the blood perpetually shed upon it, and the heads and limbs of the men he had murdered were fastened to the posts of the doors.

Cæculus also lived by plunder and robbery. He was so called from the smallness of his eyes: it is thought the noble family of the Cæcilii at Rome derived their original from him. He was the founder of the city Præneste. [g]Others say, that the shepherds found Cæculus unhurt in the midst of the fire, as soon as he was born; from which he was thought to be the son of Vulcan.

To these servants and sons of Vulcan, add the shepherd Polyphemus, a monster not unlike them, born of Neptune. For he had but one eye in his forehead, like the Cyclops, and he procured his living by murders and robberies, like Cacus and Cæculus. [h]This monster

Solis inaccessam radiis; semperque recenti
Cæde tepebat humus; foribusque affixa superbis
Ora virùm tristi pendebant pallida tabo.
Huic monstro Vulcanus erat pater; illius atros
Ore vomens ignes, magna se mole forebat."
'Twas once a robber's den, inclos'd around
With living stone, and deep beneath the ground.
The monster Cacus, more than half a beast,
This hold, impervious to the sun, possess'd;
The pavements ever foul with human gore;
Heads, and their mangled members, hung the door.
Vulcan this plague begot; and, like his sire,
Black clouds he belch'd, and flakes of livid fire.

[g] Virg. Æn. 7.

[h] "Visceribus miserorum, et sanguine vescitur atro.
Vidi egomet, duo de numero cum corpora nostro
Prensa manu magna, medio resupinus in antro
Frangeret ad saxum, sanieque aspersa natarent.
Limina: vidi, atro cum membra fluentia tabo
Manderet, et tepidi tremerent sub dentibus artus.
Haud impunè quidem: nec talia passus Ulysses,
Oblitusque sui est Ithacus discrimine tanto.
Nam simul expletus dapibus, vinoque sepultus
Cervicem inflexam posuit, jacuitque per antrum
Immensus, saniem eructans, ac frustra cruento
Per somnum commixta mero; nos magna precati

drew Ulysses and some of his companions into his den in Sicily, and devoured them. He thought, too, that the rest of Ulysses' servants could not escape his jaws. But Ulysses made him drunk with wine, and then with a firebrand quite put out his sight, and escaped.

QUESTIONS FOR EXAMINATION.

Who was Vulcan, and where did he exercise his trade?

Whose son was he, and what accident happened to him?

How was his life saved, and how did he requite the kindness of his benefactors?

Who did he marry, and how did he treat his wife?

Did he wish to marry any one besides, and was he successful?

What were the Vulcania, and how were they celebrated?

What other feasts; and what temple was dedicated to him?

What is said of the dogs that guarded that temple?

Numina, sortitique vices, una undique circum
Fundimur, et telo lumen terebramus acuto
Ingens; quod torvâ solùm sub fronte latebat,
Argolici clypei aut Phœbeæ lampadis instar." Virg. Æn. 8.
The joints of slaughter'd wretches are his food,
And for his wine he quaffs the steaming blood.
These eyes beheld, when with his spacious hand
He seiz'd two captives of our Grecian band;
Stretch'd on his back, he dash'd against the stones
Their broken bodies and their crackling bones.
With spouting blood the purple pavement swims,
While the dire glutton grinds the trembling limbs.
Not unreveng'd Ulysses bore their fate,
Nor thoughtless of his own unhappy state;
For, gorg'd with flesh, and drunk with human wine,
While fast asleep the giant lay supine,
Snoring aloud, and belching from his maw
His undigested foam and morsels raw;
We pray, we cast the lots; and then surround
The monstrous body, stretch'd along the ground:
Each, as he could approach him, lends a hand
To bore his eyeball with a flaming brand;
Beneath his frowning forehead lay his eye,
For only one did this vast frame supply,
But that a globe so large, his front it fill'd,
Like the sun's disk, or like the Grecian shield.

What story is told of Vulcan with respect to Pandora?

Who were Vulcan's servants, and what was their business?

Repeat the lines from Virgil: in the original and also the translation—

"Alii ventosis follibus," &c.

What is said of his son Cacus?

Repeat the lines from Virgil—

"Hic Cacum," &c.

Give the description of his cave—

"Hic spelunca," &c.

What is said of Cæculos, another son?

How is Polyphemus described?

Repeat the lines from Virgil—

"Visceribus miserorum," &c.

CHAPTER IV.

ÆOLUS.

He who stands next him is [i] Æolus, the "god of the winds," begotten by Jupiter, of Acesta or Segesta, the daughter of Hippotas, from whom he is named Hippotades. He dwelt in one of those seven islands, which from him are called Æoliæ, and sometimes Vulcaniæ. He [k] was a skilful astronomer, and an excellent natural philosopher; he understood more particularly the nature of the winds; and, by observing the clouds of smoke of the Æolian islands, he was enabled to foretel winds and tempests a great while before they arose, and it was generally believed that they were under his power, so that he could raise the winds, or still them as he pleased. Hence he was styled Emperor and King of the Winds, the children of Astræus and Aurora.

[i] Ov. Met. 11.

[k] Palæphat. de incredibil. Var. et Strabo ap. Serv.

[1] Virgil describes Juno coming to him, at his palace, of which he gives a description in beautiful verse.

QUESTIONS FOR EXAMINATION.

Who was Æolus, and where did he live?
What was his character as a philosopher?
What was generally believed of him?
How was he styled in consequence of this?
Give Virgil's fine description—
"Nimborum in patriam," &c.

[1] "Nimborum in patriam, loca fœta furentibus Austris,
Æoliam venit. Hic vasto rex Æolus antro
Luctantes ventos, tempestatesque sonoras
Imperio premit, ac vinclis et carcere frœnat.
Illi indignantes magno cum murmure montis
Circum claustra fremunt. Celsa sedet Æolus arce,
Sceptra tenens; mollitque animos, et temperat iras.
Ni faciat, maria ac terras, cœlumque profundum
Quippe ferant rapidi secum, verrantque per auras.
Sed pater omnipotens speluncis abdidit atris,
Hoc metuens; molemque, et montes insuper altos,
Imposuit; regemque dedit, qui fœdere certo,
Et premere, et laxat sciret dare jussus habenas."
Thus rag'd the goddess, and, with fury fraught,
The restless regions of the storms she sought.
Where, in a spacious cave of living stone,
The tyrant Æolus, from his airy throne,
With pow'r imperial curbs the struggling winds,
And sounding tempests in dark prisons binds.
This way and that, th' impatient captives tend,
And, pressing for release, the mountains rend.
High in his hall th' undaunted monarch stands,
And shakes his sceptre, and their rage commands;
Which did he not, their unresisted sway
Would sweep the world before them in their way:
Earth, air, and seas, through empty space would roll,
And heaven would fly before the driving soul.
In fear of this, the father of the gods
Confin'd their fury to these dark abodes,
And lock'd them safe, oppress'd with mountain-loads;
Impos'd a king, with arbitrary sway,
To loose their fetters, or their force allay.

CHAPTER V.

MOMUS.

THE name of the god Momus [m] is derived from the Greek, signifying a jester, mocker, a mimick; for that is his business. He follows no particular employment, but lives an idle life, yet nicely observes the actions and sayings of the other gods, and when he finds them doing amiss, or neglecting their duty, he censures, mocks, and derides them with the greatest liberty.

Neptune, Vulcan, and Minerva may witness the truth of this. They all contended for the mastery as the most skilful artificer; whereupon Neptune made a bull, Minerva a house, and Vulcan a man: Momus was appointed judge between them; but he chid them all three. He accused Neptune of imprudence, because he did not place the bull's horns in his forehead before his eyes; for then the bull might give a stronger and a surer blow. He blamed Minerva, because her house was immoveable; so that it could not be carried away, if by chance it was placed among bad neighbours. But he said that Vulcan was the most imprudent of them all, because he did not make a window in the man's breast, that we might see what his thoughts were, whether he designed some trick, or whether he intended what he spoke.

The parents of Momus were [n] Nox and Somnus. It is a sign of a dull, drowsy, sottish disposition, when we see a man satirizing and censuring the actions of all other men, because none but GOD is wholly perfect; some imperfection attaches to every other being, so that every thing is defective, and liable to blame.

[m] Μῶμος irrisorem significat.

[n] Hesiod. in Theog.

QUESTIONS FOR EXAMINATION.

What does the name Mòmus signify?

How is he employed?

For what did Neptune, Vulcan, and Minerva contend?

What was the decision of Momus with respect to their several performances?

Who were the parents of Momus?

What does a satirical temper indicate?

CHAPTER VI.

OF THE TERRESTRIAL GODDESS VESTA.

[o] VESTA, whom you see sitting and holding a drum, is the wife of Cœlum, and the mother of Saturn. She is the eldest of the goddesses, and is placed among the terrestrial goddesses, because she is the same with Terra, and has her name from [p] clothing, plants and fruits being the garments of the earth. Or, [q] according to Ovid, the earth is called Vesta from its stability, because it supports itself. She sits, [r] because the earth is immoveable, and was supposed to be placed in the centre of the world. Vesta has a drum, because the earth contains the boisterous winds in its bosom; and divers flowers weave themselves into a crown, with which her head is crowned. Several kinds of animals creep about and fawn upon her. Because the earth is round, Vesta's temple at Rome was also round, and some say that the image of Vesta was orbicular in some places, but

[o] Virg. Æn. 9. [p] Quòd plantis frugibusque terra vestiatur.

[q] "Stat vi terra sua, vistando Vesta vocatur." Fast. 6.

By its own strength supported Terra stands;
Hence it is Vesta nam'd.

[r] Var. ap. Aug. de Civ. Dei. 7. Cic. de Somno Hecat. Miles. general. Phurnutius.

Ovid says her image was rude and shapeless.[s] And hence round tables were anciently called [t] *vestæ*, because, like the earth, they supply all necessaries of life for us. [u] It is no wonder that the first oblations in all sacrifices were offered to her, since whatever is sacrificed springs from the earth. And the [w] Greeks both began and concluded their sacrifices with Vesta, whom they esteemed as the mother of all the gods.

There were two Vestas, the elder and the younger. The first, of whom I have been speaking, was the wife of Cœlum and the mother of Saturn. The second was the daughter of Saturn by his wife Rhea. And as the first is the same with Terra, so the other is the same with Ignis: and [x] her power was exercised about altars and houses. The word *vesta* is often put for *fire* itself, for it is derived from a [y] Greek word which signifies a chimney, a house, or household goods. [z] She is esteemed the president and guardian of houses, and one of the household deities, not without reason, since she invented the art of building houses: and therefore an image of Vesta, to which they sacrificed every day, was placed before the doors of the houses at Rome: and the places where these statues were set up were called *vestibula*, from Vesta.

This goddess was a [a] virgin, and so great an admirer of virginity, that when Jupiter her brother gave her liberty of asking what she would, she begged that she might always be a virgin, and have the first oblations in all sacrifices. She not only obtained her desire, but received this further honour [b] among the Romans, that

[s] "Effigiem nullam Vesta nec ignis habet." Fast. 6.
No image Vesta's shape can e'er express,
Or fire's ———

[t] Plut. in Sympos. [u] Hom. in Hymn.

[w] Ap. Lil. Gyr. 1. Strabo.

[x] Hujus vis omnis ad aras et focos pertinet. Cic. de Nat. Deor. 2.

[y] Ducitur à Græco nomine ἑστία quod *focum, penatem, domum* significat.

[z] Hom. in Hymn. Virg. Æn. 2. et Geo. 1. Eugráphius in And. Terent. act. 4. sc. 3. [a] Aristot. l. 2. Aristoph. in Vespis.

[b] Liv. 5. dec. 1. Val. Max. l. 4. c. 4. Pap. Stat. l. 4. Syl. 3.

a perpetual fire was kept in her temple, among the sacred pledges of the empire; not upon an altar, or in the chimnies, but in earthen vessels, hanging in the air; which the vestal virgins tended with so much care, that if by chance this fire was extinguished, all public and private business was interrupted, and a vacation proclaimed till they had expiated the unhappy prodigy with incredible pains; [c] and if it appeared that the virgins were the occasion of its going out, by carelessness, they were severely punished, and sometimes with rods.

In recompense for this severe law, the vestals obtained extraordinary privileges and respect: they had the most honourable seats at games and festivals: the consuls and magistrates gave way whenever they met them: their declarations in trials were admitted without the form of an oath; and, if they happened to encounter in their path a criminal going to the place of execution, he immediately obtained his pardon. Upon the calends of March, every year, though it was not extinguished, they used to renew it, with no other fire than that which was produced by the rays of the sun. Ovid mentions both the elder and the younger Vesta, [d] in the sixth book of his Fasti.

It has been conjectured, that when the poets say that Vesta is the same with fire, the fire of Vulcan's forge is not understood, nor yet the dangerous flames of Venus, but a pure, unmixed, benign flame, so necessary for us, that human life cannot possibly subsist without it; whose heat, being diffused through all the parts of the body, quickens, cherishes, refreshes, and nourishes it: a flame really sacred, heavenly, and divine; repaired daily by the food which we eat, and on which the safety and welfare of our bodies depend. This flame moves and actuates the whole body; and cannot be extinguished but when life itself ceases with it.

[c] Idem, c. 1. Ovid. Fast. 3.

[d] "Vesta eadem est, et Terra; subest vigil ignis utrique,
Significant sedem Terra focusque suam."
Vesta and Earth are one; one fire they share,
Which does the centre of them both declare.

QUESTIONS FOR EXAMINATION.

Who was Vesta?

Why is she placed among the terrestrial goddesses?

What reasons are assigned for the ornaments with which she is decked?

Why is Vesta's temple round?

What were the Vestæ?

Why were the first sacrifices offered to Vesta?

Why did the Greeks begin and conclude their sacrifices with Vesta?

Who were the two Vestas?

For what is the word "vesta" put?

Why is she esteemed the president and guardian of houses; and why was her image placed before the doors of the houses at Rome?

What favour did she ask of Jupiter; and what other honour did she obtain among the Romans?

What was the duty of the vestal virgins?

What was the punishment inflicted on them if they suffered the fire to go out?

What respect was paid them, by way of recompense for the severity of this law?

When and how was the vestal fire renewed?

What is understood by the vestal fire?

CHAPTER VII.

SECT. 1.—CYBELE. HER IMAGE. HER NAMES.

CYBELE is the goddess not of cities only, but of all things which the earth sustains. [e] She is the *Earth itself.* On the earth are built many towers and castles, so on her head is placed a crown of towers. In her hand she carries a key, [f] for in winter the earth locks up those treasures which she brings forth and dispenses with so much plenty in summer. She rides in a chariot,

[e] Serv. in Æn. 3 et 10. [f] Isid. l. 8.

because the earth hangs suspended in the air, balanced and poised by its own weight. But that chariot is supported by wheels, since the earth is a revolving body, and turns round; [g] and it is drawn by lions, because nothing is so fierce, so savage, or so ungovernable, but a motherly piety and tenderness is able to tame it, and make it submit to the yoke. I need not explain why her [h] garments are painted with diverse colours, and figured with the images of several creatures, since everybody sees that such a dress is suitable to the earth.

[i] She is called Cybele, and Ops, and Rhea, and Dyndymena, and Berecynthia, and Bona Dea (the good goddess), and Idæa, and Pessinuntia, and Magna Deorum Mâter (the great mother of the gods), and sometimes also Vesta. All these names, for different reasons, were given to the same goddess, who was the daughter of Cœlum by the elder Vesta, and Saturn's wife.

She is called Cybele, [k] from the mountain Cybelus in Phrygia, where sacrifices were first instituted to her. Or the name was given her from the behaviour of her priests, who used [l] to dance upon their heads, and toss about their hair like madmen, foretelling things to come, and making a horrible noise. They were named Galli, and this fury and outrage in prophesying is described by [m] Lucian in his first book.

Others again derive the word Cybele from a [n] cube, because the cube, which is a body every way square, was dedicated to her by the ancients.

She is called [o] Ops, because she brings help and assistance to every thing contained in this world.

[g] Ovid. Fast. 4. [h] Martin. Lil. Gyr.

[i] Propert. l. 3 el 16. [k] Stephanus Strabo.

[l] Ἀπὸ τῦ κυβιστᾷν vel κυβιλεῖν, id est, in caput saltare. Suid. Serv. in Æn. 3.

[m] —— "Crinemque rotantes
Sanguineum populis ulularunt tristia Galli."
Shaking their bloody tresses, some sad spell
The priests of Cybel to the people yell.

[n] Ἀπὸ τῦ κύβυ. Festus. [o] Quòd opem ferat.

Her name [p] Rhea is derived from the abundance of benefits, which, without ceasing, flow from her on every side.

[q] Dyndymene and Dindyme, is a name given her from the mountain Dindymus, in Phrygia.

Virgil calls her [r] *mater* Berecynthia, from Berecynthus, a castle in that country; and in the same place describes her numerous and happy offspring.

She was by the Greeks called [s] Pasithea; that is, as the Romans usually named her, the mother of all the gods; and from the [t] Greek word, signifying a mother. Her sacrifices were named Metroa, and to celebrate them was called Metrazein, in the same language.

Her name Bona Dea [u] implies that all good things necessary for the support of life proceed from her. She is also called Fauna, [w] because she is said to favour all creatures; and Fatua, [x] because it was thought that new born children never cried till they touched the ground. [y] It is said, that this Bona Dea was the wife of king Faunus; who beat her with myrtle rods till she died, because she disgraced herself, and acted very unsuitable to the dignity of a queen, by drinking so much wine that she became drunk. But the king afterwards,

[p] A ῥέω, fluo, quòd bonis omnibus circumfluat.
[q] Horat. l. 1. Carm.

[r] —— "Qualis Berecynthia mater
Invehitur curru Phrygiæ turrita per urbes
Læta Deum partu, centum complexa nepotes,
Omnes cœlicolas, omnes supera alta tenentes." Æn. 6.
High as the mother of the gods in place,
And proud, like her, of an immortal race;
Then, when in pomp she makes the Phrygian round,
With golden turrets on her temples crown'd,
A hundred gods her sweeping train supply,
Her offspring all, and all command the sky.

[s] Pasithea, id est, πᾶσι θεοῖς μητὴρ, omnibus diis mater. Luc. l. 2.
[t] A μητὴρ, mater, derivantur μητρῶα Cybeles sacra, et μητράζειν sacra ea celebrare. Cœl. Rhod. l. 8. c. 17.
[u] *Bona* quòd omnium nobis ad victum *bonorum* causa sit. Labeo. ap. Lil. Syntag. 4. p. 143.
[w] *Fauna* quòd animantibus *favere* dicatur.
[x] *Fatua* à *fando*, quòd infantes non prius vocem emittere crederentur quam terram ipsam attigissent. [y] Sext. Clod. apud. Lactant.

repenting of his severity, deified his dead wife, and paid her divine honours. This is the reason assigned why it was forbidden that any one should bring myrtle into her temple. [z] In her sacrifices, the vessels of wine were covered; and when the women drank out of them they called it milk, not wine. [a] The modesty of this goddess was so extraordinary, that no man ever saw her except her husband; or scarce heard her name: wherefore her sacrifices were performed in private, [b] and all men were excluded from the temple. From the great privacy observed by her votaries, the place in which her sacrifices were performed was called [c] Opertum, and the sacrifices themselves were styled [d] Opertanea, for the same reason that Pluto is by the poets called [e] Opertus. Silence was observed in a most peculiar manner in the sacrifices [f] of Bona Dea, as it was in a less degree in all other sacrifices; according to the doctrine of the Pythagoreans and Egyptians, who [g] taught, that GOD was to be worshipped in silence, since from this, at the first creation, all things took their beginning. To the same purpose, Plutarch says, "[h] Men were our masters to teach us to speak, but we learn silence from the gods: from those we learn to hold our peace, in their rites and initiations."

She was called [i] Idæa Mater, from the mountain Ida,

[z] Plut. in Probl. [a] Juvenal. sat. 9.

[b] "Sacra bonæ maribus non adeunda Deæ." Tib. 1. el. 6.
No men admitted were to Cybele's rites.

[c] Cic. 1. ad atticum et in Paradox. [d] Plin. l. 10 c 56.

[e] "Nosse domos Stygias, arcanaque Ditis Operti." Luc. l. 6.
To hear hell's secret counsels, and to know
Dark Pluto's rites and mysteries below.

[f] "Hinc mater cultrix Cybele Corybantiaque æra,
Idæumque nemus: hinc fida silentia sacris,
Et functi currum Dominæ subiêre Leones." Æneid. l. 3.
Here Cybele, the mother of the gods,
With tinkling cymbals charm'd th' Idæan woods.
She secret rites and ceremonies taught,
And to the yoke the savage lions brought.

[g] Ap. de la Cerda in Æneid. 3. [h] Loquendi magistros homines habemus, tacendi Deos: ab illis silentium accipientes in initiationibus et mysteriis. Plut. de Loquac. [i] Luc. l. 2.

in Phrygia, or Crete, for she was at both places highly honoured: as also at Rome, whither they brought her from the city Pessinus in Galatia, by a remarkable miracle. For when the ship, in which she was carried, stopped in the mouth of the Tiber, the vestal Claudia (whose fine dress and free behaviour made her modesty suspected) easily drew the ship to shore with her girdle, where the goddess was received by the hands of virgins, and the citizens went out to meet her, placing censers with frankincense before their doors; and when they had lighted the frankincense, they prayed that she would enter freely into Rome, and be favourable to it. And because the Sibyls had prophesied that Idæa Mater should be introduced by the "best man among the Romans, the senate [k] was a little busied to pass a judgment in the case, and resolve who was the best man in the city: for every one was ambitious to get the victory in a dispute of that nature more than if they stood to be elected to any commands or honours by the voices either of the senate or people. At last the senate resolved that P. Scipio, the son of Cneus, who was killed in Spain, a young gentleman who had never been quæstor, was the best man in the whole city."

She was called Pessinuntia, [l] from a certain field in Phrygia, into which an image of her fell from heaven; from this [m] the place was called Pessinus, and the goddess Pessinuntia. And here the Phrygians first began to celebrate the sacrifices Orgia to this goddess, near the river Gallus, from which her priests were called [n] Galli. When these priests desired that great respect and adoration should be paid to any thing, they pretended that it fell from heaven; and they called those

[k] Haud parvæ rei judicium senatum tenebat, qui vir optimus in civitate esset: verum certe victoriam ejus rei sibi quisque mallet, quàm ulla imperia, honoresve, suffragio seu Patrum, seu Plebis, delatos. Patres Conscripti P. Scipionem, Cnei filium ejus, qui in Hispania occidebat, adolescentem, nondum Quæstorum, judicaverunt in tota civitate virum optimum esse.

[l] Hesiod. l. l.

[m] Ἀπὸ τῦ πίπτειν, à cadendo.

[n] Festus.

images Διοπετη [*Diopete*] that is, "sent from" Jupiter. Of which sort were the [o] Ancile, the Palladium, and the effigies of this goddess, concerning which we now speak.

QUESTIONS FOR EXAMINATION.

Who was Cybele?
How is she represented?
In what does she ride; and how is she drawn?
Why are her garments of diverse colours?
Why is she called Cybele?
What were her priests called?
Why is she called Ops and Rhea?
Why and by whom is she called Dindyme and Berecynthia?
Repeat the lines from Virgil, and translation.
What was she called by the Greeks, and why?
What does the name Bona Dea imply?
Who was Bona Dea?
Why is myrtle prohibited from her temple?
What was observed in her sacrifices, and why?
What was the saying of Plutarch?
Why was Cybele called Idæa Mater?
Why was she called Pessinuntia?
Why were her priests called Galli; and under what pretence were they able to get particular respect paid to any thing?

SECT. 2.—OF THE SACRIFICES AND PRIESTS OF CYBELE.

Her sacrifices, like the sacrifices of Bacchus, [p] were celebrated with a confused noise of timbrels, pipes, and cymbals; and the sacrificants howled, as if they were mad: they profaned both the temple of their goddess, and the ears of their hearers, with their filthy words and actions. The following rites were peculiarly observed in her sacrifices: [q] her temple was opened, not by hands, but by prayers; none entered who had tasted garlic;

[o] Herod. l. 1. [p] Apulei 8. Metam. Claud. de Rap. Pros. 2.
[q] Serv. in Æn. 6. Athen. ap. Lil. Gyr. synt. 4. Lactant. p. in 8. Theb.

the priests sacrificed to her sitting, and touching the earth, and offered the hearts of the victims. And lastly, among the trees, the box and the pine were sacred to her: the box, because the pipes used in her sacrifices were made of it; [r] the pine, for the sake of Atys, Attes, or Attines, a boy that Cybele much loved, and made him president of her rights, upon condition that he always preserved his chastity inviolate. But he forgot his vow, and lost that virtue; [s] wherefore the offended goddess threw him into such a madness, that he was about to lay violent hands upon himself, but Cybele, in pity, turned him into a pine.

There was, however, a true Atys, the son of Crœsus king of Lydia. He was born dumb; but when he saw in the fight a soldier at his father's back, with a sword lifted up to kill him, the strings of his tongue, which hindered his speech, burst; and by speaking clearly, he prevented his father's destruction.

[t] The priests of Cybele were named Galli, from a river of Phrygia. Such was the nature of the water of this river, that whoever drank of it, immediately grew mad. The Galli were made eunuchs, and thence called Semiviri, and as often as they sacrificed, they furiously cut and slashed their arms with knives; and thence all furious and mad people were called Gallantes. [u] Beside the name of Galli, they were also called Curetes, Corybantes, Telchines, Cabiri, and Idæi Dactyli. Some say that these priests were different from the Galli; but most people believe them to be the same, and say that they were all priests of Cybele.

The Curetes were either Cretans, or Ætolians, or Eubœans, and had their names from [v] shaving; so that Curetes and Detonsi signify almost the same thing. For they shaved the hair of their heads before, but

[r] Serv. in Æn. 9.
[s] Aug. de Civ. Dei. 7.
[t] Lil. Gyr. p. 141.
[u] Var. apud Nonn. in verbo Castus.
[v] Ἀπὸ τῆς κουρᾶς, à tonsura Curetes dicebantur.

wore hair behind, that they might not be taken (as it has often happened) by the forelocks, by the enemy; or, perhaps, they were called Curetes, [w]because they were habited in long vests, like young maidens; or lastly, [x]because they educated Jupiter in his infancy.

Her priests were also called Corybantes; because in the sacrifices of their goddess they tossed their heads and danced, and butted with their foreheads like rams, after a mad fashion. Thus, when they initiated any one into their sacrifices, [y]they placed him in a chair, and danced about him like fools.

Another name of her priests was Telchines. These were famous magicians and enchanters; and they came from Crete to Cyprus, and thence into Rhodes, which latter island was called Telchines from them. [z]Or, if we believe others, they were deserving men, and invented many arts for the good of the public, and first set up the statues and the images of the gods.

The Cabiri, or Caberi, so called from Cabiri, mountains of Phrygia, [a]were either the servants of the gods, or gods themselves, or rather dæmons, or the same with the Corybantes; for the people's opinions concerning them are different.

The Idæi Dactyli [b]were the servants and assistants of Magna Mater; called Idæi from the mountain Ida, where they lived; and Dactyli [c]from the fingers; for these priests were ten, like the fingers: [d]they served Rhea every where, and in every thing, as if they were fingers to her. [e]Yet many affirm, that there were more than ten.

[w] Ἀπὸ τῆς κόρης, à puella, quòd puellarum stolam induebant.

[x] Ἀπὸ τῆς κοροτροφίας, ab educatione juvenum, quòd Jovem infantem aluisse perhibentur. Strabo.

[y] Ἀπὸ τοῦ κορύττειν, à cornibus feriendo, et βαίνειν incedendo. Strabo, l. 1. Plato in Euthid.

[z] Strabo, l. 1.

[a] Idem ibid.

[b] Sophocl. apud Lil. Gyr.

[c] Digiti enim Græcè dicuntur δακτυλοι.

[d] Jul. Pol. l. 1.

[e] Strabo. Diod. ap. Gyr.

QUESTIONS FOR EXAMINATION.

How were the sacrifices of Cybele celebrated?

What peculiar rites were observed in them?

Why were the box and pine sacred to Cybele?

On what condition was Atys made president of her rites, and what happened to him on his breaking his vow?

Who was the true Atys, and what is his history?

What property belonged to the river Gallus?

What is the origin of the word "gallantes?"

What other names have been given to the priests of Cybele?

From what did the Curetes derive their name?

From what circumstance were the Corybantes named?

Who were the Telchines?

Who were the Cabiri?

Who were the Idæi Dactyli?

CHAPTER VIII.

SECT. 1.—CERES. HER IMAGE AND SACRIFICES.

CERES is a tall majestic lady, who stands [f] beautified with yellow hair, and crowned with a turban composed of the ears of corn; her bosom swells with breasts as white as snow; her right hand is full of poppies and ears of corn, and in her left is a lighted torch. She is [g] the daughter of Saturn and Ops; whose singular beauty made the gods themselves her lovers and admirers. Her brothers Jupiter and Neptune fell in love with her, and betrayed her virtue. [h] She had Proserpine by Jupiter; and by Neptune it is uncertain whether she had a daughter or a horse; for, [i] as some say, when she avoided the pursuits of Neptune, who followed her, she cast herself among a drove of mares, and immediately put on the shape of a mare; which Neptune per-

[f] Ovid. Fast. 4. Arnobius. 5. contra Gentes. Martian. 2. de Nupt.
[g] Hesiod. in Theog. [h] Idem. ibid.
[i] Procl. in Georg. Virg.

ceiving, made himself a horse; and from them the horse Arion was produced. [k] Ovid himself is of this opinion: and hence I suppose the story comes which [l] Pausanias relates. Upon the mountain Æleus, in Arcadia, an altar was dedicated to Ceres; her image had the body of a woman, but the head of a horse; it remained entire and unhurt in the midst of fire. Yet others have told us, that Ceres did not bring forth a horse, but a daughter: [m] the Arcadians thought it a wicked thing to call this daughter by any other name than "[n] the lady," or "the great goddess," which were the usual names of her mother Ceres.

Ceres was greatly ashamed of this disgrace: she exceedingly lamented the loss of her honour, and testified her sorrow by the mourning clothes which she afterwards wore; whence she was named Melæna, Μελαινα *nigra:* she retired into the dark recesses of a cave, where she lay so privately that none of the gods knew where she was, till Pan, the god of the woods, discovered her by chance, and told Jupiter; who, sending the Fates to her, persuaded her at last to lay aside her grief, and rise out of the cave, which was a happy and joyful thing for all the world. For in her absence a great infection reigned throughout all sorts of living creatures, which sprang from the corruption of the fruits of the earth and the granaries every where. She is the goddess of the fruits, and her very name is derived [o] from the care which she exerts in producing or preserving them. It is supposed that she first in-

[k] "Et te, flava comas frugum mitissima mater,
Sensit equum." Met. 6.
The gold-hair'd gentle goddess Ceres knew
Thee in a horse's shape.

[l] Pausan. in Arcad. [m] Idem ibid.

[n] Δέσποινα Domina. et Magna Dea.

[o] Ceres dicitur quasi Ceres à gerendis fructibus: aut quasi Serens, vel ab antiquò verbo Cereo, quòd idem est ac Creo, quòd cunctarum frugum creatrix sit et altrix. Cic. Nat. Deo. 2. Maten. de prof. Rel. c. 18. Scaliger et Serv. in Geo. 1. Callimach. Hymn. in Cer. Plin. 7. c. 50.

vented and taught the art of tilling the earth, and sowing corn, and of making bread therewith, when before mankind only ate acorns. This may be learned from [p] Ovid, who tells us that Ceres was the first that made laws, provided wholesome food, and taught the art of husbandry, of plowing and sowing. For, before her time, the earth lay rough and uncultivated, covered with briars and unprofitable plants; when there were no proprietors of land, they neglected to cultivate it; when nobody had any ground of his own, they did not [q] care to fix landmarks; but all things were common to all men, till Ceres, who had invented the art of husbandry, taught men how to exercise it; and then they began to contend and dispute about the limits of those fields from the culture of which they reaped so much profit; and hence it was necessary that laws should be enacted to determine the rights and properties of those who contended. For this reason Ceres was named the [r] foundress of laws: and hence she is crowned with corn.

1. Ceres is beautiful and well shaped, because the earth, which she resembles, appears beautiful and delightful to the beholders; especially when it is arrayed with plants, diversified with trees, adorned with flowers, enriched with fruits, and covered with greens; when it displays the honours of spring, and pours forth the gifts of autumn with a bountiful hand.

2. Her hair is yellow, and when the ears of corn are ripe, they are adorned with that golden colour.

[p] "Prima Ceres unco glebam dimovit aratro,
Prima dedit fruges alimentaque mitia terris,
Prima dedit leges. Cereris sunt omnia munus."
Ceres was she who first our furrows plough'd;
Who gave sweet fruits, and easy food allow'd.
Ceres first tamed us with her gentle laws;
From her kind hand the world subsistence draws.

[q] "Aut signare quidem, aut partiri limite campum."
Or to make landmarks, or to balk their fields.

[r] Legifera, et Græce Θεσμόφορις; ejusque sacra dicebantur Θεσμοφόρια: Vocabatur etiam Ceres Δημήτηρ, quasi Γημήτηρ, id est, Terra mater. Virg. Æn. 3. and Servius, ibid.

3. Her breasts swell with milk, [s] whence she is styled Mammosa sometimes, [t] because after the earth is impregnated with seed, and big with the fruit thereof, it brings forth all things out of itself in abundance, and, like a mother, feeds and nourishes us; and hence she is called [u] Alma, and [w] Altrix nostra.

4. She holds a lighted torch, because when Proserpine was stolen away by Pluto, her mother [x] Ceres was greatly afflicted at the loss of her daughter, and, being very desirous to find her again, she kindled her torches with the flames which burst from the top of the mountain Ætna; and with them sought her daughter through the whole world.

5. She carries poppy, because, when through grief she could not obtain the least rest or sleep, Jupiter gave her poppy to eat; [y] for this plant is endued with a power to cause sleep and forgetfulness. Her grief was a little allayed by sleep, but she forgot not her loss, and, after many voyages and journeys, she at last heard where Proserpine was; as we shall hear in its proper place.

We often see a young man sitting in a chariot drawn by flying serpents. It is Triptolemus, in the chariot which Ceres gave him. He was the son of Celeus, king of Eleusis in Attica. Ceres brought him up from his infancy, upon this occasion: While she was seeking Proserpine by sea and land, [z] upon the way she came into the city Eleusis, where king Celeus entertained her; whose kindness she requited by bringing up his young son, whom, in the day-time she fed [a] with celestial and divine milk, but in the night covered him all over with fire. The child in a few days became a beautiful young man by this extraordinary manner of education. Meganira his mother, greatly wondering at this speedy progress, was very desirous to know how Ceres dealt

[s] Lil Gyr. synt. 14. [t] Cic. Nat. Deor. 2 and 3.
[u] Virg. Geo. 1. [w] Cic. Nat. Deor. 2. [x] Cic. in Verrem.
[y] Serv. in Geo. 1. [z] Callimach. Hymn. in Cer.
[a] Serv. in Geo. 1.

with her son; she therefore looked through a small hole, and saw Ceres cover her son Triptolemus with burning coal. This affrighted her so, that she cried out that Ceres was murdering her son; and ran into the room to save him. Ceres punished her imprudent curiosity with death; then putting Triptolemus into a splendid chariot, she sent him throughout the world, to show mankind the use of corn. He executed her commands so faithfully, and taught men the art of husbandry, of sowing, reaping, and of thrashing the corn so well, that hence he obtained his name [b] Triptolemus. [c] Ovid gives us an excellent description of this in the fifth book of his Metamorphoses.

Ceres once changed a boy into a newt: for, being very weary with travelling, and thirsty, she came to a cottage, and begged a little water, to wash her mouth, of an old woman that lived there; the old woman not only gave her water, but also barley-broth; which when the goddess took greedily, the woman's son, Stellio, a saucy boy, mocked her. This raised Ceres' indignation, that, in a rage, she flung some of the broth into the boy's face, [d] who was thereby changed into an evet or newt.

[b] Triptolemus dicitur quasi τρίψας τὰς ὔλας, id est, hordeum terens. Hygin. fab. 147.

[c] —— "Geminos dea fertilis angues
Curribus admovit: frænisque coërcuit ora;
Et medium cœli, terræque per aëra vecta est:
Atque levem currum Tritonida misit in arcem
Triptolemo; partimque rudi data semina jussit
Spargere humo, partim post tempora longa recultæ."
Ceres her chariot mounts: yok'd dragons stand,
Tame and obedient to her gentle hand:
With stretch'd-out wings, through yielding air they fly,
Till Ceres sends her chariot from the sky,
To good Triptolemus, her Athenian friend;
Triptolemus, whose useful cares intend
The common good: seed was the chariot's load,
Which she on him for public use bestow'd:
Part she for fallow fields new plough'd design'd,
And part for land by frequent tilth refined.

[d] "Fugit anum, latebramque petit, aptumque colori
Nomen habet, variis stellatus corpora guttis."
Flies the old wife, and creeps into a hole,
And from his speckled back a name he gets.

We may notice here Erisichthon, who, in contempt of the sacrifices of Ceres, defiled her groves, and cut down one of her oaks; for which he was punished with perpetual hunger: so that, when he has devoured all the meat and food which he can by any ways procure, he is forced to eat his own flesh to support his body; and to bring upon himself a horrible death, the better to sustain his life.

Among all the Cerealia, or sacrifices instituted to the honour of Ceres, these which follow are the chief: Eleusinia (by which name the [e] goddess herself was also known) were so called, because they were first celebrated in the city Eleusis. [f] Of these were two sorts; the Majora, consecrated to Ceres, and the Minora, to Proserpine. [g] It was a custom, that those who were initiated in the Majora, never pulled off the clothes which they then wore, till they fell into rags. [h] In both the Majora and Minora, a perpetual and wonderful silence was kept: to publish any thing concerning them was a crime; whence came the proverb concerning silent persons, Αττικα Ελευσινι [*Attica Eleusinia*], and the word *mysterium* signifies a "religious rite," from μυω [*muo*] *os claudo*. Lighted torches were used in their sacrifices, [i] because Ceres with them sought Proserpine: and up and down the streets and the highways they cried out "Proserpine!" till they had filled all places with their dismal howlings. Games were celebrated in these sacrifices, in which the victors [k] were honoured with a barley crown.

The [l] Thesmophoria were instituted by Triptolemus; and those women who vowed perpetual chastity were initiated in them. For some days a fast was kept; and wine was [m] altogether banished from her altar; whence this expression came, *Cereri nuptias facere*, which

[e] Pausan. in Attic. [f] Plut. in Demetrio. [g] Aristoph. in Pluto.
[h] Seneca, l. 7. nat. quæst. c. 31.
[i] "Nocturnisque Hecate triviis ululata per urbes" Æn. 4. vide Servium.
And Hecate by night adored with shrieks.
[k] Pindar. in Isthm. [l] Pliny, l. 24. [m] Serv. in Æn. 3.

p. 100.

H. Moses del. et sculp.

CERES

Published by Wilkie & Robinson, Paternoster Row, May [illegible]

(among the ancients) signifies a feast where there was no wine. Swine were sacrificed to this goddess, [n] because they hurt the fruits of the earth. And garlands, [o] composed of ears of corn, were offered to her.

Ambarvalia were instituted to purge the fields, and to beg fruitfulness and plenty. They were so called [p] because the sacrifices were led about the fields; as the suburbs [*amburbia*] were esteemed sacred, because the sacrifice was carried round the city. These sacrifices were performed by husbandmen, [q] who carried a sow big with young, or a cow-calf, through the corn and the hay, in the beginning of harvest, thrice; the countrymen following him with dancing and leaping, and acclamations of joy, till all the fields rung with the noise. In the mean time, one of them, adorned with a crown, sung the praises of Ceres; and after they had offered an oblation of wine mixed with honey and milk before they began to reap, they sacrificed the sow to her. [r] The rites of the Ambarvalia are beautifully described by Virgil.

[n] "Prima Ceres avidæ gavisa est sanguine porcæ,
Ulta suas meritâ cedæ nocentes opes." Ovid. Fast. 1.
Ceres with blood of swine we best atone,
Which thus requite the mischiefs they have done.

[o] "Flava Ceres, tibi sit nostro de rure corona
Spicea, quæ templi pendeat ante fores." Tibullus.
To thee, fair goddess, we'll a garland plait
Of ears of corn, t' adorn thy temple gate.

[p] Quod victima ambiret arva. Serv. in Geo. 1.

[q] Virg. Ecl. 3.

[r] "Cuncta tibi Cererem pubes agrestis adoret:
Cui tu lacte favos, et miti dilue Baccho,
Terque novas circum felix eat hostia fruges;
Omnis quam chorus et socii comitantur evantes,
Et Cererum clamore vocent in tecta: neque ante
Falcem maturis quisquam supponat aristis,
Quàm Cereri, torta redimitus tempora quercu,
Det motus incompositos, et carmina dicat." Geo. 1.
Let ev'ry swain adore her power divine,
And milk and honey mix with sparkling wine:
Let all the choir of clowns attend this show,
In long procession, shouting as they go;
Invoking her to bless their yearly stores,
Inviting plenty to their crowned floors.

QUESTIONS FOR EXAMINATION.

How is Ceres represented?

Who is she, and who were her brothers?

What story is told of her with regard to Neptune?

What kind of altar was dedicated to her on the mountain Æleus?

What were the usual names of her mother Ceres?

Why was she named Melæna?

Where did she conceal herself; who discovered her; and who persuaded her to come out of her retirement?

What happened to the world during her absence?

What inventions are inscribed to her?

Repeat the lines from Ovid, and also the translation.

In what respects does she resemble the earth?

Why does she hold a lighted torch in her hand?

Why does she carry a poppy?

What is the history of Triptolemus?

Give the lines from Ovid.

What is the history of Stellio?

What is the story of Erisichthon?

What were the Eleusinia, and what was the custom of those who were initiated in the Majora?

From what is the word "mystery" derived?

Why were lighted torches used in their sacrifices?

Who instituted the Thesmophoria, and who were initiated in them?

Why were the Ambarvalia instituted?

Repeat the lines from Virgil in which these sacrifices are described.

> Thus in the spring, and thus in summer's heat,
> Before the sickles touch the rip'ning wheat,
> On Ceres call; and let the lab'ring hind
> With oaken wreaths his hollow temples bind:
> On Ceres let him call, and Ceres praise,
> With uncouth dances, and with country lays.

CHAPTER IX.

SECT. 1.—THE MUSES. THEIR IMAGE, NAMES, AND NUMBER.

THE Muses are nine virgins, crowned with palms; their dress is decent and becoming. They sit together in the shade of a laurel arbour. Some of them play on the harp, some upon the cithern, some upon the pipe, some upon the cymbal, and some harmoniously sing and play at once. Methinks I hear them with united minds, voices, and hands, make an agreeable concord arise from their different instruments, governing their several voices in such a manner, as to produce the most noble harmony.

They are [s] the mistresses of all the sciences, the presidents of the musicians and poets, and the governors of the feasts and solemnities of the gods. [t] Jupiter begat them of the nymph Mnemosyne, who afterward brought them forth upon the mountain Pierius. [u] Some affirm that they had other parents, and [w] ancients writers say, that they lived before Jupiter, and were the daughters of Cœlum. They are called the daughters of Jupiter and Mnemosyne (which in Greek signifies "memory"), because all students and scholars ought not only to have great ingenuity, but ready memories.

The Musæ were formerly called Mosæ, and were so named from a [x] Greek word that signifies "to inquire," because men, by inquiring of them, learn the things of which they were before ignorant. But others say, they had their name from [y] their resemblance, because there is a similitude, and an affinity and relation between all the sciences; in which they agree, and are united with

[s] Orph. in Hymn. Mus.
[t] Hesiod. in Theog.
[u] Tzetzes Chil. 6. hist. 50.
[w] Mus. ap. Lil. Gyr.
[x] Ἀπὸ τῦ μῶσαι, id est, ab inquirendo. Plato in Cratylo.
[y] Μῦσαι, quasi ὁμοιοῦσαι, id est similes. Cassiodor.

one another. Wherefore the Muses are often painted with their hands joined, dancing in a ring: in the middle of them sits Apollo, their commander and prince. The pencil of nature described them in that manner upon the agate which Pyrrhus, who made war against the Romans, wore in a ring; for in it was a representation of the nine Muses, and Apollo holding a harp: and these figures were not delineated by art, but by the [z] spontaneous handywork of nature: and the veins of the stone were formed so regularly, that every Muse had her particular distinction.

They had each a name derived from some particular accomplishment of their minds or bodies.

The first, Calliope, was so called from [a] the sweetness of her voice; she presides over rhetoric, and is esteemed the most excellent of all the nine.

The second, Clio, is so named from [b] glory. For she is the historical muse, and takes her name from the excellence of the things she records.

The third, Erato, has her name from [c] love, because she sings of amours, or because learned men are beloved and praised by others. She is also called Soltatrix; for she first invented the art of dancing, over which she presided. She was also the inventress of poetry.

The fourth, Thalia, from [d] her gaiety, briskness, and pleasantry: because she sings pleasantly and wantonly. Some ascribe to her the invention of comedy, others of geometry.

The fifth, Melpomene, from [e] the excellency of her song, and the melody she makes when she sings. She is supposed to have presided over tragedy, and to have invented sonnets.

[z] Plin. l. 37. c. 1.

[a] Ἀπὸ τῆς καλῆς ὀπῆς à suavitate vocis.

[b] Ἀπὸ τῦ κλέυς, à gloria sc. rerum gestarum quas memorat. Schol. Ap 1.

[c] Ἀπὸ τῦ ἔρωτος, ab amore. Ovid. Art. Am. 2.

[d] Ἀπὸ τῦ Θαλλειν, id est, virere, germinare, et florere. Procl. in Hesiod.

[e] Α μέλπομαι canto et modulor, vel ἀπὸ τῦ μέλος ποιεῖν concentum facere.

The sixth, Terpsichore, has her name from [f] the pleasure she takes in dancing, because she delights in balls. Some call her Citharistria.

The seventh, Euterpe, or Euterpia, from [g] the sweetness of her singing. Some call her Tibicina, because, according to them, she presides over the pipes: and some say logic was invented by her.

The eighth, Polyhymnia, or Polymnia, or Polymneia, from [h] her excellent memory: and therefore [i] the invention of writing history is attributed to her, which requires a good memory. It was owing to her, [k] that the songsters add to the verses that they sing, hands and fingers which speak more than the tongue; an expressive silence; a language without words; in short, gesture and action.

The ninth, [l] Urania, was so called either because she sings of divine things; or because, through her assistance, men are praised to the skies; or because, by the sciences, they become conversant in the contemplation of celestial things.

Bahusius, a modern poet, has comprised the names of all the Muses in a [m] distich; that is, he has made the nine Muses to stand, which is something strange, but upon eleven feet. Perhaps you will remember their names better, when they are thus joined together in two verses.

The most remarkable of the names which are common to them all are:

Heliconide, or Heliconiades, from the mountain Helicon, in Bœotia.

Parnassides, from the mountain Parnassus, in Phocis,

[f] Ἀπὸ τέρπεσθαι τοῖς χόροις quod choreis delectetur.
[g] Ab εὐτερπής, jucunda nempe in concentu.
[h] A πολυς multus et μνεία memoria. Plu. in Sympos.
[k] Quod carminibus additæ sint orchestrarum loquacissimæ manus, linguosi digiti, silentium clamosum, expositio tacita, uno verbo gestus et actio. [l] Ἀπὸ τοῦ οὐρανοῦ, à cœlo.

[m] "Calliope, Polymneia, Erato, Clio, atque Thalia,
Melpomene, Euterpe, Terpsichore, Urania." L. 4. ep. 1.

which has two heads, [n] where, if any person slept, he presently became a poet. It was anciently called Larnassus, from Larnace, the ark of Deucalion, which rested here, and was named Parnassus after the flood, from an inhabitant of this mountain so called.

Citherides, or Citheriades, from the mountain Citheron, where they dwelt.

Aonides, from the country Aonia.

Pierides, or Pieriæ, [o] from the mountain Pierus, or Pieria, in Thrace; or from the daughters of Pierius and Anippe, who, daring to contend with the Muses, were changed into pies.

Pegasides and Hippocrenides, from the famous fountain Helicon, which by the Greeks is called [p] Hippocrene, and by the Latins [q] Caballinus, both which words signify the horse's fountain: it was also named Pegaseius, from Pegasus, the winged horse, [r] which, by striking a stone in this place with his foot, opened the fountain, [s] and the waters of it became vocal.

Aganippides, or Aganippeæ, from the fountain Aganippe.

Castalides, from the fountain Castalius, at the foot of Parnassus.

Some [t] write, that they were but three in the beginning; because sound, out of which all singing is formed, is naturally threefold: either made by the voice alone; or by blowing, as in pipes, or by striking, as in citherns and drums. Or it may be, because there are three tones of the voice or other instruments, the bass, the tenor, and the treble. [u] Or lastly, because all the sciences are distributed into three general parts, philosophy, rhetoric, and mathematics; and each of these parts is subdivided into three other parts; philosophy into logic, ethics, and physics; rhetoric into the demonstrative, deliberative, and judicial kind; mathematics into music,

[n] Persius in Procemio. [o] Idem ibid. [p] Ab ἵππος equus, et κρήνη fons [q] Caballinus, à Caballus, id est, equus.
[r] Ovid. Met. 5. [s] Sidonius Apollin. [t] Var. apud August.
[u] Phur. de Deorum Natura.

geometry, and arithmetic: and hence it came to pass, that they reckoned not only Three Muses, but Nine.

Others give us a different reason why they are Nine. [w] When the citizens of Sicyon appointed three skilful artificers to make the statues of the Three Muses, promising to choose those three statues out of the nine which they liked best, they were all so well made that they could not tell which to prefer; so that they bought them all, and placed them in the temples: and Hesiod afterward assigned to them the names mentioned above.

[x] Some affirm that they were virgins, and others deny it, who reckon up their children. Let no person, however, despise the Muses, unless he design to bring destruction upon himself by the example of Thamyras or [y] Thamyris; who, being conceited of his beauty and skill in singing, presumed to challenge the Muses to sing, upon condition, that if he was overcome, they should punish him as they pleased. And after he was overcome, he was deprived at once both of his harp and his eyes.

QUESTIONS FOR EXAMINATION.

Who are the Muses, and how are they dressed?

What is their employment?

Over what do they preside?

Who were their parents, and why are they called daughters of Jupiter and Mnemosyne?

Why were they formerly called Mosæ?

How were the Muses represented on Pyrrhus' ring?

From what were their names derived?

How did Calliope derive her name?

Who is Clio?

What does Erato derive her name from?

Why is Thalia so called?

What are the peculiar excellencies of Melpomene and Terpsichore?

[w] Var. apud August. ex Lil. Gyr.
[x] Plato ap. eundem. Vide Nat. Com.
[y] Hom. Iliad. 2. Plut. de Musica.

In what does Euterpe excel?

From what does Polyhymnia derive her name?

Why was Urania so named?

Repeat the distich of Bahusius.

Give some account of the names common to all the Muses.

How many Muses were there at first, and how were the Three converted into Nine?

What other reason is given?

What should the example of Thamyris teach?

CHAPTER X.

THEMIS, ASTRÆA, NEMESIS,

ARE three goddesses, who contrive and consult together on affairs of great moment.

Themis, the first of them, [z] is the daughter of Cœlum and Terra. According to the [a] signification of her name, her office is to instruct mankind to do things honest, just, and right. [b] Therefore her images were brought and placed before those who were about to speak to the people, that they might be admonished thereby to say nothing in public but what was just and righteous. Some say, [c] she spoke oracles at Delphi, before Apollo; though [d] Homer says, that she served Apollo with nectar and ambrosia. There was another Themis, of whom Justice, Law, and Peace, are said to be born. Hesiod, by way of eminence, calls her [e] modest, because she was ashamed to say any thing that was done against right and equity. Eusebius calls her Carmenta; [f] because by her verse and precepts she

[z] Hesiod. in Theog. [a] Θέμις enim significat fas. [b] Ex. Lil. Gyr.
[c] Ovid Met. 1. [d] Hymn. in Apollinem. [e] Ἀιδοίην, id est, pudibundam. Hesiod. in Theog.
[f] Quòd carminibus edictisque suis præcipiat unicuique quod justum est. Euseb. Præp. Evang. l. 3.

directs every one to that which is just. But here he means a different Carmenta from the Roman Carmenta, who was the mother of Evander, otherwise called Themis Nicostrata, a prophetical lady. [g]She was worshipped by the Romans, because she prophesied; and was called Carmenta, either [h]from the verse in which she uttered her predictions, or [i]from the madness which seemed to possess her when she prophesied. To this lady an altar was dedicated near the gate Carmentalis, by the Capitol; and a temple was also built to her honour upon this occasion: When [k]the senate forbad the married women the use of litters or sedans, they combined together, and resolved, that they would never bring children, unless their husbands rescinded that edict: they kept to this agreement with so much resolution, that the senate was obliged to change their sentence, and yield to the women's will, and allow them all sedans and chariots again. And when their wives conceived and brought forth fine children, they erected a temple in honour of Carmenta.

Astræa, [l]the daughter of Aurora and Astræus the Titan (or, as others rather say, the daughter of Jupiter and Themis), was esteemed [m]the princess of Justice. The poets feign, that in the Golden Age she descended from heaven to the earth; and being offended at last by the wickedness of mankind, [n]she returned to heaven again, after all the other gods had gone before her. She is many times directly called by the name of Justitia; as particularly by [o]Virgil. And when she had

[g] Solinus in descriptione Romæ. [h] A Carmine. Ovid. Fast.
[i] Quasi carens mente. [k] Vide Ovid. in Fast. l. 2.
[l] Hesiod in Theog. [m] Justitiæ antistita.

[n] "Victa jacet pietas, et virgo cæde madentes
Ultima cœlestûm terras Astræa reliquit."
All duty dies, and wearied justice flies
From bloody earth at last, and mounts the skies.

[o] ——— "Extrema per illos
Justitia excedens terris vestigia fecit." Geo. 2.
Justice last took her flight from hence, and here
The prints of her departing steps appear.

returned to heaven again, she was placed where we now see the constellation [p] Virgo.

The parents of Nemesis were [q] Jupiter and Necessity; or, according to others, Nox and Oceanus. She was the goddess that rewarded virtue, and punished vice: and she taught men their duty, so that she received her name [r] from the distribution that she made to every body. Jupiter enjoyed her, as the story says, in the shape of a goose; [s] and afterward she brought forth an egg, which she gave to a shepherd whom she met, to be carried to Leda. Leda laid up the egg in a box, and Helena was soon after produced of that egg. But others give us quite different accounts of the matter. The Romans certainly sacrificed to this goddess, when they went to war; whereby they signified that they never took up arms unless in a just cause. She is called by another name, Adrastæa, from Adrastus, a king of the Argives, who first built an altar to her; or, perhaps, from [t] the difficulty of escaping from her: because no guilty person can flee from the punishment due to his crime, though Justice sometimes overtakes him late. She has indeed [u] wings, but does not always use them; but then [w] the slower her foot is, the harder is her hand. Rhamnusia is another name of this goddess, from Rhamnus, a town in [x] Attica, where she had a temple, in which [y] there was a statue of her made of one stone, ten cubits high; she held the bough of an apple-tree in her hand, and had a crown upon her head, in

[p] Bocca. Gen. Deor. 4.

[q] Pausan. in Arcad.

[r] Ἀπὸ τῆς ἑκάστῳ ἐπινεμήσεως, à distributione quæ unicuique sit. Plato de Legibus Dial.

[s] Apollod. l. 3. Biblioth.

[t] Ab α non, et διδράσκω fugio, quòd videlicet nemo nocens effugere queat pœnam suis sceleribus debitam.

[u] Pausan. in Attic.

[w] "Ad scelerum pœnas ultrix venit ira tonantis,
Hoc graviore manu, quo graviore pede.
Vengeance divine to punish sin moves slow.
The slower is its pace, the surer is its blow.

[x] Strabo, l. 2.

[y] In Atticis.

which many images of deer were engraven. [z]She had also a wheel, which denoted her swiftness when she avenges.

QUESTIONS FOR EXAMINATION.

Who are the goddesses that are consulting together on important business?

Who was Themis; what was her business? and why were her images placed before public speakers?

Who were the children of the other Themis?

Why was Themis styled modest by Hesiod; and Carmenta by Eusebius?

Why was a temple erected in honour of Carmenta?

Who was Astræa?

What does Virgil say of her?

Who were the parents of Nemesis?

When did the Romans sacrifice to her?

Why was she called Adrastæa?

Why is she named Rhamnusia?

CHAPTER XI.

THE GODS OF THE WOODS, AND THE RURAL GODS.

PAN. HIS NAMES, DESCENT, ACTIONS, &c.

WE are now come to the images of the gods and goddesses of the woods. Here you may see the gods Pan, Silvanus, the Fauni, the Satyri, Silenus, Priapus, Aristæus, and Terminus.

And there you see the goddesses, Diana, Pales, Flora, Feronia, Pomona, and an innumerable company of Nymphs.

[z] "Sed Dea, quæ nimiis obstat Rhamnusia votis,
Ingemuit, flexitque rotam." Claudian.
Th' avenging goddess, t' our desires unbent,
First groan'd, then turned her wheel.

Pan is called by that name, either, as some tell us, [a]because he was the son of Penelope by all her wooers; or, [b]because he exhilarated the minds of all the gods with the music of the pipe, which he invented; and by the harmony of the cithern, upon which he played skilfully as soon as he was born. Or, perhaps, he is called Pan, [c]because he governs the affairs of the universal world by his mind, as he represents it by his body.

The Latins called him Inuus and Incubus, the "nightmare;" and at Rome he was worshipped, and called [d]Lupercus and Lyceus. To his honour a temple was built at the foot of the Palatine hill, and festivals called Lupercalia were instituted, in which his priests, the Luperci, ran about the streets naked.

His descent is uncertain: but the common opinion is, that he was born of Mercury and Penelope. [e]For when Mercury fell violently in love with her, and tried in vain to move her, at last, by changing himself into a very white goat, he obtained his desire, and begat Pan when she kept the sheep of her father Icarius in the mount Taygetus. Pan, after he was born, [f]was wrapt up in the skin of a hare, and carried to heaven.

He is represented as a [g]horned half goat, that resembles a beast rather than a man, much less a god. He has a smiling ruddy face, his nose is flat, his beard comes down to his breast, his skin is spotted, and he has the tail, thighs, legs, and feet of a goat; his head is crowned or girt about with pine, and he holds a crooked staff in one hand, and in the other a pipe of uneven reeds, with the music of which he can cheer even the gods themselves.

When the Gauls, under Brennus their leader, made an irruption into Greece, and were just about to plunder the city Delphi, Pan, so terrific in appearance,

[a] A Πᾶν omne, quòd ex omnium procorum congressu cum Penelope sit natus Samius. [b] Hom. in Hymn. [c] Phurnut.
[d] Justin. l. 43. [e] Herod. in Euterpe. [f] Hom. in Hymn.
[g] Lucian. in Bacch.

alarmed them to such a degree, that they all betook themselves to flight, though nobody pursued them. Whence we proverbially say, that men are in [h] panic fear, when we see them affrighted without a cause.

Now hear what the image of Pan signifies. Pan is a symbol of the world. [i] In his upper part he resembles a man, in his lower part a beast; because the superior and celestial part of the world is beautiful, radiant, and glorious: as is the face of this god, whose horns resemble the rays of the sun, and the horns of the moon: the redness of his face is like the splendor of the sky; and the spotted skin that he wears, is an image of the starry firmament. In his lower parts he is shagged and deformed, which represents the shrubs, and wild beasts, and trees, of the earth below: his goats' feet signify the solidity of the earth; and his pipe of seven reeds, that celestial harmony which is made by the seven planets. He has a sheephook, crooked at the top, in his hand, which signifies the turning of the year into itself.

The nymphs dance to the music of his pipe; [k] which instrument Pan first invented. You will wonder when you hear the relation which the poets give of this pipe, namely, [l] as oft as Pan blows it, the dugs of the sheep are filled with milk: for he is the god of the shepherds and hunters, the captain of the nymphs, the president of the mountains and of a country life, and the [m] guardian of the flocks that graze upon the mountains. Although his aspect is so deformed, yet when he changed himself into a white ram, he pleased and gratified Luna, [n] as it is reported. The nymph Echo fell also in love

[h] Terrores Panici eorum sunt qui sine causâ perterrentur Pausan. Plutarch. [i] Serv. in Ecl. 3.

[k] "Pan primus calamos cerâ conjungere plures
Instituit." Virg. Ecl. 2.
Pan taught to join with wax unequal reeds

[l] Orph. in Hymn. Ibicus, Poëta Græcus.

[m] —— "Pan curat oves, oviumque magistros." Virg Ecl. 2.
Pan loves the shepherds, and their flocks he feeds.

[n] "Munere sic niveo lanæ, si credere dignum est,
Pan Deus Arcadiæ captam te, Luna fefellit." Virg Geo. 3.

with him, and brought him a daughter named Iringes, who [o] gave Medea the medicines with which she charmed Jason. [p] He could not but please Dryope, to gain whom, he laid aside his divinity, and became a shepherd. But he did not court the nymph Syrinx with so much success: for she ran away to avoid her filthy lover; till coming to a river (where her flight was stopped), she prayed the Naïades, the nymphs of the waters, because she could not escape her pursuer, to change her into a bundle of reeds, just as Pan was laying hold of her, [q] who therefore caught the reeds in his arms instead of her. [r] The winds moving these reeds backward and forward occasioned mournful but musical sounds, which Pan perceiving, he cut them down, and made of them reeden pipes. But [s] Lucretius ascribes the invention of

'Twas thus with fleeces milky white (if we
May trust report) Pan, god of Arcady,
Did bribe thee, Cynthia, nor didst thou disdain,
When call'd in woody shades, to ease a lover's pain.

[o] Theætet. Poeta Græcus. [p] Hom. in Hymn.

[q] "Hic se mutarent liquidas oràsse sorores:
Panaque cum prensam sibi jam Syringa putaret
Corpore pro nymphæ calamos trivisse palustres." Ovid. Met. 1.
When, that she might avoid a lustful rape,
She begg'd her sister nymphs to change her shape:
Pan thought h' had hugg'd his mistress, when indeed
He only hugg'd a truss of moorish reed.

[r] "Dumque ibi suspirat, motos in arundine ventos
Effecisse sonum tenuem similemque querenti.
Arte novâ, vocisque Deum dulcedine captum,
Hoc mihi concilium tecum, dixisse, manebit;
Atque ita disparibus calamis compagine ceræ
Inter se junctis nomen tenuisse puellæ."
He sighs, his sighs the tossing reeds return
In soft small notes, like one that seem'd to mourn.
The new, but pleasant notes the gods surprise,
Yet this shall make us friends at last, he cries:
So he this pipe of reeds unequal fram'd
With wax, and Syrinx from his mistress nam'd.

[s] —— "Zephyri cava per calamorum sibila primum
Agrestes docuere cavas inflare cicutas;
Inde minutatim dulces didicere querelas,
Tibia quas fundit digitis pulsata canentum:
Avia per nemora ac sylvas saltusque reperta,
Per loca pastorum deserta, atque otia Dia." Lucr. l. 5.

H. Moses del. et sculp.

PAN

Published by Wilkie & Robinson, Paternoster Row, May 1. 1810.

these pipes not to Pan, but to some countrymen, who had observed, on another occasion, the whistling of the wind through reeds. In the sacrifices of this god, [t] they offered to him milk and honey in a shepherd's bottle. He was more especially worshipped in Arcadia, for which reason he is so often called [u] Pan, Deus Arcadiæ.

Some derive from him [w] Hispania, Spain, formerly called Iberia; for he lived there, when he returned from the Indian war, to which he went with Bacchus and the Satyrs.

QUESTIONS FOR EXAMINATION.

From what does Pan derive his name?

What was he called by the Latins; and under what titles was he worshipped at Rome?

What is the origin of Pan?

How is he represented?

What is the origin of the phrase "panic-struck?"

What does the image of Pan signify?

What instrument did he invent, and what occurs when he blows his pipe?

What is said of his amours?

What happened to him in his courtship of Syrinx?

Repeat the lines of Ovid—

"Dumque ibi suspirat," &c.

What does Lucretius say of the invention of the pipes?

Repeat the lines.

What were used in the sacrifices of Pan?

Whence is he derived?

And while soft ev'ning gales blew o'er the plains,
And shook the sounding reeds, they taught the swains;
And thus the pipe was fram'd, and tuneful reed:
And while the tender flocks securely feed,
The harmless shepherds tune their pipes to love,
And Amaryllis sounds in ev'ry grove.

[t] Theocr. in Viator. [u] Virg. Geo. 3. et Ecl. 4. [w] Lil. Gyr.

CHAPTER XII.

SILVANUS AND SILENUS.

ALTHOUGH many writers confound the Silvani, Fauni, Satyri, and Sileni, with Pan, yet, as others distinguish them, we shall treat of them separately, and begin with Silvanus.

Silvanus, who is placed next to Pan, with the feet of a goat, and the [x] face of a man, of little stature. [y] He holds cypress in his hand stretched out. He is so called from *silvæ*, the woods; for he presides over them. [z] He mightily loved the boy Cyparissus, who had a tame deer, in which he took great pleasure. Silvanus by chance killed it; upon which the youth died for grief. [a] Therefore Silvanus changed him into a cypress-tree, and carried a branch of it always in his hand, in memory of his loss. There were many other Silvani, who endeavoured to violate the chastity of women. St. [b] Augustin says, that they and the Fauni (commonly called Incubi) were exceedingly mischievous and licentious.

Silenus follows next, with a flat nose, bald head, large ears, and with a small flat body: he derives his name [c] from his jocular temper, because he perpetually jests upon people. He sits upon a [d] saddlebacked ass; but when he walks, he leans upon a staff. He was foster-father to Bacchus his master, and his perpetual com-

[x] Ælian. Hist. Variæ. [y] Martin. de Nuptiis. [z] Serv in Æn. et Geo.

[a] "Et teneram à radice ferens, Silvane, cupressum." Geo. I.
A tender cypress plant Silvanus bears.

[b] Eos cum Faunis (quos vulgo Incubos vocant) improbos sæpè extitisse mulieribus, et earum appetisse, et peregisse concubitum. Civ Dei. l. 15. c. 23. [c] Ἀπὸ τοῦ σιλλαίνειν, id est, dicteria in aliquem dicere. Ælian. 3. Var. Hist. c. 10. [d] Pando Asello.

panion, and consequently almost always drunk, as we find him described [e] in the sixth Eclogue of Virgil. The cup which he and Bacchus used, was called Cantharus; and the staff with which he supported himself, [f] Ferula: this he used when he was so drunk, as it often happened, that he could not sit, [g] but fell from his ass.

The Satyrs were not only constant companions of Silenus, but very assistant to him; for they held him in great esteem, and honoured him as their father; and, [h] when they became old, they were called Sileni too. And concerning Silenus' ass, they say, that [i] he was translated into heaven, and placed among the stars; because in the giants' war, Silenus rode on him, and helped Jupiter very much.

[k] When Silenus was asked, "What was the best thing that could befal man?" he, after long silence, answered, "It is best for all never to be born, but being born, to die very quickly." Which expression Pliny reports nearly in the same words: [l] There have been

[e] "Silenum pueri somno videre jacentem,
Inflatum hesterno venas, ut semper, Iaccho;
Serta procul, tantum capiti delapsa jacebant,
Et gravis attritâ pendebat cantharus ansâ."
—— Two Satyrs, on the ground,
Stretch'd at his ease, their sire Silenus found;
Dos'd with his fumes and heavy with his load,
They found him snoring in his dark abode;
His rosy wreath was dropp'd not long before,
Borne by the tide of wine, and floating on the floor.
His empty can, with ears half worn away,
Was hung on high, to boast the triumph of the day

[f] "Quinque senex ferula titubantes ebrius artus
Sustinet, et pando non fortiter hæret asello." Ovid. Met. 4.
His staff does hardly keep him on his legs,
When mounted on his ass, see how he swags.

[g] "Ebrius ecce senex, pando delapsus asello,
Clamarunt Satyri, surge, age, surge, pater." Ov. Art. Am. 2.
Th' old soker's drunk, from 's ass he's got a fall,
Rouse, father, rouse, again the Satyrs bawl.

[h] Pausan. in Attic. [i] Aratus in Phænomen. [k] Rogatus quidnam, esset hominibus optimum? respondit omnibus esse optimum non nasci, et natos quam citissime interire. Plut. in Consolatione Apol.

[l] Multi extitere qui non nasci optimum censerunt, aut quam citissime aboleri. In Præfat. l. 7.

many who have judged it happy never to have been born, or to die immediately after one's birth.

QUESTIONS FOR EXAMINATION.

How is Silvanus represented?

From what is his name derived?

Why is he represented with a branch of cypress in his hand?

What character does St. Augustin give of the Silvani?

How is Silenus represented?

How is he described by Virgil?

What are his cup and staff called?

Who were his companions?

What became of his ass?

What was the decision of Silenus with respect to the best thing that can befal man?

CHAPTER XIII.

THE SATYRS, FAUNS, PRIAPUS, ARISTÆUS, TERMINUS.

BEHOLD! [m] Those are Satyrs who dance in lascivious motions and postures, under the shade of that tall and spreading oak; they have heads armed with horns, and goats' feet and legs, crooked hands, rough hairy bodies, and tails not much shorter than horses' tails. There is no animal in nature more salacious and libidinous than these gods. Their [n] name itself shows the filthiness of their nature: and Pausanias gives a proof of it, by relating a story of some mariners, who were drove upon a desert island by storm, and saw themselves surrounded by a flock of Satyrs; the seamen were frightened, and betook themselves to their ships, and the Satyrs left the men, but they seized the women, and committed all manner of wickedness with them.

[m] Pausan. in Attic. Euseb. Præp. Evan.

[n] Satyrus derivatur ἀπὸ τῆς σαθῆς a veretro.

The Fauns, whom you see joined with the Satyrs, differ from them in the name only; at least they are not unlike them in their looks: [o] for they have hoofs and horns, and are [p] crowned with the branches of the pine. When they meet drunken persons, they stupify them with [q] their looks alone. The boors of the country call them the [r] "rural gods;" and pay them the more respect, because they are armed with horns and nails, and painted in terrible shapes.

Faunus, or Fatuellus, [s] was the son of Picus king of the Latins. [t] He married his own sister, whose name was Fauna or Fatuella: he consecrated and made her priestess, after which she had the gift of prophecy. History likewise tells us that this Faunus was the father and prince of the other fauns and satyrs. [u] His name was given him from his skill in prophesying; and thence also *fatus* signifies both persons that speak rashly and inconsiderately, and enthusiasts; because they who prophesy, deliver the mind and will of another, and speak things which themselves, many times, do not understand.

Priapus, painted with a sickle in his hand, was the son of Venus and Bacchus, born at Lampsacus; from whence he was banished, till by the oracle's command he was recalled, and made god of the gardens, and crowned with garden herbs. He carries a sickle in his hand, to cut off from the trees all superfluous boughs, and to drive away thieves and beasts, and mischievous birds; whence he is called Avistupor. His image is usually placed in gardens, as we may learn from [w] Ti-

[o] Ovid. Fast. 2.
[p] Idem in Epist. Oenones. [q] Idem. in Epist. Phædræ.
[r] Dii agrestes. Virg. Geo. 1. [s] Serv. Æn. 6.
[t] Nat. Comes. l. 5. [u] Faunus dicitur à *fando* seu vaticinando. Serv. in Æn. 7. Isid. Hisp. Episcopus.
[w] "Pomosisque rubor custos ponatur in hortis,
Arceat ut sævâ falce Priapus aves."
With the swarthy guardian god our orchards grace;
With his stiff sickle he the birds will chace.

bullus, [x] Virgil, and [y] Horace. He is called Hellespontiacus by the poets; because the city of Lampsacus, where he was born, was situate upon the Hellespont. He was very deformed, which misfortune was occasioned by the ill usage that his mother suffered, while pregnant, from Juno. He was named Priapus, Phallus, and Fascinum, from his deformity. All these names savour of obscenity; though by some [z] he is called Bonus Dæmon, or Genius.

Aristæus, whom you see busied in that nursery of olives, supporting and improving the trees, is employed in drawing oil from the olive, which art he first invented. He also found out the use of honey, and therefore you see the rows of bee-hives near him. [a] For which two profitable inventions, the ancients paid him divine honours.

He was otherwise called Nomius and Agræus, and was the son of [b] Apollo by Cyrene; or, as Cicero says, the son of Liber Pater, educated by the nymphs, and taught by them the art of making oil, honey, and cheese. He fell in love with Euridice, the wife of Orpheus, and pursued her into a wood, where a serpent stung her so that she died. On this account the nymphs hated him, and destroyed all his bees to revenge the death of Euridice. The loss was exceedingly deplored by him; and asking his mother's advice, he was told by the

[x] "Et custos furum atque avium cum falce saligna
Hellespontiaci servet tutela Priapi." Geo. 1.
Beside the god obscene, who frights away,
With his lath sword, the thieves and birds of prey.

[y] "Olim truncus eram ficulnus, inutile lignum,
Cum faber incertus, scamnum faceretne Priapum,
Maluit esse Deum. Deus inde ego furum aviumque
Maxima formido." Sat. 8.
Till artists doubting which the log was good
For, stool or god; resolv'd to make a god:
So I was made; my form the log removes:
A mighty terror I to birds and thieves.

[z] Vide Phurnutium.

[a] Pausan. in Arcad.

[b] Apollon. l. 6. in Verr.

oracle, that he ought by sacrifices to appease Euridice. Wherefore he sacrificed to her four bulls and four heifers, and his loss was supplied; for suddenly a swarm of bees burst forth from the carcases of the bulls.

Another god, greatly honoured in the city of Rome, is Terminus, because they imagine that the boundaries and limits of men's estates are under his protection. His name, and the divine honours paid to him by the ancients, are mentioned by [c] Ovid, [d] Tibullus, and [e] Seneca. The statue of this god [f] was either a square stone, or a log of wood planed; which they usually perfumed with ointment, and crowned with garlands.

And indeed the Lapides Terminales (that is, "landmarks") were esteemed sacred; [g] so that whoever dared to move, or plough up, or transfer them to another place, his head became devoted to the Diis Terminalibus, and it was lawful for any body to kill him.

And further, though they did not sacrifice the lives of animals to those stones, because they thought that it was not lawful to stain them with blood; yet they offered wafers made of flour to them, and the first fruits of corn, and the like: and upon the last day of the year they always observed festivals to their honour, called Terminalia.

QUESTIONS FOR EXAMINATION.

How are the Satyrs represented?

What does Pausanias relate of some Satyrs?

[c] "Termine sive lapis, sive es desertus in agro
Stipes, ab antiquis tu quoque nomen habes." Fast. 3.
Terminus, whether stump or stone thou be,
The ancients gave a godhead too to thee.

[d] "Nam veneror, seu stipes habet desertus in agris,
Seu vetus in triviis florida serta lapis."
For I my adoration freely give,
Whether a stump forlorn my vows receive,
Or a beflower'd stone my worship have.

[e] —— "Nullus in campo sacer
Divisit agro arbiter populis lapis." Hippol. act. 2.
The sacred landmark then was quite unknown.

[f] Arnobius contra Gentes, l. 1. Clemens Alex. Strom. 7.

[g] Dion. Halicarn. l. 2.

How are the Fauns represented, and what are they called by the country-boors?
What does history say of Faunus?
How did he obtain his name?
Who was Priapus, and where was he born?
How is he represented, and for what is the sickle in his hands?
Why was he called Hellespontiacus?
Where is his image placed?
What is Aristæus's employment?
What did he invent?
Why was he called Nomius?
What is the story of Euridice?
How did Terminus derive his name?
What was his statue?
What is said of the Lapides Terminales?
What did the ancients offer as sacrifices to these stones?

CHAPTER XIV.

THE GODDESSES OF THE WOODS.

DIANA.

HERE comes a goddess, [h]taller than the other goddesses, in whose virgin looks we may ease our eyes, which have been wearied with the horrid sight of those monstrous deities. Welcome, Diana! [i]your hunting habit, the bow in your hand, and the quiver full of arrows, which hangs down from your shoulders, and the skin of a deer fastened to your breast, discover who you are. [k]Your behaviour, which is free and easy, but modest and decent; your garments, which are handsome and yet careless, show that you are a virgin. Your [l]name indicates your modesty and honour. I wish that

[h] Virg. Æn. 1. [i] Idem ibid.
[k] Pausan. in Arcad. [l] Ἄρτεμις, ab ἀρτεμής, perfectus, pudicitiam integritatemque Dianæ indicat. Strabo, l. 14.

you, who are the tallest of the goddesses, [m] to whom women owe their stature, would implant in them also a love of your chastity.

Actæon, the son of Aristæus, [n] the famous huntsman, looking impudently upon you, as you were naked in the fountain, was changed into a deer, which was afterward torn in pieces by his own dogs.

Further honour is due to you; because you represent the Moon, [o] the glory of the stars, and the only goddess [p] who observed perpetual chastity.

Nor am I ignorant of that famous and deserving action which you did, to avoid the flames of Alpheus, [q] when you so hastily fled to your nymphs, who were all together in one place; and so besmeared both yourself and them with dirt, that when he came he did not know you: whereby your honest deceit succeeded according to your intentions; and the dirt, which injures every thing else, added a new lustre to your virtue. Welcome once again, O [r] guardian of the mountains! by whose kind assistance women in child-bed are preserved from death.

Diana is called [s] Triformis and Tergemina. First, because though she is but one goddess, yet she has three different names, as well as three different offices.

[m] Hom. Odyss. 20. [n] Ovid. Met. 4.
[o] Astrorum decus. Virg. Æn. 9.
[p] "Æternum telorum et virginitatis amorem
Intemerata colit." Virg. Æn. 11
—— Herself untainted still,
Hunting and chastity she always lov'd.
[q] Pausan. in poster. Eliac.
[r] "Montium custos, nemorumque virgo,
Quæ laborantes utero puellas
Ter vocata audis admisque letho.
Diva triformis." Hor. Carm. l. 3.
Queen of the mountains and the groves!
Whose hand the teeming pain removes,
Whose aid the sick and weak implore,
And thrice invoke thy threefold pow'r.
[s] Nat. Cic. Deor. 3.

In the heavens she is called Luna; on the earth she is named Diana; and in hell she is styled Hecate or Proserpine. In the heavens she enlightens every thing by her rays; on the earth she keeps under her power all wild beasts by her bow and her dart; and in hell she keeps all the ghosts and spirits in subjection to her by her power and authority. These several names and offices are comprised in an ingenious [t] distich. But although [u] Luna, Diana, and Hecate are commonly thought to be only three different names of the same goddess, yet [w] Hesiod esteems them three distinct goddesses. Secondly, because she has, as the poets say, three heads; the head of a horse on the right side, of a dog on the left, and a human head in the midst: whence some call her [x] three-headed, or three-faced. And [y] others ascribe to her the likeness of a bull, a dog, and a lion. [z] Virgil and [a] Claudian also mention her three countenances. Thirdly, according to the opinion of some, she is called Triformis, [b] because the Moon hath three phases or shapes: the new moon appears arched with a semicircle of light; the half moon fills a semicircle with light; and the full moon fills a whole circle or orb with its splendor. But let us examine these names more exactly.

She is named Luna [c] from shining, either because she only in the night-time sends forth a glorious light, or

[t] "Terret, lustrat, agit; Proserpina, Luna, Diana;
Ima, suprema, feras; sceptro, fulgore, sagittâ."
Dempster in Paralip.

[u] In Theogon. [w] Orpheus in Argon.

[x] Τρισσοκέφαλον καὶ τριπρόσωπον, Cornut. et Artemidor. 2. Oneirocr.

[y] Porph. ap. Ger.

[z] "Tercentum tonat ore Deos, Erebumque, Chaosque,
Tergeminamque Hecatem, tria virginis ora Dianæ." Æn. 4.
Night, Erebus, and Chaos she proclaims,
And threefold Hecate with her hundred names,
And three Dianas.

[a] "Ecce procul ternis, Hecate, variata figuris." De Rap. Pros.
Behold far off the goddess Hecate
In threefold shape advances.

[b] Ap. Lil. Gyr. [c] A lucendo, quòd una sit quæ nocta lucet. Cic. Nat. Deor. 2.

else because she shines by borrowed light, and not by her own; and therefore the light with which she shines is always [d]new light. Her chariot is drawn with a white and a black horse; or with two oxen, because she has got two horns; sometimes a mule is added, says Festus, because she is barren, and shines by the light of the sun. Some say, that Lunæ of both sexes have been worshipped, especially among the Egyptians; and indeed they give this property to all the other gods. Thus both Lunus and Luna were worshipped, but with this difference, that those who worshipped Luna were thought subject to the women, and those who worshipped Lunus were superior to them. [e]We must also observe, that the men sacrificed to Venus, under the name of Luna, in women's clothes, and the women in men's clothes.

This Luna had a gallant who was named Endymion, and he was mightily courted by her; [f]insomuch that, to kiss him, she descended out of heaven, and came to the mountain Latmus, or Lathynius, in Caria; where he lay condemned to an eternal sleep by Jupiter; because, when he was taken into heaven, he attempted to violate the modesty of Juno. In reality, Endymion was a famous astronomer, who first described the course of the moon, and he is represented sleeping, because he contemplated nothing but the planetary motions.

Hecate may be derived from ἑκαθεν [*hekathen*] *eminus;* because the moon darts her rays or arrows afar off. [g]She is said to be the daughter of Ceres by Jupiter, who being cast out by her mother, and exposed in the streets, was taken up by shepherds, and nourished by them; for which reason [h]she was worshipped in the

[d] Quòd luce aliena splendeat, unde Græcè dicitur Σελήνη ὰ σέλας νέον, id est, lumen novum. Id. ibid.

[e] Serv. in Æn. 2. Philocor. Spartian. in Imp. Caracal.

[f] Apoll Argon. 4. Plin. l. 2. c. 9. [g] Hesiod. in Theog.

[h] "Nocturnisque Hecate triviis ululata per urbes."

Virg. Æn. 9.

And Hecate by night ador'd with shrieks.

streets, and her statue was usually set before the doors of the houses, whence she took the name Propylæa. Others derive her name from ἑκατον [*hecaton*] *centum*, because they sacrificed a hundred victims to her: [i] or because, by her edict, those who die and are not buried, wander a hundred years up and down hell. However, it is certain, she is called Trivia, from *triviis*, "the streets;" for she was believed to preside over the streets and ways; so that they sacrificed to her in the streets; [k] and the Athenians, every new moon, made a sumptuous supper for her there, which was eaten in the night by the poor people of the city. [l] They say that she was excessively tall, her head covered with frightful snakes instead of hair, and her feet were like serpents. [m] She was represented encompassed with dogs; because that animal was sacred to her; and Hesychius says, that she was sometimes represented by a dog. We are told that she presided over enchantments, and that [n] when she was called seven times, she came to the sacrifices: as soon as these were finished, [o] several apparitions appeared, called from her Hecatæa.

She was called by the Egyptians, [p] Bubastis; her feasts were named Bubastæ; and the city where they were yearly celebrated was called Bubastis.

Brimo is another of the names of Hecate and Diana; which is derived from [q] the cry that she gave when Apollo or Mars offered violence to her as she was hunting.

She was called Lucina and Opis, [r] because she helps to bring children into the world, which good office she first performed to her brother Apollo; for, as soon as she herself was born, she assisted her mother Latona, and did the office of a midwife; [s] but was so affrighted

[i] Pausan. in Attic. [k] Aristoph in Pluto.
[l] Lucian. Pseudoph. [m] Apud Gyrald. Apollin.
[n] Argonaut. [o] Ovid. Met. 9. [p] Apoll Argon. 3.
[q] A βριμάω, fremo, irâ exardesco. [r] Quòd infantibus in lucem venientibus opem ferat. Aug. de Civ. Dei. 4. c. 1.
[s] Callimach. Hymn. in Dian.

with her mother's pain, that she resolved never to have children, but to live a virgin perpetually.

She is called Chitone and Chitonia, [t] because women after childbirth used first to sacrifice to Juno, and then offer to Diana their own and their children's clothes.

She was named Dictynna, not only from the [u] nets which she used, [w] for she was a huntress, and the princess of hunters (for which reason all woods were dedicated to her), but also because [x] Britomartis the virgin, when she hunted, fell into the nets, and vowed, if she escaped, to build a temple for Diana. She did escape, and then consecrated a temple to Diana Dictynna. Others relate the story thus: When Britomartis, whom Diana loved because she was a huntress, fled from Minos her lover, and cast herself into the sea, she fell into the fishermen's nets, and Diana made her a goddess. The [y] ancients thought that Diana left off hunting on the ides of August, therefore at that time it was not lawful for any one to hunt, but they crowned the dogs with garlands, and by the light of torches, made of stubble, hung up the hunting instruments near them.

We shall only adjoin, to what has been said, the two stories of Chione and Meleager.

Chione was the daughter of Dædalion, the son of Dædalus: she was defloured by Apollo and Mercury, and brought forth twins; namely, Philammon, a skilful musician, the son of Apollo; and Autolychus, the son of Mercury, who proved a famous [z] juggler, and an artful

[t] Χιτώνη, quasi tunicata à χιτών, tunica; solebant enim fœminæ partùs laboribus perfunctæ Junoni sacrificare; suas autem et infantium vestes Dianæ consecrare. Plut. 3. Symp. c. ult.

[u] Retia enim δίκτυα dicuntur. [w] Ovid. Met. 2. Lact. Plac.

[x] Schol. Aristoph.

[y] Brodæus in Anthol. ex Schol Pindari.

[z] —— "Furtum ingeniosus ad omne,
Qui facere assuêrat, patriæ non degener artis,
Candida de nigris et de candentibus atra." Ov. Met. 11.
Cunning in theft, and wily in all sleights,
Who could with subtlety deceive the sight,
Converting white to black, and black to white.

thief. She was so far from thinking this a shame, that she grew very proud; nay, openly boasted, [a] that her beauty had charmed two gods, and that she had two sons by them. Besides, she was [b] so bold as to speak scornfully of Diana's beauty, and to prefer herself before her: but Diana punished the insolence of this boaster, for she drew her bow, and shot an arrow through her tongue, and thereby put her to silence.

Meleager was punished for the fault of his father [c] Oeneus, who, when he offered his first fruits to the gods, wilfully forgot Diana; therefore she was angry, and sent a wild boar into the fields of his kingdom of Caledonia, to destroy them. Meleager, accompanied with many chosen youths, immediately undertook either to kill this boar, or to drive him out of the country. The virgin Atalanta was among the hunters, and gave the boar the first wound; and soon after Meleager killed him. He valued Atalanta more who wounded him than himself who killed him, [d] and therefore offered her the boar's skin. But the uncles of Meleager were enraged that the hide was given to a stranger, and violently took it from her; upon which Meleager killed them. As soon as his mother Althæa understood that Meleager

[a] —— "Se peperisse duos, et Diis placuisse duobus."
That she two sons had brought, by having pleased two gods.

[b] —— "Se præferre Dianæ
Sustinuit, faciemque Deæ culpavit. At illi
Ira ferox mota est, factisque placabimus, inquit.
Nec mora curvavit cornu, nervusque sagittam
Impulit, et meritam trajecit arundine linguam."
She to Diana's durst her face prefer,
And blame her beauty. With a cruel look,
She said, Our deed shall right us. Forthwith took
Her bow, and bent it; which she strongly drew,
And through her guilty tongue the arrow flew.

[c] Ovid. Met. 8

[d] ——— "Exuvias, rigidis horrentia setis
Terga dat, et magnis insignia dentibus ora.
Illi lætitiæ est cum munere muneris auctor,
Invidêre alii, totoque erat agmine murmur."
Then gave the bristled spoil, and ghastly head
With monstrous tushes arm'd, which terror bred.
She in the gift and giver pleasure took:
All murmur, with preposterous envy struck.

Pl. XIX. p. 183.

H. Moses del. et sculp.

DIANA.

Published by Wilkie & Robinson, Paternoster Row, May 1, 1810.

had killed her brothers, she sought revenge like a mad woman. In Althæa's chamber was a billet, which, when Meleager was born, [e] the Fates took, and threw into the fire, saying, The new-born infant shall live as long as this stick remains unconsumed. The mother snatched it out of the fire and quenched it, and laid it in a closet. But now, moved with rage, she goes to her chamber, and fetching the stick [f] she threw it into the fire: as the log burned, Meleager, though absent, felt fire in his bowels, which consumed him in the same manner that the wood was consumed; and when at last the log was quite reduced to ashes, and the fire quenched, Meleager at the same time expired, and turned to dust.

QUESTIONS FOR EXAMINATION.

How is Diana described?

What is said of Actæon?

Why does Diana represent the moon?

What is said of her with regard to Alpheus?

Repeat the verse from Horace.

Why is she called Triformis?

How is she named in the heavens, in the earth, and in hell; and why so?

Repeat the Latin distich.

What does Hesiod say of these names?

Why is she named Lunæ?

[e] "Tempora, dixerunt, eadem lignoque tibique,
O modo nate, damus: quo postquam carmine dicto,
Excessere Deæ; flagrantem mater ab igne
Eripuit ramum, sparsitque liquentibus undis;
Servatusque diu juvenis servaverat annos."
O lately born, one period we assign
To thee and to the brand. The charm they weave
Into his fate, and then the chamber leave.
His mother snatch'd it with a hasty hand
Out of the fire, and quench'd the flaming brand.
This in an inward closet closely lays,
And by preserving it prolongs his days.

[f] —— "Dextraque aversa trementi,
Funereum torrem medios conjecit in ignes.
—— With eyes turn'd back, her quaking hand
To trembling flames expos'd the fun'ral brand.

How was Lunæ worshipped among the Egyptians?

What is said of Endymion?

What is said of Hecate?

Why was she called Trivia?

Why is she represented as encompassed with dogs?

Why is she called Bubastæ; and why Brimo?

Why was she called Lucina and Opis?

Why was she called Chitone?

Why was she named Dictynna?

Why did the ancients esteem it unlawful to hunt after the first of August?

Give some account of the stories of Chione and Meleager.

Repeat the lines—

"Tempora, dixerunt," &c.

CHAPTER XV.

PALES, FLORA, FERONIA, POMONA.

THAT old lady, whom you see [g] surrounded by shepherds, is Pales, the goddess of shepherds and pastures. Some call her Magna Mater and Vesta. To this goddess they sacrificed milk, and wafers made of millet, that she might make the pastures fruitful. They instituted the feasts called Palilia, or Parilia, to her honour, which were observed upon the eleventh or twelfth day of the calends of May by the shepherds in the field, on the same day in which Romulus laid the foundation of the city. These feasts were celebrated to appease this goddess, that she might drive away the wolves, and prevent the diseases incident to cattle. The solemnities observed in the Palilian feasts were many: the shepherds placed little heaps of straw in a particular order, and at a certain distance; then they danced and leaped over them; then they purified the sheep and the rest of

[g] Virg. Eclog

the cattle with the fume of rosemary, laurel, sulphur, and the like; as we learn from Ovid, [h] who gives a description of these rites.

[i] Flora, so dressed and ornamented, is the goddess and president of flowers. The Romans gave her the honour of a goddess; but in reality she was a woman of infamous character, who, by her abominable trade, heaped up a great deal of money, and made the people of Rome her heir. She left a certain sum, the yearly interest of which was settled, that the games, called Florales, or Floralia, might be celebrated annually, on her birth-day. But because this appeared impious and profane to the senate, they covered their design, and worshipped Flora, under the title of "goddess of flowers;" and pretended that they offered sacrifice to her, that the plants and trees might flourish.

Ovid follows the same fiction, and relates, [k] that Chloris, an infamous nymph, was married to Zephyrus, from whom she received the power over all the flowers. But let us return to Flora, and her games. Her image, as we find in Plutarch, was exposed in the temple of Castor and Pollux, dressed in a close coat, and holding in her right hand the flowers of beans and peas. [l] For while these sports were celebrated, the officers, or ædiles, scattered beans and other pulse among the people. These games were proclaimed and begun by sound of trumpet, as we find mentioned in [m] Juvenal,

[h] "Alma Pales, faveas pastoria sacra canenti,
Prosequar officio si tua facta meo.
Certè ego de vitulo cinerem, stipulamque fabulam
Sæpe tuli, læva, februa tosta, manu.
Certe ego transilui positas ter in ordine flammas,
Virgoque rorales laurea misit aquas."
Great Pales help; the past'ral rites I sing,
With humble duty mentioning each thing.
Ashes of calves, and bean-straw oft I've held,
With burnt purgations in a hand well fill'd.
Thrice o'er the flames, in order rang'd, I've leapt,
And holy dew my laurel twig has dript.

Lactant. l. 1. c. 24. [k] Ovid. in Fastis. [l] Val. Max. l. 2. c. 5.

[m] —— "Dignissima certè
Florali matrona tubâ." Sat. 6.

Feronia, the [n] goddess of the woods, is justly placed near Flora, the goddess of flowers. She is called Feronia, from the care she takes in [o] producing and propagating trees. The higher place is due to her, because fruits are more valuable than flowers, and trees than small and ignoble plants. It is said she had a grove sacred to her, under the mountain Soracte: this was set on fire, and the neighbours were resolved to remove the image Feronia thence, when on a sudden the grove became green again. [p] Strabo reports, that those who were inspired by this goddess, used to walk barefoot upon burning coals without hurt. Though many believed, that by the goddess Feronia, that kind of virtue only is meant, by which fruit and flowers were produced.

Pomona is the goddess, the guardian, the president, not of the [q] apples only, but of all the fruit and the product of trees and plants. As you see, she follows after Flora and Feronia, in order; but in the greatness of her merit she far surpasses them; and has a priest who only serves her, called Flamen Pomonalis.

Once when Pomona was very busy in looking after her gardens and orchards with great care, and was wholly employed in watering and securing the roots, and lopping the over-grown branches; [r] Vertumnus, a principal god among the Romans (called so because he had power to turn himself into what shape he pleased), fell in love with Pomona, and counterfeited the shape of an old gray-headed woman. He came [s] leaning on a staff into the gardens, admired the fruit and beauty of them, and commending her care about them, he saluted her. He viewed the gardens, and from the observations he

——— A woman worthy sure
Of Flora's festal trumpet.

[n] Virg. Æn. 7. [o] Feronia à ferendis arboribus dicta.

[p] Geogr. l. 5. [q] Pomona à pomis dicitur.

[r] Vertumnus à vertendo, quod in quas vellet figuras sese vertere poterat.

[s] "Innitens baculo, positis ad tempora canis." Ov. Met. 14.
With gray-hair'd noddle, leaning on a staff.

Pl. XX. p. 182.

H. Moses del. et sculp.

FLORA

Published by Wilkie & Robinson Paternoster Row May 1. 1810.

had made, he began to discourse of marriage, telling her that it would add to the happiness even of a god, to have her to wife. Observe, says he, the trees which creep up this wall: how do the apples and plums strive which shall excel the other in beauty and colour! whereas, if they had not [t] props or supports, which like husbands hold them up, they would perish and decay. All this did not move her, till Vertumnus [u] changed himself into a young man; and then she began also to feel the force and power of love, and submitted to his wishes.

QUESTIONS FOR EXAMINATION.

Who is Pales, and what did they sacrifice to her?

Why were these feasts observed?

What solemnities were observed in the Palilian feasts?

Who was Flora?

Was she really a goddess?

How were the Floralia instituted; when were they celebrated; and under what pretence did they worship Flora?

[t] "At si staret, ait, cælebs sine palmite truncus,
Nil præter frondes, quare peteretur, haberet;
Hæc quoque, quæ juncta vitis requiescit in ulmo,
Si non juncta foret, terræ acclinata jaceret:
Tu tamen exemplo non tangeris arboris hujus."
Yet, saith he, if this elm should grow alone,
Except for shade, it would be priz'd by none;
And so this vine in am'rous foldings wound,
If but disjoin'd, would creep upon the ground:
Yet art not thou by such examples led,
But shunn'st the pleasures of a happy bed.

[u] —— "In juvenem reddit; et anilia demit
Instrumenta sibi: talisque apparuit illi,
Qualis ubi oppositas nitidissima solis imago
Evicit nubes, nullâque obstante reluxit:
Vimque parat; sed vi non est opus, inque figura
Capta Dei Nymphe est, et mutua vulnera sensit."
——— Again himself he grew;
Th' infirmities of heatless age depos'd;
And such himself unto the nymph disclos'd,
As when the sun, subduing with his rays
The muffling cloud, his golden brow displays:
He force prepares; of force there was no need,
Struck with his beauty, mutually they bleed.

How is her figure represented?

Who is Feronia; what is her occupation; and why is more honour due to her than to Flora?

What does Strabo say of Feronia?

Who is Pomona, and what was her priest called?

What story was related of Vertumnus?

Repeat the lines—

"At si staret," &c.

Repeat also the lines—

"In juvenem reddit," &c.

CHAPTER XVI.

THE NYMPHS.

Now observe that great company of neat, pretty, handsome, beautiful, charming virgins, who are very near the gardens of Pomona. Some run about the woods, and hide themselves in the trunks of the aged oaks; some plunge themselves into the fountains, and some swim in the rivers. They are called by one common name, [w] nymphs, [x] because they always look young, or [y] because they are handsome: yet all have their proper names beside, which they derive either from the places where they live, or the offices which they perform; they are especially distributed in three classes, celestial, terrestrial, and marine.

The celestial nymphs were those genii, those souls and intellects, [z] who guided the spheres of the heavens, and dispensed the influences of the stars to the things of the earth.

Of the terrestrial nymphs, some preside over the woods, and were called Dryades, from a Greek [a] word,

[w] Phurnut.

[x] Ἀπὸ τοῦ ἀεὶ νέας φαίνεσθαι quòd semper juvenes appareant.

[y] Ἀπὸ τοῦ φαίνειν splendere, quòd formæ decore præfulgeant.

[z] Ex. Plut. Macrob. Procl.

[a] Δρῦς, id est, quercus. Virg. Geo. 4.

which principally signifies an oak, but generally any tree whatever. These Dryades had their habitations in the oaks. Other nymphs were called [b] Hamadryades, for they were born when the oak was first planted, and when it perishes they die also. The ancients held strange opinions concerning oaks: they imagined that even the smallest oak was sent from heaven. The [c] Druidæ, priests of the Gauls, esteemed nothing more divine and sacred than the excrescence which sticks to oaks. Others of those nymphs were called [d] Oreades or Orestiades, because they presided over the mountains. Others, [e] Napææ, because they had dominion over the groves and vallies. Others [f] Limoniades, because they looked after the meadows and fields. And others, [g] Meliæ, from the ash, a tree sacred to them; and these were supposed to be the mothers of those children, who were accidentally born under a tree, or exposed there.

Of the marine nymphs, those [h] which preside over the seas were called Nereïdes or Nerinæ, from the sea god Nereus, and the sea nymph Doris, their parents; which Nereus and Doris were born of Tethys and Oceanus, from whom they were called Oceanitides and Oceaniæ. Others of those nymphs preside over the fountains, and were called [i] Naïdes or Naïades: others inhabit the rivers, and were called Fluviales or [k] Potamides: and others preside over the lakes and ponds, and were called [l] Limnades.

All the gods had nymphs attending them. Jupiter speaks of his [m] in Ovid. Neptune had many nymphs, insomuch that Hesiod and Pindar call him [n] Nympha-

[b] Ab ἅμα, simul, et δρυς, quercus. [c] Lil. Gyr. synt. 1.
[d] Ab ὄρος, mons. [e] A νάπη, saltus vel vallis.
[f] A λειμών, pratum. [g] A μελία, fraxinus. [h] Orph. in Hymn.
[i] A νάω, fluo. [k] Πόταμος, fluvius. [l] A λίμνη, lacus.

[m] "Sunt mihi Semidei, sunt rustica numina Fauni,
Et Nymphæ, Satyrique, et monticolæ Sylvani." Met. 1.
Half gods and rustic Fauns attend my will,
Nymphs, Satyrs, Sylvans, that on mountains dwell.

[n] Νυμφαγέτης, id est, Nympharum dux. Hesiod. et Pind. in Isthm.

getes, that is, the captain of the nymphs: the poets generally gave him fifty. Phœbus likewise had nymphs called Aganippidæ and Musæ. Innumerable were the nymphs of Bacchus, who were called by different names, Bacchæ, Bassarides, Eloides, and Thyades. Hunting nymphs attended upon Diana; sea nymphs, called Nereïdes, waited upon Tethys; and [o] fourteen very beautiful nymphs belonged to Juno. Out of all which I will only give you the history of two.

Arethusa was one of Diana's nymphs: her virtue was as great as her beauty. The pleasantness of the place invited her to cool herself in the waters of a fine clear river: Alpheus, the god of the river, assumed the shape of a man, and arose out of the water: he first saluted her with kind words, and then approached near to her: but away she flies, and he follows her; and when he had almost overtaken her, she was dissolved with fear, by the assistance of Diana, whom she implored, into a fountain. [p] Alpheus then resumed his former shape of water, and endeavoured to mix his stream with hers, but in vain; for to this day Arethusa continues her flight, and by her passage through a cavity of the [q] earth she goes under ground into Sicily. Alpheus also follows by the like subterraneous passages, till at last he unites and marries his own streams to those of Arethusa in that island.

Echo [r] was a nymph formerly, though nothing of her

[o] —— "Bis septem præstanti corpore Nymphæ."
Virg. Æn. 1.

Twice seven the charming daughters of the main
Around my person wait, and bear my train.

[p] —— "Sed enim cognoscit amatas
Amnis aquas; positoque viri, quod sumpserat, ore,
Vertitur in proprias, ut se illi misceat, undas." Ov. Met. 5.

The river his beloved waters knew;
And putting off th' assumed shape of man,
Resumes his own, and in a current ran.

[q] Virg. Æn. 3.

[r] "Corpus adhuc Echo, non vox erat; et tamen usum
Garrula non alium, quam nunc habet, oris habebat;
Reddere de multis ut verba novissima posset." Ov. Met. 3.

but her voice remains now, and even when she was alive, she was so far deprived of her speech, that she could only repeat the last words of those sentences which she heard. [s] Juno inflicted this punishment on her for her talkativeness: for when she came down to discover Jupiter's amours with the nymphs, Echo detained her very long with her tedious discourses, that the nymphs might have an opportunity to escape, and hide themselves. This Echo by chance met Narcissus rambling in the woods; and she so admired his beauty that she fell in love with him: she discovered her love to him, courted him, followed him, and embraced the proud youth in her arms; but he broke from her embraces, and hastily fled from her sight: upon which the despised nymph hid herself in the woods, and pined away with grief, [t] so that every part of her but the voice was consumed, and her bones were turned into stones.

Narcissus met with as bad a fate; for though he would neither love others, nor admit of their love, yet he fell so deeply in love with his own beauty, that the love

She was a nymph, though only now a sound;
Yet of her tongue no other use was found,
Than now she has; which never could be more,
Than to repeat what she had heard before.

[s] "Fecerat hoc Juno, quia cum deprendere posset
Sub Jove sæpe suo nymphas in monte jacentes,
Illa deam longo prudens sermone tenebat,
Dum fugerent nymphæ."

This change impatient Juno's anger wrought,
Who, when her Jove she o'er the mountains sought,
Was oft by Echo's tedious tales misled,
Till the shy nymphs to caves and grottos fled.

[t] "Vox tantum, atque ossa supersunt·
Vox manet: ossa ferunt lapidis traxisse figuram;
Inde latet sylvis, nulloque in monte videtur,
Omnibus auditur: sonus est qui vivit in illa."

Her flesh consumes and moulders with despair,
And all her body's juice is turn'd to air;
So wond'rous are th' effects of restless pain,
That nothing but her voice and bones remain;
Nay, ev'n the very bones at last are gone,
And metamorphos'd to a thoughtless stone,
Yet still the voice does in the woods survive;
The form's departed, but the sound's alive.

of himself proved his ruin. His thirst led him to a [u] fountain, whose waters were clear and bright as silver: when he stooped down to drink, he saw his own image; he stayed gazing at it, was wonderfully pleased with the beauty of it, insomuch that he fell passionately in love with it. A [w] little water only separated him from his beloved object. He continued a [x] long time admiring this beloved picture, before he discovered what it was that he so passionately adored; but at length [y] the unhappy creature perceived that the torture he suffered was from the love of his own self. In a word, his passion conquered him, and the power of love was greater than he could resist, so that, by degrees, [z] he wasted away and consumed, and at last, by the favour of the gods, was turned into a daffodil, a flower called by his own name.

[u] "Fons erat illimis nitidis argenteus undis." Ovid. Met. 3.
There was by chance a living fountain near,
Whose unpolluted channel ran so clear,
That it seem'd liquid silver.
[w] "Exiguâ prohibetur aquâ"——
A little drop of water does remove,
And keep him from the object of his love.
[x] —— "Sed opaca fusus in herba
Spectat inexpleto mendacem lumine formam.
Perque oculos perit ipse suos."
He lies extended on the shady grass,
Viewing with greedy eyes the pictur'd face,
And on himself brings ruin.
[y] —— "Flammas, inquit, moveoque, feroque:
Quod cupio mecum est: inopem me copia fecit.
O utinam à nostro secedere corpore possem!
Votum in amante novum est, vellem quod amamus abesset."
My love does vainly on myself return,
And fans the cruel flames with which I burn.
The thing desir'd I still about me bore,
And too much plenty has confirm'd me poor.
O that I from my much-lov'd self could go;
A strange request, yet would to God 'twere so!
[z] —— "Attenuatus amore
Liquitur, et cæco paulatim carpitur igne."
No vigour, strength, nor beauty does remain,
But hidden flames consume the wasting swain.

QUESTIONS FOR EXAMINATION.

Who are the Nymphs; how are they engaged; and from whence do they derive their general name?

From what do they get their peculiar names, and into what classes are they divided?

Who are the celestial Nymphs?

Give some account of the terrestrial Nymphs.

Over what did the marine Nymphs preside?

Whom did the Nymphs attend?

What is said of Arethusa?

Who was Echo, and what is her history?

What is the history of Narcissus?

CHAPTER XVII.

THE INFERIOR RURAL DEITIES.

RUSINA, the goddess to whose care all the parts of the country are committed.

Collina, she who reigns over the hills.

Vallonia, who holds her empire in the vallies.

Hippona, [a] who presides over the horses and stables. [b] This was the name also of a beautiful woman, begotten by Fulvius from a mare.

Bubona, who hath the care of the oxen.

Seia, [c] who takes care of the seed, while it lies buried in the earth. She is likewise called [d] Segetia, because she takes care of the blade as soon as it appears green above ground.

Runcina is the goddess of weeding. She is invoked [e] when the fields are to be weeded.

[a] Ab ἵππος, equus. Apuleius Asin. aur. l. 3.
[b] Tertullian Apol. [c] A serendo nomen habet Seia, ut.
[d] Segetia à segete. Plin. l. 8. [e] Cum *runcuntur* agri.

Occator is the god of harrowing. He is worshipped [f] when the fields are to be harrowed.

Sator and Sarritor are the gods of [g] sowing and raking.

To the god Robigus were celebrated festivals called Robigalia, which were usually observed upon the seventh of the calends of May, to avert the [h] blasting of the corn.

Stercutius, Stercutus, or Sterculius, called likewise Sterquilinius and Picumnus, is the god who first invented the art of [i] dunging the ground.

Proserpine is the goddess who presides over the corn, [k] when it is sprouted pretty high above the earth. We shall speak more of her when we discourse concerning the infernal deities.

Nodosus, or Nodotus, is the god that takes care of the [l] knots and the joints of the stalks.

Volusia is the goddess who takes care to fold the blade round the corn, before the beard breaks out, which [m] foldings of the blade contain the beard, as pods do the seed.

Patelina, who takes care of the corn [n] after it is broken out of the pod and appears.

The goddess Flora presides over the ear when it [o] blossoms.

Lactura, or Lactucina, who is next to Flora, presides over the ear when it begins [p] to have milk.

And Matura takes care that the ear comes to a just maturity.

Hostilina was worshipped that the ears of the corn might grow [q] even, and produce a crop proportionable to the seed sown.

[f] Cum *occantur* agri Serv. in Geo. 1. Plin. l. 18. c. 29.

[g] Ita dicti à *serendo* et *sarriendo*

[h] Ad vertendam à satis *rubiginem*.

[i] Ita dicitur à *stercore*.

[k] Cum super terram seges *proserpserit*.

[l] Præponitur *nodis* geniculisque culmorum.

[m] Folliculorum *involucris* præficitur.

[n] Cum spica *patet* postquam è folliculis emersit.

[o] Cum *florescit*.

[p] Cum *lactescere*.

[q] Ab *hostire*, quòd veterum linguâ significabat idem quod *æquare*. Augustinus de Civitate jam laudatus.

Tutelina, or Tutulina, hath the tutelage of corn when it is reaped.

Pilumnus invented the art of [r] kneading and baking bread. He is commonly joined with Picumnus, his brother, whom we mentioned above.

Mellona is the goddess who invented the [s] art of making honey.

And Fornax is esteemed a goddess; because, before the invention of grinding the wheat, the bread corn was parched in a furnace. Ovid [t] makes mention of this goddess.

QUESTIONS FOR EXAMINATION.

Who were Rusina, Collina, Vallonia, and Hippona?

What were the occupations of Bubona, Seia, Runcina, and Occator?

Who were the gods of sowing and raking?

On what account were the Robigalia instituted?

Who invented the art of dunging the land?

Over what does Proserpine preside?

Who were Nodosus, Volusia, and Patellina?

Over what does Flora, Lactura, and Matura preside?

Why was Hostilena worshipped?

What was the office of Tutelina?

What did Pilumnus invent?

Who is Mellona?

Why is Fornax esteemed a goddess?

[r] A *pilando*, id est, condensando et farinam subigendo. Vid. Serv. in Æn. 9.

[s] Artem mellificii excogitavit.

[t] "Facta Dea est Fornax, læti fornace coloni
Orant, ut vires temperet illa suas." Fast. 6.
A goddess Fornax is, and her the clowns adore,
That they may 've kindly batches by her pow'r.

PART III.

OF THE GODS OF THE SEA.

CHAPTER I.

SECT. I.—NEPTUNE. HIS NAME AND DESCENT, ACTIONS AND CHILDREN.

NEPTUNE, the king of the waters, is represented with black hair and blue eyes, holding a sceptre in his right hand like a fork with three tines, and beautifully arrayed in a mantle of blue, clasping his left hand round his queen's waist. He stands upright in his chariot, which is a large escalop shell, drawn by sea-horses, and attended by odd kind of animals, which resemble men in the upper parts, and fish in the lower. His name is derived, by the change of a few letters, from the word [a] *nubo*, which signifies "to cover;" because the sea encompasses, embraces, and, as it were, covers the land. Or, as others believe, he is so called from an Egyptian word (*nepthen*), which signifies the coasts and promontories, and other parts of the earth which are washed by the waters. So that [b] Cicero, who derives Neptune from *nando* (swimming), is either mistaken, [c] or the place is corrupt.

Neptune is the governor of the sea, the father of the rivers and the fountains, and the son of Saturn by Ops. His mother preserved him from the devouring jaws of

[a] A *nubendo*, quod mare terras obnubat. Varro.
[b] De Nat. Deor. 2. [c] Lipsius et Bochartus.

Saturn, who ate up all the male children that were born to him, by giving Saturn a young foal to eat in his stead. In the Greek he is called Ποσειδον [*Poseidon*], because he so binds our feet that we are not able to walk within his dominions, that is, on the water.

When he came of age, Saturn's kingdom was divided by lot, and the maritime parts fell to him. He and Apollo, by Jupiter's command, were forced to serve Laomedon, in building the walls of Troy; because he and some other gods had plotted against Jupiter. Then he took [e] Amphitrite to wife, who refused a long time to hearken to his courtship, and comply with his desires: but at last, by the assistance of a dolphin, and by the power of flattery, he gained her. To recompense which kindness, the dolphin was placed among the stars, and made a constellation. Amphitrite had two other names; Salacia, so called from *salum*, the sea, [f] or the salt water, toward the lower part and bottom of the sea; and Venilia, so named from *veniendo*, because the sea goes and comes with the tide, or ebbs and flows by turns.

The poets tell us, that Neptune produced a [g] horse in Attica out of the ground, [h] by striking it with his trident; whence he is called [i] Hippius and Hippodromus, and he is esteemed the president over the horse-races. At his altar, in the Circus of Rome, games were instituted, in which they represented [k] the ancient Romans by violence, carrying away the Sabine virgins. His altar was under ground, and sacrifices were offered to him by the name of [l] Consus, the god of counsel;

[d] Qui ποσὶ δεσμὸν, hoc est, pedibus vinculum injicit, ne pedibus aquas ambulemus. Plato in Cratyl.

[e] Dicitur ἀμφιτρίτη παρὰ τὸ ἀμφιτρίβειν, à circumterendo, quod erram mare circumterat. [f] Aug. de Civ. Dei.

[g] Soph. in Œdip.

[h] ——— "Magno tellus percussa tridenti." Virg. Geo. 1.
With his huge trident having struck the ground.

[i] Ab ἵππος equus, et δρόμος cursus. Pindar. ode 1. Isth. Var. ap. Lil. Gyr. [k] Dion. Halic. l. 2.

[l] A consilio dando. Serv. in Æn. 8.

which for the most part ought to be given privately; and therefore the god Consus was worshipped in an obscure and private place. The solemn games [m] Consualia, celebrated in the month of March, were instituted in honour of Neptune. At the same time, the horses left working, and the mules were adorned with garlands of flowers.

Hence it also happens, that the chariot of Neptune is drawn by *hippocampi*, or sea horses, as well as sometimes by dolphins. Those sea horses had the tails of fishes, and only two feet, which were like the fore feet of a horse, according to the description given of them in [n] Statius; and this is the reason why [o] Virgil calls them two-footed horses: Neptune guides them, and goads them forward with his trident, as it is expressed in [p] Statius.

It was therefore Neptune's peculiar office, [q] not only to preside over, and govern horses both by land and by sea, but also the government of ships was committed to his care, which were always safe under his protection; for whenever he rides [r] upon the waters, the weather immediately grows fair, and the sea calm.

[m] Plut. in Romulo. Dion. Halic. l. 2.

[n] "Illic Ægeo Neptunus gurgite fessos
In portam deducit equos, prior haurit habenas
Ungula, postremi solvuntur in æquora pisces." Theb. 2.
Good Neptune's steeds to rest are set up here,
In the Ægean gulf, whose fore parts harness bear,
Their hinder parts fish-shap'd.

[o] —— "Magnum qui piscibus æquor,
Et juncto bipedum curru metitur equorum." Geo. 4.
—— Through the vast sea he glides,
Drawn by a team half fish half horse he rides.

[p] —— "Triplici telo jubet ire jugales:
Illi spumiferos glomerant à pectore fluctus,
Pone natant, delentque pedum vestigia caudâ." Achil. 1.
Shaking his trident, urges on his steeds,
Who with two feet beat from their brawny breasts
The foaming billows; but their hinder parts
Swim, and go smooth against the curling surge.

[q] Hom. in Hymn. Sil. Ital. l. 1.

[r] ——— "Tumida æquora placat,
Collectasque fugat nubes, solemque reducit." Virg. Æn. 1.

The most remarkable of his children were Triton, Phorcus or Proteus. Of the first we shall speak in another place.

Phorcus or Phorcys was his son [s] by the nymph Thesea. He was vanquished by Atlas, and drowned in the sea. His surviving friends said that he was made a sea god, and therefore they worshipped him. We read of another Phorcus, [t] who had three daughters; they had but one eye among them all, which they all could use. When either of them desired to see any thing, she fixed the eye in her forehead, in the same manner as men fix a diamond in a ring; and having used it, she pulled the eye out again, that her sisters might have it: thus they all used it, as there was occasion.

Proteus, his son by the nymph Phœnice, was the [u] keeper of the sea calves. [w] He could convert himself into all sorts of shapes: sometimes he could flow like the water, and sometimes burn like the fire; sometimes he was a fish, a bird, a lion, or whatever he pleased.

Nor was this wonderful power enjoyed by Proteus alone; for Vertumnus, one of the gods of the Romans, possessed it; his [x] name shows it, as we observed before in the story of Pomona. From this god, Vertumnus, comes that common Latin expression *bene* or *male vertat*, may it succeed well or ill: because it is the

——— He smooth'd the sea,
Dispell'd the darkness, and restor'd the day.
——— "Æquora postquam
Prospiciens genitor, cæloque invectus aperto,
Flectit equos, curruque volans dat lora secundo." Virg. Æn. 1.
——— Where'er he guides
His finny coursers, and in triumph rides,
The waves unruffle, and the sea subsides.
"Subsidunt undæ, tumidumque sub axe tonanti
Sternitur æquor aquis, fugiunt vasto æthere nimbi." Æn. 5.
High on the waves his azure car he guides.
Its axles thunder, and the sea subsides;
And the smooth ocean rolls her silent tides.

[s] Var. ad Nat. Com. [t] Palæphat. in fab.
[u] Phocarum seu vitulorum marinorum pastor. Tzetz. chil. 2. hist. 44.
[w] Ovid. Met. 8. [x] Vertumnus dictus est à vertendo.

business of Vertumnus to [y] preside over the turn or change of things, which happen according to expectation; though oftentimes what we think good is found in the conclusion [*male vertere*] to be worse than was expected; as that [z] sword was which Dido received from Æneas, with which she afterward killed herself.

Neptune [a] endued Periclymenus, Nestor's brother, with the same power; and he was killed by Hercules when in the shape of a fly: for when Hercules fought against Neleus, a fly tormented him and stung him violently; and on Pallas discovering to him that this fly was Periclymenus, he killed him.

Neptune gave the same power to Metra, Mestra, or Mestre, the daughter of Erisichthon, by which [b] she was enabled to succour her father's insatiable hunger.

For the same cause Cænis, a virgin of Thessaly, obtained the same, or rather a greater power, from Neptune; for he gave her power to change her sex, and made her invulnerable: she therefore turned herself into a man, and was called Cæneus. [c] She fought against the Centaurs, till they had overwhelmed her with a vast load of trees, and buried her alive; after which, she was changed into a bird of her own name.

QUESTIONS FOR EXAMINATION

How is Neptune represented?

From what is his name derived?

Whose son was Neptune, and how was his life preserved?

What is his name in Greek, and why?

What task was imposed on him for his rebellion against Jupiter?

Why was the dolphin made a constellation?

[y] Rebus ad opinata revertentibus præesse. Donatus in Terent.

[z] ——— " Ensemque recludit
Dardanium, non hos quæsitum munus in usus." Virg. Æn. 4.
——— The Trojan sword unsheath'd,
A gift by him not to this use bequeath'd.

[a] Hom. in Odyss. 11.

[b] " Nunc equa, nunc ales, modo bos, modo servus abibat,
Præbebatque avido non justa alimenta parenti." Ov. Met. 8.

[c] Ovid. Met.

What were Amphitrite's names, and from what were they derived?

Why is Neptune called Hippius and Hippodromus?

What games were instituted at his altar, and what sacrifices were offered him?

What were the Consualia, and how were they kept?

What were the Hippocampi?

What was Neptune's peculiar office?

Who were Neptune's children?

What is the history of Phorcus?

Who was Proteus, and what particular power had he?

What is said of Vertumnus?

What is the history of Periclymenus?

Who was Mestra, and what did she do?

What power did Neptune grant to Cænis?

CHAPTER II.

TRITON, AND THE OTHER MARINE GODS.

TRITON was the [d] son of Neptune by Amphitrite; he was his father's [e] companion and [f] trumpeter Down to his navel he resembles a man, but his other part is like a fish: his two [g] feet are like the fore feet of a horse, his tail is cleft and crooked, like a half moon, and his hair resembles wild parsley. Two princes of Parnassus, [h] Vir-

[d] Hesiod. in Theog. 2. [e] Stat. Theb. 6. [f] Virg. Æn. 1.
[g] Apollon. Argon. 4.

[h] "Hunc vehit immanis Triton, et cærula concha
Exterrens freta; cui laterum tenus hispida nanti
Frons hominem præfert, in pristim definit alvus,
Spumea pestifero sub pectore murmurat unda." Æn. 10.
Him and his martial train the Triton bears,
High on his poop the sea-green god appears;
Frowning, he seems his crooked shell to sound,
And at the blast the billows dance around.
A hairy man above the waist he shows;
A porpoise tail beneath his belly grows,

gil and [i] Ovid, give most elegant descriptions of him.

Oceanus, another of the sea gods, [k] was the son of Cœlum and [l] Vesta. He, by the ancients, was called the "Father," not only of all the rivers, but of the animals, and of the very gods themselves; for they imagined, that all the things in nature took their beginning from him. It is said, he begot of his wife Tethys three thousand sons, the most eminent of which was

[m] Nereus, who was nursed and educated by the waves, [n] and afterward dwelt in the Ægean Sea, and became a famous prophesier. He [o] begat fifty daughters by his wife Doris, which nymphs were called, after their father's name, Nereïdes.

Palæmon, and his mother Ino, are also to be reckoned among the sea deities. They were made sea gods on this occasion: Ino's husband, Athamas, was distracted, and tore his son Learchus into pieces, and dashed him against the wall: Ino saw this, and fearing lest the same fate should come upon herself and her other son Melicerta, she took her son, and with him threw herself into the sea: where they were made sea deities. Nothing perished in the waters but their names. Though their former names were lost in the waves, yet they

And ends a fish · his breasts the waves divide,
And froth and foam augment the murm'ring tide

[i] "Cæruleum Tritona vocat; conchaque sonaci
Inspirare jubet; fluctusque et flumina signo
Jam revocare dato. Cava buccina sumitur illi
Tortilis, in latum quæ turbine crescit ab imo:
Buccina, quæ medio concepit ut aëra ponto,
Littora voce replet sub utroque jacentia Phœbo." Met. 1.
Old Triton rising from the deep he spies,
Whose shoulders rob'd with native purple rise,
And bids him his loud-sounding shell inspire,
And give the floods a signal to retire.
He his wreath'd trumpet takes (as given in charge)
That from the turning bottom grows more large;
This, when the Numen o'er the ocean sounds,
The east and west from shore to shore rebounds.

[k] Hesiod. in Theog. [l] Orph. in Hymn. Hesiod. ibid.
[m] Horat. Carm. 1. [n] Eurip. in Iphig. [o] Apol. 4.

found new ones: she was called Leucothea, and he Palæmon by the Greeks, and Portumnus by the Latins.

Glaucus, the fisherman, became a sea god by a more pleasant way: for when he pulled the fishes which he had caught out of his nets, and laid them on the shore, he observed, that by touching a certain [p] herb, they recovered their strength, and leaped again into the water. He wondered at so strange an effect, and had a desire to taste this herb. [q] When he had tasted it, he followed his fishes, and, leaping into the water, became a god of the sea.

To these we may add the story of Canopus, a god of the Egyptians, who, by the help of water, gained a memorable victory over the god of the Chaldeans. [r] When these two nations contended about the power and superiority of their gods, the priests consented to bring two gods together, that they might decide their controversy. The Chaldeans brought their god Ignis (*Fire*), and the Egyptians brought Canopus: they set the two gods near one another to fight. Canopus was a great pitcher filled with water, and full of holes, but so stopped with wax, that nobody could discern them: when the fight began, Fire, the god of the Chaldeans, melted the wax, which stopped the holes; so that Canopus, with rage and violence, assaulted Ignis with streams of water, and totally extinguished, vanquished, and overcame him.

QUESTIONS FOR EXAMINATION.

Who was Triton, and how is he described?
Give Virgil's description in Latin and English.
Give Ovid's account.
Who was Oceanus?
What is said of Nereus?
Give the history of Palæmon.
How was Glaucus transformed to a sea god?
What story is told of Canopus?

[p] Strabo l. 9. [q] Ovid. Met. 13. [r] Ruffin. l. 11. c. 26.

CHAPTER III.

THE MONSTERS OF THE SEA.

THE SIRENS, SCYLLA, AND CHARYBDIS.

THERE were three Sirens, whose parentage is uncertain, though some say [s] that they were the offspring of the river Achelous, and the muse Melpomene. [t] They had the faces of women, but the bodies of flying fishes: they dwelt near the promontory Peloris in Sicily (now called Capo di Faro), or in the islands called [u] Sirenusæ, which are situate in the extreme parts of Italy; where, with the sweetness of their singing, they allured all the men to them that sailed by those coasts: and when by their charms they brought upon them a dead sleep, they drowned them in the sea, and afterward took them out and devoured them. Their names were Parthenope (who died at Naples, for which reason that city was formerly called Parthenope), Ligæa, and Leucosia.

That their charms might be more easily received, and make the greater impression on the minds of the hearers, they used musical instruments with their voices, and [w] adapted the matter of their songs to the temper and inclination of their hearers. [x] With some songs they enticed the ambitious, with others the voluptuous, and with other songs they drew on the covetous to their destruction.

History mentions only two passengers, *viz.* Ulysses and Orpheus, who escaped. [y] The first was forewarned of the danger of their charming voices by Circe: there-

[s] Nicand. Met. 3. [t] Ovid. Met. 3. [u] Strabo, l. 5 Idem. l. 1. [w] Hom. Odyss.

[x] Monstra maris Sirenes erant, quæ voce canora
Quaslibet admissas detinuere rates." Ov. Art. Am. 3.
Sirens were once sea monsters, mere decoys,
Trepanning seamen with their tuneful voice.

[y] Hom. Odyss. 1.

fore he stopped the ears of his companions with wax, and was himself fast bound to the mast of the ship, by which means he safely passed the fatal coasts. [z] But Orpheus overcame them in their own art, and evaded the temptations of their murdering music, by playing upon his harp, and singing the praises of the gods so well, that he outdid the Sirens. The Fates had ordained that the Sirens should live till somebody who passed by heard them sing, and yet escaped alive. When, therefore, they saw themselves overcome, they grew desperate, and threw themselves headlong into the sea, and were turned into stones. Some write, that they were formerly virgins, Proserpine's companions, who sought every-where for her when she was stolen away by Pluto; but when they could not find her, they were so grieved, that they cast themselves into the sea, and from that time were changed into sea monsters. [a] Others add, that by Juno's persuasion they contended in music with the Muses, who overcame them, and, to punish their rashness, cut off their wings, with which they afterward made for themselves garlands.

The poets teach by this fiction, that the "[b] minds of men are deposed from their proper seat and state by the allurements of pleasure." It corrupts them; and there is not a more deadly plague in nature to mankind than voluptuousness. Whoever addicts himself altogether to pleasures, loses his reason, and is ruined; and he that desires to decline their charms, must stop his ears and not listen to them; but hearken to the music of Orpheus, that is, he must observe the precepts and instructions of the wise.

The description of Scylla is very various: for some say, that [c] she was a most beautiful woman from the breasts downward, but had six dogs' heads: and others say, that in her upper parts she resembled a woman, in her lower, a serpent and a wolf. But whatever her

[z] Apollon. Argon. 3. [a] Pausan. in Bœot.

[b] Voluptatum illicebris mentem è suâ sede et statu dimoveri. Cic. de Senectute. [c] Hom. Odyss.

picture was, [d] all acknowledge that she was the daughter of Phorcus. She was courted by Glaucus, and received his embraces; upon which Circe, who passionately loved Glaucus, and could not bear that Scylla should be preferred before her by Glaucus, [e] poisoned with venomous herbs those waters in which Scylla used to wash herself: Scylla was ignorant of it, and according to her custom, went into the fountain; and when she saw that the lower parts of her body were turned into the heads of dogs, being extremely grieved that she had lost her beauty, she cast herself headlong into the sea, where she was turned into a rock, famous for the many shipwrecks that happen there. This rock is still seen in the sea that divides Italy from Sicily, between Messina, a city of Sicily, and Rhegium (now Reggio) in Calabria. It is said to be surrounded with dogs and wolves, which devour the persons who are cast away there: but by this is meant, that when the waves, by a storm, are dashed against this great rock, the noise a little resembles the barking of dogs, and the howling of wolves.

There was another Scylla, [f] the daughter of king Nisus, in love with Minos, who besieged her father in the city of Megara. She betrayed both her father and her country to him, by cutting off the fatal lock of purple hair, in which were contained her father's and her country's safety, and sent it to the besieger. Minos gained the city by it, but detested Scylla's perfidiousness, and hated her. She could not bear this misfortune, but was changed into a lark. Nisus, her father, was likewise changed into a sparhawk, which is called *nisus*, after his name, and, as if he still sought to punish his daughter's baseness, pursues the lark with great fury to devour her.

Charybdis is a vast whirlpool in the same Sicilian Sea, over against [g] Scylla, which swallows whatsoever comes within its circle, and throws it up again. They say;

[d] Apollon. Argon. 3. [e] Myro Prian. l. 3. Rerum Messan. [f] Pausan. in Attic. [g] Virg. Geo. 5.

that this Charybdis was formerly a very ravenous woman, who stole away Hercules' oxen: for which theft Jupiter struck her dead with thunder, and then turned her into this gulf. [h] Virgil gives an elegant description of these two monsters, Scylla and Charybdis.

The fables of Scylla and Charybdis represent lust and gluttony, vices which render our voyage through this world extremely hazardous and perilous. Lust, like Scylla, engages unwary passengers by the beauty and pomp of her outside; and when they are entangled in her snares, she tortures, vexes, torments, and disquiets them with rage and fury, which exceeds the madness of dogs, or the ravenousness of wolves. Gluttony is a Charybdis, a gulf or whirlpool that is insatiable: it buries families alive, devours estates, consumes lands and treasures, and sucks up all things.

QUESTIONS FOR EXAMINATION.

Who were the Sirens, and how are they described?

What were their names?

How did they entice the unwary?

Who escaped their machinations, and how did they effect it?

[h] "Dextrum Scylla latus, lævum implacata Charybdis
Obsidet: atque imo barathri ter gurgite vastos
Sorbet in abruptum fluctus, rursusque sub auras
Erigit alternos, et sidera verberat undâ,
At Scyllam cæcis cohibet spelunca latebris
Ora exertantem, et naves in saxa trahentem.
Prima hominis facies, et pulchro pectore virgo
Pube tenus: postrema immani corpore pistris,
Delphinum caudas utero commissa luporum." Æn. 3.
Far on the right her dogs foul Scylla hides:
Charybdis roaring on the left presides,
And in her greedy whirlpool sucks the tides;
Then spouts them from below: with fury driv'n,
The waves mount up, and wash the face of heav'n.
But Scylla, from her den, with open jaws
The sinking vessel in her eddy draws;
Then dashes on the rocks. A human face
And virgin bosom hide the tail's disgrace:
Her parts obscene below the waves descend,
With dogs inclos'd, and in a dolphin end.

What became of the Sirens afterwards?
What moral is to be drawn from this story?
What is the history of Scylla?
What is said of the other Scylla?
Give the history of Charybdis.
Repeat Virgil's description.
What is the moral of the fable?

PART IV.

OF THE INFERNAL DEITIES.

CHAPTER I.

A VIEW OF HELL. CHARON. RIVERS OF HELL. CERBERUS.

WE are now in the confines of Hell. Prithee come along with me; I will be the same friend to you that the [a] Sibyl was to Æneas. Nor shall you need a golden bough to present to Proserpine. You see here painted those regions of hell, of which you read a most elegant description in [b] Virgil. The passage that leads to these infernal dominions was a wide dark cave, through which you pass by a steep rocky descent till you arrive at a

[a] Virg. Æn. 6.

[b] "Spelunca alta fuit, vastoque immanis hiatu,
Scrupea, tuta lacu nigro nemorumque tenebris;
Quam super haud ullæ poterant impune volantes
Tendere iter pennis: talis sese halitus atris
Faucibus effundens supera ad convexa ferebat;
Unde locum Graii dixerunt nomine Avernum." Æn. 6.
Deep was the cave, and downward as it went
From the wide mouth, a rocky rough descent;
And here th' access a gloomy grove defends;
And there th' unnavigable lake extends,
O'er whose unhappy waters, void of light,
No bird presumes to steer his airy flight,
Such deadly stenches from the depth arise,
And steaming sulphur, which infects the skies;
Hence do the Grecian bards their legends make,
And give the name Avernus to the lake.

gloomy grove, and an unnavigable lake, called [c] Avernus, from which such poisonous vapours arise, that no birds can fly over it, for in their flight they fall down dead.

The monsters [d] at the entrance of hell are those fatal evils, which bring destruction and death upon mankind, by means of which the inhabitants of these dark regions are greatly augmented; and those evils are care, sorrow, diseases, old-age, frights, famine, want, labour, sleep, death, sting of conscience, force, fraud, strife, and war.

Charon is an old, decrepid, long-bearded fellow: he is the ferryman of hell; his [e] name denotes the ungracefulness of his aspect. In the Greek language, he is called Πορθμεὺς [*Porthmeus*], that is, *portitor*, "ferryman." You see his image, but you may read a more beautiful and elegant picture of him drawn by the pen of [f] Virgil.

[c] Avernus dicitur quasi ἄορνος, id est, sine avibus. Quòd nullæ volucres lacum illum, ob lethiferum halitum, prætervolare salvæ possent.

[d] "Vestibulum ante ipsum, primisque in faucibus Orci,
Luctus et ultrices posuêre cubilia Curæ;
Pallentesque habitant Morbi, tristesque Senectus,
Et Metus, et malesuada Fames, et turpis Egestas,
(Terribiles visu formæ) Lethumque Laborque.
Tum consanguineus Lethi Sopor, et mala mentis
Gaudia, mortiferumque adverso in limine Bellum,
Ferreique Eumenidum thalami, et Discordia demens
Vipereum crinem vittis innexa cruentis." Æn. 6.
Just in the gate, and in the jaws of Hell,
Revengeful Care and sullen Sorrow dwell;
And pale Diseases, and repining Age,
Want, Fear, and Famine's unresisted rage:
Here Toil and Death, and Death's half brother, Sleep
(Forms terrible to view), their sentry keep.
With anxious Pleasures of a guilty mind,
Deep Fraud before, and open Force behind:
The Furies' iron beds, and Strife that shakes
Her hissing tresses, and unfolds her snakes.

[e] Charon, quasi Acharon, id est, sine gratiâ, ab α non, et χάρις gratia.

[f] "Portitor has horrendus aquas et flumina servat
Terribili squalore Charon: cui plurima mento
Canities inculta jacet; stant lumina flammâ,
Sordidus ex humeris nodo dependet amictus.
Ipse ratem conto subigit, velisque ministrat,

He is waiting to take and carry over to the other side of the lake the souls of the dead, which you see flocking on the shores in troops. Yet he takes not all promiscuously who come, but such only whose bodies are buried when they die; for the [g] unburied wander about the shores a hundred years, and then are carried over. But first they pay Charon his fare, [h] which is at least a halfpenny.

There are three or four rivers to be passed by the dead. The first is Acheron, [i] which receives them when they come first. This Acheron was the son of Terra or Ceres, born in a cave, and conceived without a father; and because he could not endure light, [k] he ran down into hell and was changed into a river, whose waters are extremely bitter.

The second is Styx, which is a lake rather than a river, [l] and was formerly the daughter of Oceanus, and the mother of the goddess Victoria by Acheron. When Victoria was on Jupiter's side in his war against the Giants, she obtained this prerogative for her mother, that no oath that was sworn among the gods by her name should ever be violated: for if any of the gods broke an oath sworn by Styx, they were banished from the nectar and the table of the gods [m] a year and nine days. This

Et ferrugineâ subvectat corpora cymbâ,
Jam senior; sed cruda Deo viridisque senectus." Æn. 6.
There Charon stands, who rules the dreary coasts;
A sordid god: down from his hoary chin
A length of beard descends, uncomb'd, unclean;
His eyes like hollow furnaces on fire;
A girdle foul with grease binds his obscene attire.
He spreads his canvas, with his pole he steers;
The freights of flitting ghosts in his thin bottom bears.
He look'd in years; yet in his years were seen
A youthful vigour, and autumnal green.

[g] "Centum errant annos, volitant hæc litora circum:
Tum demum admissi stagna exoptata revisunt." Virg. Æn. 6.
A hundred years they wander on the shore,
At length, their penance done, are wafted o'er.

[h] Lucian. de Luct. [i] Plato in Phædone. [k] Pausan. in Attic.
[l] Hesiod. in Theog. [m] Serv. in Æn. 6.

is the Stygian Lake, by which [n] when the gods swore, they observed their oath with the utmost scrupulousness.

The third river, Cocytus, flows out of Styx with a lamentable groaning noise, and imitates the howling, and increases the exclamations of the damned.

Next comes [o] Phlegethon, or Puriphlegeton, so called because it swells with waves of fire, and all its streams are flames.

When the souls of the dead have passed over these four rivers, they were afterward carried to the palace of Pluto, where the gate is guarded by Cerberus, a dog with three heads, whose body is covered in a terrible manner with snakes, instead of hair. This dog is the porter of hell, [p] begotten of Echidna, by the giant Typhon, and is described by [q] Virgil and by [r] Horace.

QUESTIONS FOR EXAMINATION.

Give Virgil's description of hell, and the translation.
How is it described in the text?

[n] "Dii cujus jurare timent et fallere numen." Virg. Æn. 6.
The sacred stream which heaven's imperial state
Attests in oaths, and fears to violate.

[o] A φλέγω ardeo, quòd undis intumeat ignis, flammeosque fluctus evolvat.

[p] Hesiod. in Theog.

[q] "Cerberus hæc ingens latratu regna trifauci
Personat adverso recubans immanis in antro." Æn. 6.
Stretch'd in his kennel, monstrous Cerb'rus round
From triple jaws made all these realms resound.

[r] "Cessit immanis tibi blandienti
Janitor aulæ
Cerberus; quamvis furiale centum
Muniant angues caput ejus; atque
Spiritus teter, saniesque manat
Ore trilingui." L. 3. od. 11.
Hell's grisly porter let you pass,
And frown'd and listen'd to your lays;
The snakes around his head grew tame,
His jaws no longer glow'd with flame,
Nor triple tongue was stain'd with blood;
No more his breath with venom flow'd.

What is said of the monsters at the entrance?

Give Virgil's description.

Who is Charon?

What is his business?

Repeat Virgil's description.

Does Charon take all, promiscuously?

What is said of Acheron?

What is Styx?

How are Cocytus and Phlegethon described?

What becomes of the souls of the dead after they have passed these rivers?

Repeat Virgil's description of Cerberus.

Likewise the description of Horace.

CHAPTER II.

PLUTO. PLUTUS.

PLUTO is the king of hell, [s] begotten of Saturn and Ops, and the brother of Jupiter and Neptune. He had these infernal dominions allotted to him, not only because in the division of his father's kingdom the western parts fell to his lot; but also, [t] because the invention of burying, and of honouring the dead with funeral obsequies, proceeded from him: for the same reason he is thought to exercise a sovereignty over the dead. Look upon him: he sits on a throne covered with darkness, and discover, if you can, his habit, and the ensign of his majesty more narrowly. He holds a [u] key in his hand, instead of a sceptre, and is [w] crowned with ebony.

Sometimes he is crowned with a diadem; and [x] sometimes with the flowers of *narcissus*, or white daffodils, and sometimes with cypress leaves; because those plants

[s] Diodor. Sicul. 4. Bibl.
[t] Idem apud Lil. Gyr. Eurip. in Phœn.
[u] Pausan. in pr. Iliac.
[w] Marian.
[x] Lil. Gyr.

greatly please him, and especially the *narcissus*, since he stole away Proserpine when she gathered that flower. Very often a [y] rod is put into his hand in the place of a sceptre, with which he guides the dead to hell: and [z] sometimes he wears a headpiece, which makes him [a] invisible. His chariot and horses are of a black colour, and [b] when he carried away Proserpine, he rode in his chariot. But if you would know what the key signifies which he has in his hand, the answer is plain, that when once the dead are received into his kingdom, the gates are locked against them, and [c] there is no regress thence into this life again.

His Greek name [d] Plouton or Pluto, as well as his Latin name Dis, signifies wealth. The reason why he is so called is, because all our wealth comes from the lowest and most inward bowels of the earth; and because, as Cicero observes, [e] all the natural powers and faculties of the earth are under his direction; for all things proceed from the earth, and go thither again.

The name Ἅδης [*Hades*], by which he is called among the Greeks, [f] signifies dark, gloomy, and melancholy; or else, [g] as others guess, invisible; because he sits in darkness and obscurity: his habitation is melancholy and lonesome, and he seldom appears to open view.

He is likewise called [h] Agesilaus, because he leads

[y] Varr. apud eund. [z] Pind. in Od. [a] Hom. Iliad. 5. Hygen. Astron. Poet. [b] Ovid. Met. 5.

[c] ——— "Facilis descensus Averni:
Noctes atque dies patet atri janua Ditis;
Sed revocare gradum, superasque evadere ad auras,
Hoc opus, hic labor est."——— Virg. Æn. 6.
To th' shades you go a downhill easy way;
But to return, and re-enjoy the day,
That is a work, a labour.———

[d] Πλοῦτος, divitiæ.

[e] Terrena vis omnis ac natura ipsi dicata credebatur. Cic. de Nat. Deor. 2.

[f] Ἅδης ἀειδὴς, id est, triste, tenebrosum.

[g] Aut quasi ἀόρατος, quòd videri minimè possit, aut ab α privante, et ἰδεῖν videre. Socr. ap. Plut. Phurnut. Gaza. ap. Lil. Gyr.

[h] Παρὰ τὸ ἄγειν τοὺς λαοὺς, à ducendis populis ad inferos.

people to the infernal regions; and sometimes [i] Agelastus, because it was never known that Pluto laughed.

His name Februus comes from the old word *februo*, to purge by sacrifice, because purgations and lustrations were used at funerals: whence the month of [k] February receives also its appellation: at which time especially, the sacrifices called Februa were offered by the Romans to this god.

He is also called Orcus or Urgus, and Ouragus, as some say, [l] because he excites and hastens people to their ruin and death: but others think that he is so named, [m] because, like one that brings up the rear of an army, he attends at the last moments of men's lives.

He is called Summanus, that is, the chief [n] of all the infernal deities; the principal governor of all the ghosts and departed spirits. The thunder that happens in the night is attributed to him: whence he is commonly styled also, the Infernal Jupiter, the Stygian Jupiter, the Third Jupiter; as Neptune is the Second Jupiter.

The Fates will tell you that Pluto [o] presides over life and death; that he not only governs the departed spirits below, but also can lengthen or shorten the lives of men here on the earth, as he thinks fit.

Though Plutus be not an infernal god, I join him to Pluto, because their names and office are very similar:

[i] Ab α non, et γελάω rideo, quòd sine risu sit.

[k] Ovid. Fast. 2.

[l] Orcus quasi Urgus et Ouragus ab urgendo, quòd homines urgeat in interitum. Cic. in Verrem. 6.

[m] Οὐραγὸς, eum significat qui agmen claudit; simili modo Pluto postremum humanæ vitæ actum excipit. Guth. l. i. c. 4. de Jur. Man.

[n] Quasi summus Deorum manium. Aug. de Civ. Dei. l. 4.

[o] ——— "O maxime noctis
Arbiter, umbrarumque potens, cui nostra laborant
Stamina, qui finem cunctis et semina præbes,
Nascendique vices alternâ morte rependis,
Qui vitam lethumque regis." Claud. de Rap. Pros.
Great prince o' th' gloomy regions of the dead,
From whom we hourly move our wheel and thread,
Of nature's growth and end thou hast the sway,
All mortals' birth with death thou dost repay,
Who dost command 'em both.

they are both of them gods of riches, which are the root of all evil, and which Nature, our common parent, hath placed near hell; and, indeed, there is not a nearer way to hell than to hunt greedily after riches.

Plutus was the son of [p] Jason, or Jasius, by Ceres: he was blind and lame, injudicious, and mighty timorous. And truly these infirmities are justly ascribed to him; for, if he were not blind and injudicious, he would never pass over good men, and heap his treasures upon the bad. He is lame, because great estates come slowly. He is fearful and timorous, because rich men watch their treasures with a great deal of fear and care.

QUESTIONS FOR EXAMINATION.

Who is Pluto, and how did he become possessed of his dominions?

How is he painted?

What does the key signify?

What does his name Pluto signify, and why is he so called?

What does the name Hades signify?

Why is he called Agesilaus?

From what does his name Februus come?

Why is he called Orcus?

Why is he called Summanus, and what else is he styled?

Over what does Pluto preside?

Repeat the lines—

——— "O maxime noctis," &c.

In what respects is Plutus like Pluto?

Who was Plutus, and how is he represented?

[p] Hesiod. in Theog.

CHAPTER III.

PROSERPINE. THE FATES. THE FURIES.

She who sits next to Pluto is the queen of hell, [q] the Infernal Juno, [r] the "lady" (as the Greeks commonly call her), and the most beloved wife of Pluto, [s] the daughter of Ceres and Jupiter. She is called both Proserpine and Libera.

When all the goddesses refused to marry Pluto, because he was so deformed, he was vexed at this contempt and scorn, and troubled that he was forced to live a single life; wherefore, in a rage, he seated himself in a chariot, and arose on a sudden from a den in Sicily, where [t] he saw a company of very beautiful virgins gathering flowers in the fields of Enna, a beautiful place, situate about the middle of the island, and therefore called the Navel of Sicily. One of them, Proserpine, pleased him above the rest, for she surpassed them all in beauty. He came raging with love, and carried her with him from that place; and on a sudden he sunk into the earth near Syracuse. In the place where he descended, a lake arose: and [u] Cicero says, the people of Syracuse keep yearly festivals, to which great multitudes of both sexes resort.

The nymphs, her companions, were grievously affrighted, and fled away. In the mean time Ceres, the mother of Proserpine, seeks her daughter among her acquaintance a long time, but in vain. She next kindled torches by the flames which burst out from the top of the mountain Ætna, and went with them, to seek her daughter, throughout the whole world; neither did she give over her vain labour, till the nymph Arethusa fully assured her, that Proserpine was stolen by Pluto, and

[q] Virg. Æn. 6.
[r] Δέσποινα, domina. Paus. in Arcad.
[s] Hesiod. in Theog.
[t] Cic. in Verrem. 6.
[u] Ibid.

carried down into his kingdom. In great anger, she immediately hastened and expostulated with [w] Jupiter concerning the violence that was offered her daughter; and the god promised to restore Proserpine again, if she had not yet tasted any thing in hell. Ceres went joyfully down, and Proserpine, full of triumph and gladness, prepared to return into this world; when Ascalaphus discovered, that he saw Proserpine, while she walked in Pluto's orchard, pluck a pomegranate, and eat some grains of it; therefore Proserpine's journey was immediately stopped. Ceres being amazed at this new misfortune, and incensed at the fatal discovery of Ascalaphus, turned him into an owl, a bird said to be of an ill omen, and unlucky to all that see it: but at last, by the importunity of her prayers to Jupiter, she extorted this favour from him, that he should permit [x] Proserpine to live half the year, at least, with her in heaven, and the other half below in hell with her husband. Proserpine afterwards loved this disagreeable husband so much, that she was jealous, and changed Mentha, who was his mistress, into mint, a herb of her own name.

Let us now turn our eyes toward the tribunal of Pluto; where you see, in that dismal picture, continual trials: and all persons, as well the accusers as the offenders, who have been formerly wicked in their lives, receive their deaths impartially from the three Fates; after death they receive their sentence impartially from the three judges; and after condemnation, their punishment impartially from the three Furies.

The Fates are represented by three ladies: their [y] garments are made of ermine, white as snow, and bordered with purple. They were born either of [z] Nox and Ere-

[w] Serv. in Geo. 1.

[x] "Et Dea regnorum numen commune duorum,
Cum marte est totidem, totidem cum conjuge menses."
Ov. Met. 5.

The goddess now in either empire sways,
Six months with Ceres, six with Pluto stays.

[y] Catullus in Epith. Thet. [z] Hesiod. in Theog.

bus, or of [a] Necessity, or of the [b] Sea, or of that rude and indigested mass which the ancients called Chaos.

They are called Parcæ in Latin; because, as [c] Varro thinks, they distributed good and bad things to persons at their birth; or, as the common and received opinion is, [d] because they spare nobody. They are likewise called Fatum, "fate;" and are three in number, [e] because they order the past, present, and future time. Fate, says [f] Cicero, is all that which GOD hath decreed and resolved shall come to pass, and which the Grecians call Εἱμαρμένη [*Eimarmene*]. [g] Fatum is derived from the word *fari*, to pronounce or declare; because when any one is born, these three sisters pronounce what fate will befal him; as we saw in the story of Meleager.

Their names and offices are as follow: the name of one is [h] Clotho; the second is called [i] Lachesis; the third [k] Atropos, because she is unalterable, unchangeable. These names the Grecians give them: [l] the Romans call them Nona, Decima, and Morta.

To them is intrusted the management of the fatal thread of life: for Clotho draws the thread between her fingers; Lachesis turns about the wheel; and Atropos cuts the thread spun with a pair of scissors. That is, Clotho gives us life, and brings us into the world; Lachesis determines the fortunes that shall befal us here; and Atropos concludes our lives. [m] One speaks, the other writes, and the third spins.

The Furies have the faces of women. Their looks are full of terror; they hold lighted torches in their hands; snakes and serpents lash their necks and shoulders.

[a] Plato de Republ. 10. [b] Lycophron. [c] Parcæ dicuntur à partu, quòd nascentibus hominibus bona malaque conferre censeantur. [d] Aut à parcendo per Antiphrasin, quòd nemini parcant. Serv. in Æn. 1. [e] Euseb. Præp. Evang. 6.

[f] Est autem Fatum id omne quòd à Deo constitutum et designatum est ut eveniat, quòd Græci εἱμαρμένη appellant. De Fato et Divinat.

[g] Var. ap. Lil. Gyr. [h] A verbo κλωθω, id est, neo.

[i] Ab λαγχάνω, sortior. [k] Ab α privativâ particulâ, et τρέ τω verto, quòd verti et flecti nequeat. [l] Censen. Vind. ap. Lil. Gyr.

[m] Una loquitur, altera scribit, tertia fila ducit. Serv. in Æn. 1.

They are called in Latin sometimes Furiæ; [n] because they make men mad by the stings of conscience which guilt produces. They are also called [o] Diræ, [p] Eumenides, and [q] Canes; and were the offspring of [r] Nox and [s] Acheron. Their proper names are Alecto, Tisiphone, and Megæra; [t] and they are esteemed virgins; because, since they are the avengers of all wickedness, nothing can corrupt and pervert them from inflicting the punishment that is due to the offender.

There are only three Furies, because there are three [u] principal passions of the mind, anger, covetousness, and lust, by which mankind are chiefly hurried into all sorts of wickedness: for anger begets revenge, covetousness provokes us to get immoderate wealth by right or wrong, and lust persuades us to pursue our pleasures at any rate. Indeed some add a [w] fourth Fury, called Lisso; that is, rage and madness; but she is easily reduced to the other three: as also Erinnys, a name common to them all.

The office of the Furies is to observe and punish the crimes of bad men, and to torment the consciences of secret offenders; whence they are commonly also entitled [x] "the goddesses, the discoverers and revengers of evil actions." They punish and torment the wicked, by frightening and following them with burning torches. You see the picture of them there, and you will find them beautifully [y] described in the twelfth book of Virgil's [z] Æneid.

[n] Quòd sceleratos in furorem agant. [o] Virg. Æn. 3.
[p] Ibid. 8. [q] Ibid. 4. [r] Ibid. 6. [s] Ibid. 11.
[t] Suidas et Orph. in Hymn. [u] Isidor. ap. Gyr.
[w] Eurip. in Hercule furente. [x] Deæ speculatrices et vindices Facinorum.

[y] "Dicuntur geminæ pestes, cognomine Diræ,
Quas et Tartaream Nox intempesta Megæram
Uno eodemque tulit partu, paribusque revinxit
Serpentum spiris, ventosasque addidit alas."
Deep in the dismal regions, void of light,
Two daughters at a birth were born to Night:
These their brown mother, brooding on her care,
Endued with windy wings to fleet in air,
With serpents girt alike, and crown'd with hissing hair,
In heaven the Diræ call'd.

[z] Sua enim quemque fraus et suus terror maximè vexat: suum quem-

QUESTIONS FOR EXAMINATION.

Who was Proserpine?
How did Pluto obtain her for his wife?
What steps did Ceres take to recover her daughter?
What favour did Ceres obtain for Proserpine?
What do the *Fates*, the *Judges*, and the *Furies* determine?
Who are the Fates?
Why are they called Parcæ?
What is fate, according to Cicero?
From what is the word "fate" derived?
What are the names and offices of the Fates?
How are the Furies described?
What are their common and what their proper names?
Why are they esteemed virgins?
Why are there only three Furies?
What is the office of the Furies?

CHAPTER IV.

NIGHT. DEATH. SLEEP. THE JUDGES OF HELL.

Nox is, of all the gods, the most ancient: she was the sister of Erebus, and the daughter of the first Chaos; and of these two, Nox and Erebus, Mors [*Death*] was born. She is represented as a skeleton, dressed usually with a speckled garment and black wings: but there are no temples nor sacrifices, nor priests consecrated to Mors; because she is a goddess whom no [a] prayers can move, or sacrifices pacify.

Somnus [*Sleep*] [b] is the brother of Death, and [c] he

que scelus exagitat, amentiaque afficit: suæ malæ cogitationes conscientiæ quæ animi terrent. Hæ sunt impiis assiduæ domesticæ Furiæ, quæ dies noctesque pœnas à sceleribus repetunt. Or. pro Roscio Am.

[a] Horat. 2. Sermonum. [b] Orph. in Hymn.

[c] Hom. Iliad. 14. Virg. Æn. 5.

also hath wings, like her. Iris, who was sent by Juno to the palace of this god, mentions the great benefits that he bestows on mankind; such as [d] quiet of mind, tranquillity, freedom from care, and refreshment of the spirits, by which men are enabled to proceed in their labours. In his palace there are [e] two gates, out of which dreams pass and repass: one of these gates was made of clear ivory, through which false dreams pass; the other was made of transparent horn, and through that gate true visions come to men. [f] Morpheus, the servant of Somnus, who can put on any shape or figure, presents these dreams to those who sleep; and these dreams were brought from a great spreading elm in hell, under whose shade they usually sit.

Near the three Furies and the three Fates, [g] you see the three judges of hell, Minos, Rhadamanthus, and Æacus, who are believed to be judges of the souls of the dead; because they exercised the offices of judges in Crete with the greatest prudence, discretion, and justice. The first two were the sons of Jupiter by Europa: the last was the son of Jupiter by Ægina. When all the subjects of queen Ægina were swept away in a plague, beside Æacus, he begged of his father, that he would repair the race of mankind, which was almost extinct: Jupiter heard his prayer, and turned [h] a great mul-

[d] "Somne, quies rerum, placidissime Somne Deorum,
Pax animi, quem cura fugit, qui corpora duris
Fessa ministeriis mulces reparasque labori." Ov. Met. 11.
"Thou rest o' th' world, Sleep, the most peaceful god,
Who drivest care from the mind, and dost unload
The tired limbs of all their weariness,
And for new toil the body dost refresh.

[e] "Sunt geminæ Somni portæ, quarum altera fertur
Cornea, qua veris facilis datur exitus umbris:
Altera candenti perfecta nitens elephanto;
Sed falsa ad cœlum mittunt insomnia manes." Virg. Æn. 6.
Two gates the silent house of Sleep adorn;
Of polish'd iv'ry this, that of transparent horn:
True visions through transparent horn arise;
Through polish'd iv'ry pass deluding lies.

[f] Ovid. Met. 11. Virg. Æn. 6. [g] Hom. Odyss. 2.

[h] Ovid. Met. 7. Plato in Georg.

titude of ants, which crept about a hollow old oak, into men, who afterward were called Myrmidones, from μυρμηξ [*murmex*], which word signifies an ant.

These three had their particular province assigned by Pluto in this manner: Rhadamanthus was appointed to judge the Asiatics, and Æacus the Europeans, each holding a staff in his hand; but Minos holds a golden sceptre and sits alone, and oversees the judgments of Rhadamanthus and Æacus; and if in their courts there arose a case that was ambiguous and difficult, then Minos used to take the cognizance thereof, and decide it. [i] Cicero adds to these a fourth judge, Triptolemus; but we have already discoursed of him in his proper place.

QUESTIONS FOR EXAMINATION.

Who is Nox, and how was Mors produced?
How is Mors, or Death, represented?
Who is Somnus, and what benefits does he bestow on mankind?
Repeat the lines from Ovid and Virgil.
Who is Morpheus and Somnus?
Who are the judges of hell, and whose sons were they?
What is the origin of the Myrmidones?
What was the province of each of the judges?

CHAPTER V.

THE MOST FAMOUS OF THE CONDEMNED IN HELL.

FROM the judges let us proceed to the criminals, whom you see represented there in horrid colours. It will be enough if we take notice of the most celebrated of them, and notice their crimes, and the punishments inflicted on them.

The [k] Giants were the sons of Terra (*the earth*) when

[i] Tusc. Quæst. l. 1.

[k] Hesiod. in Theog.

she was impregnated by the blood of Cœlum, which flowed from that dishonourable wound given him by his son Saturn. They are all very tall in stature, with horrible dragons' feet; their looks and their bodies are altogether full of terror. Their impudence [l] was so great, that they strove to depose Jupiter from the possession of heaven; and when they engaged with the celestial gods, they [m] heaped up mountains upon mountains, and thence darted trees, set on fire, against the gods and heaven. [n] They hurled also prodigious massy stones and solid rocks, some of which, falling upon the earth again, became mountains; others fell into the sea, and became islands. This [o] battle was fought upon the Phlegræan plains, near the borders of Campania, [p] which country is called Phlegra, from φλεγω [*phlego*] *uro*, for it abounds in subterraneous fires, and hot baths flowing continually. The Giants were beaten, and all cut off, either by Jupiter's thunder, Apollo's arrows, or by the arms of the rest of the gods. And some say, that out of the blood of the slain, which was spilt upon the earth, serpents and such envenomed and pernicious animals were produced. The most eminent of those Giants were,

Typhœus, or Typhon, the son of Juno, conceived by her without a father. So vast was his magnitude, that he touched the east with one hand and the west with the other, and the heavens with the crown of his head. A hundred dragons' heads grew from his shoulders; his body was covered with feathers, scales, rugged hair, and adders; from the ends of his fingers snakes issued, and his two feet had the shape and folds of a serpent's body; his eyes sparkled with fire, and his mouth belched out flames. He was at last overcome, and thrown down; and, lest he should rise again, [q] the whole island of Sicily was laid upon him. This island was also called Trina-

[l] Hom. Odyss. 12. [m] Ovid. Met. 1.
[n] Duris Samius. [o] Nat. Comes, l. 6.
[p] Hom. Hymn. in Apollin.
[q] " Nititur ille quidem, pugnatque resurgere sæpe;
Dextra sed Ausonio manus est subjecta Peloro;

cria, because it bears the shape of a triangle, in the corners of which are the three promontories, Pelorus, Pachynus, and Lilybæus: Pelorus was placed on his right hand, Pachynus on his left, and Lilybæus lay upon his legs.

Ægeon was another prodigious and cruel giant: [r] Virgil tells us he had fifty heads and a hundred hands, from which he was called Centumgeminus, and [s] by the Grecians, Briareus. He hurled a hundred rocks against Jupiter at one throw; yet Jupiter dashed him down, bound him in a hundred chains, and [t] thrust him under the mountain Ætna; where, as often as he moves his side, the mountain casts forth great flames of fire.

Tityus was the son of [u] Jupiter and Elara, born in a subterraneous cave, in which Jupiter hid his mother, fearing the anger of Juno. She brought forth a child of so prodigious a bulk, that the earth was rent to give him a passage out of the cave; and thence he was believed to be the son of the earth. Juno afterward persuaded this giant to accuse Latona of adultery; for which Jupiter struck him with thunder down into hell: [w] there

Læva, Pachyne, tibi? Lilybæo crura premuntur;
Prægravat Ætna caput." Ovid. Met. 5.
He struggles oft, and oft attempts to rise;
But on his right hand vast Pelorus lies;
On 's left Pachynus; Lilybæus spreads
O'er his huge thighs; and Ætna keeps his heads.

[r] "Ægeon qualis, centum qui brachia dicunt,
Centenasque manus, quinquaginta oribus ignem
Pectoribusque arsisse: Jovis cum fulmina contra
Tot paribus streperet clypeis, tot stringeret enses." Æn. 10.
And as Ægeon, when with heaven he strove,
Stood opposite in arms to mighty Jove,
Moved all his hundred hands, provoked to war,
Defied the forky lightning from afar:
At fifty mouths his flaming breath expires,
And flash for flash returns, and fires for fires;
In his right hand as many swords he wields,
And takes the thunder on as many shields.

[s] Hom. Iliad. 1. [t] Callimachus in Lavacr. Deli. [u] Apol. 1.

[w] "Necnon et Tityon, terræ omniparentis alumnum,
Cernere erat; cui tota novem per jugera corpus
Porrigitur, rostroque immanis vultur obunco
Immortale jecur tundens, fœcundaque pœnis

he lies stretched out, covering nine acres of ground with his body; and a vulture continually gnaws his liver, which grows again every month.

To these we may add the Titans, [x] the sons of Terra and Cœlum; the chief of whom was Titanus, Saturn's eldest brother. They made war against Saturn, because the birth of Jupiter was concealed, and conquered him; but they were afterward overcome by Jupiter, and cast down into hell.

Phlegyas, who was king of the Lapithæ in Thessalia, and the father of the nymph Coronis. When he heard that Apollo had debauched his daughter, he went in anger and fired the temple of Apollo at Delphi: for which the enraged god shot him through the body with an arrow, and inflicted on him the following punishment: [y] A great stone hangs over his head, which he imagines every moment will fall down and crush him to pieces: thus he sits, perpetually fearing what will never come to pass; which makes him frequently call out to men, [z] to observe the rules of justice and the precepts of religion.

Ixion was the son of this Phlegyas: he killed his own sister, and obtained his pardon from the gods, who ad-

Viscera, rimaturque epulis, habitatque sub alto
Pectore: nec fibris requies data ulla renatis." Virg. Æn. 6.
There Tityus tortured lay, who took his birth
From heaven, his nursing from the fruitful earth;
Here his gigantic limbs, with large embrace,
Infold nine acres of infernal space:
A rav'nous vulture, in his open side
Her crooked beak and cruel talons tried;
Still for the growing liver digg'd his breast,
The growing liver still supplied the feast;
Still are the entrails fruitful to their pains,
Th' immortal hunger lasts, th' immortal food remains.

[x] Æschyl. in Prometheo.

[y] "Quos super atra silex jamjam lapsura, cadentique
Imminet assimilis." Virg. Æn. 6.
——— A massy stone,
Ready to drop, hangs o'er his cursed head.

[z] "Discite justitiam moniti, et non temnere Divos."
Learn justice hence, and don't despise the gods.

vanced him to heaven; and his prosperity made him so wanton, that he attempted to violate the chastity of Juno. This insolent attempt was discovered to Jupiter, who sent a cloud in the shape of Juno, which the deceived lover embraced, and thence those monsters the Centaurs were born: he was then thrown down to the earth again; where, because he boasted every where that he had familiarly known the queen of the gods, he was struck with thunder down into hell, and tied fast to a wheel, which turns about continually.

Salmoneus was king of Elis: his ambition was not satisfied with an earthly crown, for he desired divine honours; and, that the people might esteem him a god, he built a brazen bridge over the city, and drove his chariot upon it, imitating, by this noise, Jupiter's thunder: he also threw down lighted torches, and those who were struck by them were taken and killed. Jupiter would not suffer so great insolence, therefore threw the proud man from his stage headlong into hell, where Æneas, when he visited the infernal regions, saw him punished as [a] Virgil relates.

Sisyphus was a famous robber, killed by Theseus: [b] he is condemned in hell to roll [c] a great and unwieldy stone to the top of a high hill, and as oft as the stone almost touches the top of the mountain, it slides down again.

The Belides were fifty virgin-sisters, so called from their grandfather Belus; and named also Danaïdes, from their father Danaüs, who married them to the fifty sons of his brother. The oracle foretold that Danaüs should be slain by his son-in-law; wherefore he commanded his daughters to provide daggers, and on their wedding-night to kill their husbands. The daughters performed

[a] "Vidi crudeles dantem Salmonea pœnas,
Dum flammas Jovis et sonitus imitatur Olympi." Æn. 6.
Salmoneus suffering cruel pains I found,
For emulating Jove; the rattling sound
Of mimic thunder, and the glittering blaze
Of pointed lightnings, and their forked rays.

[b] Hesiod. Argon. [c] Ingens et non exsuperabile saxum. Virg.

their promises, and killed their husbands, except Hypermnestra, for she spared Lynceus, her husband, who afterward killed Danaüs, and took his kingdom. This great impiety was thus punished: [d] they were condemned to draw water out of a deep well, and fill a tub that (like a sieve) is full of holes: the water runs out of the tub as fast as it is put in, so that they are tormented with a perpetual and unprofitable labour.

Tantalus, another remarkable criminal, was the [e] son of Jupiter by the nymph Plota. He invited all the gods to a feast, to get a plain and clear proof of their divinity: when they came, he killed and quartered his own son Pelops, and boiled him, and set the joints before them to eat. All the gods abstained from such horrid diet, except Ceres, who, being melancholy and inattentive from the recent loss of her daughter, eat one of the child's shoulders. Afterward the gods sent Mercury to recal him to life, and gave him an ivory shoulder, instead of the shoulder which Ceres had [f] eaten. This Pelops was the husband of Hippodamia, who bore him Atreus and Thyestes; the latter of whom was banished, because he corrupted Ærope his brother Atreus's wife; and, when he was recalled from banishment, he eat up those children that he had by her; for Atreus killed them, and had them served in dishes to the table, where he and Thyestes dined together. It is said that the sun could not endure so horrible a sight, and turned his course back again to the east. But as Tantalus' crime was greater, so was his punishment; [g] for he is tormented with eternal hunger and thirst in the midst of plenty both of meat and drink: he stands in water up to his lips, but cannot reach it; and fruit is placed just to his mouth, which he cannot take hold of. [h] Ovid mentions

[d] "Assiduas repetunt quas perdunt Belides undas." Ov. Met. 4.
They hourly fetch the water that they spill.

[e] Euseb. Præp. Evang. [f] Pindar. in Olymp.

[g] Hom. Odyss. 11.

[h] "Quærit aquas in aquis, et poma fugacia captat
Tantalus, hoc illi garrula lingua dedit."

the punishment of Tantalus, but assigns another reason for it; namely, because he divulged the secrets of the gods to men.

Now this fable of Tantalus represents the condition of a miser, who in the midst of plenty suffers want, and wants as much the things which he has, as those which he has not; as Horace rightly says, where he applies this fable of Tantalus to the real wants of the covetous man.

QUESTIONS FOR EXAMINATION.

Who were the Giants?
How are they and their actions described?
How were they subdued?
Who was Typhæus or Typhon, and how is he described?
What became of him?
Who was Ægeon, and what were his other names?
Repeat the lines from Virgil.
What became of him when he was subdued?
Who was Tityus?
What became of him?
Who were the Titans, and what is said of their chief?
Repeat the lines from Virgil.
Who was Phlegyas; what was his crime; and what his punishment?
What is said of Ixion?
What is said of Salmoneus?
Who was Sisyphus; and what was his punishment?
Who were the Belides?
What is the history of Tantalus?
What are the lines of Horace descriptive of Tantalus?

"Tantalus à labris sitiens fugientia captat,
Flumina... Quid rides? mutato nomine, de te
Fabula narratur." Serm. I. I.
Though Tantalus, you've heard, does stand chin deep
In water, yet he cannot get a sip:
At which you smile; now all on't would be true,
Were the name changed, and the tale told of you.

CHAPTER VI.

MONSTERS OF HELL. ELYSIUM. LETHE.

THERE are many strange pictures of these infernal monsters, but the most deformed are the Centaurs, who were the ancient inhabitants of Thessalia, and the first who tamed horses, and used them in war. Their neighbours, who first saw them on horseback, thought that they had partly the members of a man, and partly the limbs of a horse. But the poets tell us another story; for they say that Ixion begat them of a cloud, which he believed to be Juno. Whence they are called [k] Nubigenæ; and Bacchus is said to have overcome them.

Geryon, because he was the king of three islands called Balearides, [l] is feigned to have three bodies; or, it may be, because there were three brothers of the same name, whose minds and affections were so united, that they seemed to be governed and to live by one soul. They add that Geryon kept oxen, which devoured the strangers that came to him: they were guarded by a dog with two heads, and a dragon with seven. Hercules killed the guards, and drove the oxen away.

The Harpies, so called [m] from their rapacity, were born of Oceanus and Terra. They had the faces of virgins, and the bodies of birds; their hands were armed with claws, and their habitation was in the islands. Their names were Aello, Ocypete, and Celeno; which last brought forth Zephyrus, the "west wind," and Balius and Xanthus, the horses of Achilles. Virgil gives us an [n] elegant description of these three sisters.

[k] Virg. Æn. 6. [l] Tricorporem et tergeminum fuisse.
[m] Ab αρπάζω, rapio.
[n] "At subitæ horrifico lapsu de montibus adsunt
Harpyæ; et magnis quatiunt clangoribus alas:
Sive Deæ, seu sunt Diræ, obscœnæque volucres.
Tristius haud illis monstrum est, nec sævior ulla

To the three Harpies add the three Gorgons, Medusa, Stheno, and Euryale, who were the daughters of Phorcus and Cete. Instead of hair, their heads were covered with vipers, which so terrified the beholder, that they turned him presently into a stone. Perhaps they intended to represent, by this part of the fable, the extraordinary beauty of these sisters; which was such, that whoever saw them were amazed, and stood immoveable like stones. There were other Gorgons beside, born of the same parents, who were called Lamiæ, or Empusæ. [o] They had only one eye and one tooth, common to them all: they kept this tooth and eye at home in a little vessel, and whichever of them went abroad, she used them. [p] They had the faces of women, and also the necks and breasts; but below they were covered with scales, and had the tails of serpents. They used to entice men, and then devour them.

The Chimæra [q] was a monster, [r] which vomited forth fire: he had the head and breast of a lion, the belly of a goat, and the tail of a dragon, as it is expressed [s] in a known verse, and described by [t] Ovid. A volcano in

Pestis et ira Deûm, Stygiis sese extulit undis.
Virginei volucrum vultus, fœdissima ventris
Proluvies, uncæque manus, et pallida semper
Ora fame." Æn. 3.

When from the mountain-tops, with hideous cry
And clattering wings, the filthy harpies fly:
Monsters more fierce offended heaven ne'er sent,
From hell's abyss, for human punishment.
With virgin faces, but with wombs obscene;
Foul paunches, and with ordure still unclean;
With claws for hands, and looks for ever lean.

[o] Æschyl. in Prometh.
[p] Dion. Hist. Libyæ.
[q] Hom. Iliad. 14.
[r] Hesiod. in Theog.
[s] "Prima leo, postrema draco, media inde capella."
A lion's head and breast resemble his,
His waist a goat's, his tail a dragon's is.
[t] "Quoque Chimæra jugo, mediis in partibus hircum,
Pectus et ora leæ, caudam serpentis habebat." Met. 9.
—— And on the craggy top
Chimæra dwells, with lion's face and mane,
A goat's rough body, and a serpent's train.

Lycia occasioned this fable; for in the top of the mountain were lions; in the middle, where was pasture, goats lived; and the bottom of it abounded with serpents. [x] Bellerophon made this mountain habitable, and therefore is said to have killed the Chimæra.

The monster Sphynx was begotten [y] of Typhon and Echidna. She had the head and breast of a woman, the wings of a bird, the body of a dog, and the paws of a lion. She lived in the mountain Sphincius, assaulted all passengers, and infested the country about Thebes; insomuch that the oracle of Apollo was consulted concerning her, and answer was made, that unless somebody did resolve the riddle of Sphynx, there would be no end of that great evil. Many endeavoured to explain it, but were overcome, and torn in pieces by the monster. Creon, at that time king of Thebes, published an edict through all Greece, in which, if any one could explain the riddle of Sphynx, he promised that he would give him to wife his own sister Jocasta. The riddle was this: [z] "What animal is that, which goes upon four feet in the morning, upon two at noon, and upon three at night?" Oedipus, encouraged with the hopes of the reward, undertook it, and happily explained it; so that the Sphynx was enraged, and cast herself headlong from a rock, and died. He said, that the animal was a man, who in his infancy creeps upon his hands and feet, and so may be said to go on four feet; when he grows up, he walks on two feet; but when he grows old, he uses the support of a staff, and so may be said to walk on three feet.

This Oedipus was the son of Laius, [a] king of Thebes. Soon after his birth, Laius commanded a soldier to carry his son Oedipus into a wood, and then destroy him; because it had been foretold by the oracle, that he should be killed by his own son. But the soldier was moved with pity toward the child, and afraid to imbrue his

[x] Pausan. in Corinth. [y] Vide Nat. Com.
[z] Quidnam animal mane quadrupes, meridie bipes, vesperi tripes esset?
[a] Stat. 1. Theb. Plutarch. Ælian. et alii.

hands in royal blood; wherefore he pierced his feet with a hook, and hanged him upon a tree to be killed with hunger. One of the shepherds of Polybius, king of Corinth, found him, and brought him to the queen, who, because she had no children, educated him as her own son, and from [b] his swollen feet called him Oedipus. When Oedipus came to age, he knew that king Polybius was not his father, and therefore resolved to find out his parents: he consulted the oracle, and was told that he should meet his father in Phocis. In his journey he met some passengers, among whom was his father, but he knew him not: a quarrel arose, and in the fray he by chance killed his father. After this, he proceeded on his journey, and arrived at Thebes, where he overcame Sphynx, and for his reward married Jocasta, whom he knew not to be his mother then, but discovered it afterward. He had by her two sons, Eteocles and Polynices, and two daughters, Antigone and Ismena. [c] Afterwards, when he found, by clear proof, that he had killed his father, and married his mother, he was seized with so great madness, that he pulled out his own eyes, and would have killed himself, if his daughter Antigone (who led him about after he was blind) had not hindered him.

Eteocles and Polynices, the sons of Oedipus and Jocasta, [d] succeeded their father in the government; and they agreed to reign a year each in their turns. Eteocles reigned the first year, and then refused to admit his brother Polynices to the throne; upon which a war arose, and the two brothers, in a duel, killed each other. Their enmity lasted longer than their lives; for when their bodies were placed on the same pile to be burnt by the same fire, the flames refused to unite, but divided themselves into two parts.

There is a place in the infernal dominions abounding

[b] Puerum Œdipum vocavit à tumore pedum, οἰδέω enim tumeo et ποῦς pedem significat.

[c] Senecæ Œdip. [d] Stat. Theb.

with pleasures and delights, which is called the Elysium; [e] because thither the souls of the good resort, after they are loosed from the chains of the body, and have been purged from the light offences that they had contracted in this world. [f] Æneas received the account from one of the inhabitants of it, as Virgil tells us, [g] who describes this place as abounding with all the delights that the most pleasant plains, the most verdant fields, the shadiest groves, and the finest and most temperate air can produce.

There is a river in hell called Lethe, [h] from the forgetfulness which it causes. For if any body drinks this water, he immediately forgets all things past; so that when the souls of the pious have spent many ages in the Elysian fields, [i] they drink the water of Lethe, and are believed to pass into new bodies, and return into the world again: and it is necessary they should forget both the pleasures they have received in Elysium, and the miseries they did formerly endure in this life, that they

[e] Ἀπὸ τῆς λύσεως, a solutione; quòd Animæ piorum corporeis solutæ vinculis, loca illi petant postquam purgatæ sunt à levioribus noxis quas contraxerant.

[f] "Quisque suos patimur manes; exinde per amplum
Mittimur Elysium, et pauci læta arva tenemus." Æn. 6.
All have their manes, and those manes bear:
The few, who 're cleansed, to those abodes repair,
And breathe in ample fields the soft Elysian air.

[g] "Devenere locos lætos, et amœna vireta
Fortunatorum nemorum, sedesque beatas.
Largior hic campos æther et lumina vestit
Purpureò: solemque suum, sua sidèra norunt."
These holy rites perform'd, they took their way,
Where long-extended plains of pleasure lay.
The verdant fields with those of heaven may vie,
With ether vested, and a purple sky:
The blissful seats of happy souls below,
Stars of their own, and their own sun they know.

[h] Ἀπὸ τῆς λήθης, ab oblivione.

[i] ——— "Animæ quibus altera fato
Corpora debentur, Lethæi ad fluminis undam
Securos latices et longa oblivia potant." Virg. Æn. 6.
——— Souls that by fate
Are doom'd to take new shapes, at Lethe's brink
Quaff draughts secure, and long oblivion drink.

may willingly return into it again. These souls went out from Elysium by an ivory gate, in the lower part of the wall.

QUESTIONS FOR EXAMINATION.

What is said of the Centaurs?
What is the history of Geryon?
Who were the Harpies?
Repeat the lines from Virgil, and their translation.
What is said of the Gorgons?
What is said of the Chimæra, and what was the occasion of this fable?
What is the history of Sphynx?
What was the riddle proposed by Sphynx?
Who explained it?
Give the history of Œdipus.
What is the Elysium, and how is it described?
Repeat the lines from Virgil.
What is said of the river Lethe?
Repeat the lines from Virgil.

PART V.

OF THE

DII MINORUM GENTIUM:

OR,

THE SUBORDINATE DEITIES.

CHAPTER I.

THE PENATES. THE LARES.

THE fifth division of this *Fabulous Pantheon* contains the inferior or subordinate gods: the Latins generally called them Dii Minorum Gentium, and sometimes Semones, Minuti, Plebeii, and Patellarii.

The Penates are so called from the Latin word *penus;* which word, [k] Cicero says, includes every thing that men eat. Or they have perhaps this name from the place allotted to them in the heavens, [l] because they are placed in the most inward and private parts of the heavens, where they reign: hence, they call them Penetrales, and the place of their abode Penetrale. They entirely govern us by their reason, their heat, and their spirit, so that we can neither live nor use our under-

[k] Est enim penus omne quo vescuntur homines. De Nat. Deor.

[l] Quòd penitus insideant, ex quo Penetrales à Poëtis vocantur, et locus in quo servabantur eorum effigies Penetrale dictus. Varro ap. Arnob. l. 3.

standing without them; yet we know neither their number nor names. The ancient Hetrusci called them Consentes and Complices; supposing that they are Jupiter's counsellors, and the chief of the gods; and many reckon Jupiter himself, together with Juno and Minerva, among the Penates. But I will give you a more distinct and particular information in this matter.

There were three orders of the Dii Penates: 1. Those who governed [m] kingdoms and provinces, and were absolutely and solely called Penates. 2. Those who presided over cities only; and these were called the [n] "gods of the country," or the "great gods:" Æneas makes mention of them in [o] Virgil. 3. Those who presided over particular houses and families; and these were called the [p] "small gods." The poets make frequent mention of them, especially Virgil, who in one place mentions fifty maid-servants, whose business it was to look after their affairs, and [q] to offer sacrifices to the household gods: and in [r] another place he speaks of these household gods being stained and defiled by the blood of one that was killed by his brother. But it must likewise be observed, that, among the Latins, the word *Penates* not only signifies the gods, of which we have been speaking, but likewise a dwelling-house, of which we have instances in many authors, and, among the rest, in [s] Virgil, [t] Cicero, and [u] Fabius.

[w] Timæus, and from him Dionysius, says that these Penates had no proper shape or figure; but were wooden or brazen rods, shaped somewhat like trumpets.

[m] Virg. Æn. l. 5. [n] Dii Patrii θεοὶ πατρῷοι. Macrob. 3. Saturn. 14. Plut. 4. Symp. 1.

[o] "Tu, genitor, cape sacra manu, patriosque Penates." Æn. 2.

Our country gods, the reliques and the bands,
Hold you, my father, in your guiltless hands.

[p] Parvique Penates. Virg. Æn. 8. [q] Flammis adolere penates. Æn. 1. [r] Sparsos fraterna cæde Penates. Æn. 4.

[s] Nostris succede penatibus hospes. Æn. 8.

[t] Exterminare aliquem à suis Diis Penatibus. Pro Sexto.

[u] Liberos pellere domo, ac prohibere Penatibus. Dec. 260.

[w] Lib. 1.

But it is also thought by others, that they had the shape of young men with spears, which they held apart from another.

The Lares were children born from the stolen embraces of Mercury and the nymph Lara; for when, by her prating, she had discovered some of Jupiter's amours, he was so enraged that he cut out her tongue, and banished her to the Stygian lake: Mercury, who was appointed to conduct her thither, ravished her upon the road. [x] She grew pregnant, and in due time brought forth twins, and named them Lares.

They were made domestic gods, and accordingly presided over [y] houses, streets, and ways. On this account they were worshipped [z] in the roads and open streets, called *compita* in Latin, whence the games celebrated in their honour were called [a] Compitalitii, Compitalitia, and sometimes Compitalia. When these sports were exercised, [b] the images of men and women, made of wool, were hung in the streets; and so many balls made of wool as there were servants in the family, and so many complete images as there were children. The meaning of which custom was this: These feasts were dedicated to the Lares, who were esteemed infernal gods; the people desiring by this, that these gods would be contented with those woollen images, and spare the persons represented by them. The Roman youths used to wear a golden ornament, called *bulla*, about their necks; it was made in the shape of a heart, and hollow within: this they wore till they were fourteen years of age; then they put it off, and, hanging it up, consecrated it to the Lares; as we learn from [c] Persius. These Lares

[x] "Fitque gravis Geminosque parit qui compita servant,
Et vigilant nostra semper in æde Lares." Ovid. Fast. 2.
Her twins the Lares called. 'Tis by their care
Our houses, roads, and streets in safety are.

[y] Martial. l. 3. ep. 57. [z] Arnob. 2.

[a] Varro de Rusticâ; et 5. de Ling. Lat.

[b] Festus apud Lil. Gyr.

[c] "Bullaque succinctis Laribus donata pependit."
When fourteen years are past, the Bulla's laid
Aside, an offering to the Lares made.

sometimes [d] were clothed in the skins of dogs, and [e] sometimes fashioned in the shape of dogs; whence that creature was consecrated to them.

The place in which the Lares were worshipped was called Lararium; and in the sacrifices offered to them, [f] the first fruits of the year, [g] wine and incense, were brought to their altars, and their images adorned with chaplets and garlands. [h] The beginning of which worship came hence: that anciently the dead, [i] who were buried at home, were worshipped as gods, and called Lares. And besides, we find in [k] Pliny, that they sacrificed, with wine and incense, to the images of the emperors while they yet lived.

QUESTIONS FOR EXAMINATION.

How are the inferior gods divided?

What is said of the Penates?

Into how many orders were they divided, and what was their office?

What signification is given to the word "Penates" by the Latins?

What is related of the Penates by Timæus and Dionysius?

Who were the Lares?

Over what did they preside?

What games were celebrated in honour of them, and how were they exercised?

What custom had the Romans with respect to the Lares?

Where were the Lares worshipped?

CHAPTER II.

THE GENII. THEIR NAMES, IMAGES, SACRIFICES, AND OFFICES.

ALTHOUGH the Genii and the Lares sometimes mean the same deities, yet by Genius is commonly meant that spirit of nature which produces all things, from

[d] Plutarch in Prob. [e] Plautus. [f] Tibul. l. 1.
[g] Plaut. in Prol. Aul. [h] Juv. sat. 9. 12.
[i] Arnob. 5. ex. Var. [k] Epist. l. 10.

which [l] generative power it has its name; or else it is so called, because it assists all generations; or lastly, because it protects and defends us when we are begotten. The birth-day, and the marriage bed, had the name [m] "genial" from him; which name [n] was likewise given to all days wherein mirth, pleasure, and joys did abound. And on the same account those who live merrily, who deny themselves nothing that makes for their ease and pleasure, or that is grateful to their appetite, who entirely follow the dictates of their sensual desires, are said to live a genial life, or to indulge their genius.

The Greeks called these Genii "dæmons;" as it is thought, from the [o] terror and dread they create in those to whom they appear; or, as it is more probable, [p] from the prudent and wise answers which they gave when they were consulted as oracles. [q] Hence some think, that illustrious men, whose actions in this life gain them universal praise and applause, do after their deaths become dæmons; by which dæmons is to be understood, [r] as Plutarch says, beings of a middle kind, of a greater dignity than man, but of a nature inferior to the gods.

The images of the Genii resembled for the most part the form [s] of a serpent, according to [t] Persius and his commentators. Sometimes also they were [u] described like a boy, or a girl, or an old man; and crowned with the leaves of the plane-tree, [w] which was a tree sacred to them.

[l] A gignendo seu genendo, nam geno pro gigno olim dicebatur. Aug. de Civ. Dei. 7. Cic. de Orat. 2. et de Invent. 2.

[m] Censorin. de Dei. Nat. 3. [n] Isidor. 8. Etymol.

[o] Dæmones dicuntur à δαιμαίνω exterreo, aut pavefacio. Eusebius.

[p] Vel quasi δαήμονες, id est, periti rerumque præscii, nam responsa dabant consulentibus. Isidor. 8. Etymol.

[q] Socrates ex Hes. ap. Plat. [r] Lib. de Orac.

[s] Sat. Theb. 5.

[t] "Pinge duos angues; pueri, sacer est locus, extra
Meiete." Sat. 1.

[u] Vide La Cerdæ Commentar. in Æneid.

[w] Platanus putabatur arbor genialis.

Wine and flowers were offered up in the sacrifices to the Genii, and that especially by people on their birth-days, as we may learn from [x] Persius and [y] Horace. To these flowers and wine they added [z] incense, parched bread, and corn strewed with salt. [a] Sometimes also a swine was sacrificed; though Censorinus writes, that it was not usual to sacrifice to the Genii with the blood and slaughter of any thing, since we ought not to take life from other creatures on that day on which we received it.

The Genii were appointed the continual guardians, overseers, [b] and safe keepers of the men (as [c] the women's guardians and protectors were called Junones) from their cradles to their graves. They likewise carried the prayers of men to the gods, and interceded for them. Whence some call them Præstites, or chief governors, [d] because they are set over the management of all things.

To every person [e] were assigned two Genii, a *bonus* Genius, and a *malus* Genius: [f] Horace calls them a white and a black one. We are told by [g] Valerius Maximus, that when Cassius fled to Athens, after Antony was beaten at Actium, there appeared to him a man of a large stature, of a black swarthy complexion, with long hair, and grisly beard. Cassius asked him who he was? and the apparition answered, "I am your evil

[x] "Funde merum Genio."
To Genius consecrate a cheerful glass.

[y] ———— "piabant
Floribus et vino Genium memorem brævis ævi,
Cum sociis operum et pueris et conjuge fida." Epist. 2.
Their wives, their neighbours, and their prattling boys,
Were call'd; all tasted of their sportive joys:
They drank, they danced, they sung, made wanton sport,
Enjoy'd themselves, for life they knew was short.

[z] Plut. in Aul.
[a] Palæph. Ecl. 5. Hor. Carm. 3.
[b] Arrian. in Epictet.
[c] Polit. Miscell. c. 99.
[d] Quòd præsint gerundis omnibus. Martianus de Nupt. 2.
[e] Plut. de Iside et Osir.
[f] Genium album et nigrum, Epist. 2.
[g] Interrogatus quisquam esset respondit se esse κακοδαίμονα, L. 1, c. 7.

Genius." Virgil is thought, by his [h] commentator Servius, to mean these two Genii, by the word *manes*. Of these two Genii, the good one, which is given to every one at his birth, constantly incites him to the practice of virtue and goodness; whereas the bad one prompts him to all manner of vice and wickedness.

Nor were they assigned to men only; for several countries had their Genii, who therefore were called [i] "the deities of the place." Nay, [k] Genii were allotted to all houses, and doors, and stables, and hearths: and because the hearths were usually covered with slates, therefore the god of the hearths was called Lateranus.

QUESTIONS FOR EXAMINATION.

Who were the Genii, and from what is the term derived?

Why were they called Dæmons?

How are they represented?

What were the sacrifices offered to the Genii?

To whom were the Genii appointed guardians?

How many Genii were appointed to each person, and what were they?

What was the office of each?

Were Genii appointed to countries and places, as well as persons?

What was the god of the hearths called?

[h] Quisque suos patimur manes. Virg. Æn. 6. Vide Servium in loc.

[i] Numen loci. Virg. Æn. 7.

[k] Prud. in Symm. Laterculis extrui foci solebant. Lil. Gyr. synt. 1.

CHAPTER III.

THE NUPTIAL GODS AND GODDESSES. DEITIES PRESIDING OVER WOMEN IN LABOUR, &c.

FIVE deities were so absolutely necessary to all marriages, that none could lawfully be solemnized without them. They were [l] Jupiter *perfectus* or *adultus*, Juna *perfecta* or *adulta*, Venus, Sunda, and Diana: beside these, several inferior gods and goddesses were worshipped at all marriages.

Jugatinus joined the man and the woman together in [m] the yoke of matrimony.

Domiducus [n] guided the bride into the bridegroom's house.

Domitius was worshipped, that the bride might be [o] kept at home, to look after the affairs of the family.

Manturna was worshipped, that the wife might never leave her husband, but in all conditions of life [p] abide with him.

Then the goddess Virginensis, and also the goddess Cinxia Juno, [q] were invoked when the virgin's girdle was unloosed.

Priapus, or Mutinus, was also reckoned one of the nuptial gods, because in his lap the bride was commanded to sit.

[r] Viriplaca reconciles husbands to their wives. A temple at Rome was dedicated to her, whither the married couple usually repaired when any quarrel arose between them; and there, opening their minds freely to each other, without passion, they laid aside all anger, and returned home together friendly.

[l] Minores et Plebii Dii.
[m] A jugo matrimonii dictus. Aug. de Civ. Dei. 4.
[n] Quod sponsam in sponsi domum duceret. Idem, ibid.
[o] Ut sponsam domi teneret. [p] Ut cum marito semper maneret.
[q] August. ibid. [r] A placando viro. Val. Max. l. 2. c. 1.

Pilumnus, one of the gods of children, was so called from the [s] pestle which the ancients pounded their corn with, before they made their bread; or [t] because he keeps off those misfortunes which attend children.

Intercidona was the goddess who first taught the art [u] of cutting wood with a hatchet to make fires.

Deverra was worshipped as a goddess, because she invented brooms, by which all things are brushed clean, and those distempers prevented that proceeded [w] from nastiness.

The Sylvan gods, who were always hurtful to pregnant women, were driven away by those deities, and the mischiefs they intended were prevented. For, as neither the trees, [x] says St. Augustin, are cut down without an axe, nor bread made without a pestle, nor things preserved clean without a brush; so, since those instruments are thought signs of good housewifery, it was supposed that these wild unclean deities would never dare to enter into the chamber of a pregnant woman.

Juno Lucina, [y] the friend of women in labour, is represented with one hand empty, and ready, as it were, to receive the new-born babe; the other hand holding a lighted torch, by which that light of life was signified, which all enjoy as soon as they are born.

Diana; though [z] some make no difference between her and Lucina. Timæus speaks very handsomely, [a] when he relates that Diana's temple was burnt the same night in which Alexander was born: [b] It is (says he) no wonder she was absent from her house, when her assistance was necessary at the labour of Olympias, Alexander's mother.

Lastly, the goddess of Latona, of whom we have spoken in her place. It was thought that she very much loved a dunghill-cock, because one was present

[s] A pilo. [t] Quod mala ab infantibus pellit. Servius.
[u] Ab intercisione securis. [w] A scopis quibus verritur.
[x] De Civ. Dei. 7. [y] Nat. Comes.
[z] Catull. Carm. ad Dian. 12. [a] Cic. Nat. Deor. 1.
[b] Theocr. Idyll. 17.

when she brought forth Diana and Apollo; and thence it is imagined, that the presence of a cock renders women's labours easy.

QUESTIONS FOR EXAMINATION.

Who were the deities necessary in all marriages?

What was the business of Jugatinus, Domiducus, and Domitius?

Why were Manturna, Virginensis, and Priapus, reckoned nuptial gods?

What was the business of Viriplaca?

Who was Pilumnus?

Who was Intercidona?

Why was Deverra worshipped as a goddess?

What gods were driven away by these deities; and what are the observations of St. Augustine?

How is Juno Lucina represented?

What is said of Diana, and the burning of her temple?

CHAPTER IV.

THE DEITIES PRESIDING OVER INFANTS AT THE TIME OF THEIR BIRTH, AND AFTERWARD.

THE chief of these are as follows:

Janus, who opened the [c] door of life to them.

Opis, who [d] assisted them when they came into the world.

Nascio, or Natio, a goddess so called from a Latin word [e] signifying to be born.

Cunia, [f] who attends the cradle, and watches the infants while they lie and sleep.

Levana, [g] from lifting them up from the ground: [h] for when a child was born, the midwife constantly laid

[c] Qui aperiret vitæ januam.

[d] Quæ opem ferret.

[e] A nascendo.

[f] Quæ cunis præest.

[g] A levando.

[h] Var. 2. de vita pop. Rom.

the child on the ground, and the father, or, in his absence, somebody appointed by him, lifted it from the ground; and hence *tollere liberos* signifies "to educate children."

Carna, or Carnea, [i] who keeps the inward parts safe. To this goddess they sacrificed, upon the calends of June, bacon, and cakes made of beans. Whence those calends were called Fabariæ.

The goddess Nundina was so called from [k] the ninth day of the child's age, which was the day of the purification: in which the name was given it, if it was a boy; if it was a girl, this ceremony was performed on the eighth day.

Our several actions are supposed to be under the protection of divers gods.

Juventus, or Juventas, protects us in the beginning of our youth, [l] when we have thrown off the child's coat.

Horta is the goddess [m] who exhorts us to undertake noble enterprises. Her temple at Rome stood always open: and some call her Hora.

Quies had her temple without the city; and [n] was supposed to be the donor of peace and quietness.

The goddess Meditrina has her name from [o] healing; and her sacrifices were called Meditrinalia, in which they drank new and old wine instead of physic.

The goddess Vitula is so called from [p] leaping for joy: she is the "goddess of mirth," which mitigates the toils of life.

Sentia was worshipped, that children might imbibe at first just and honourable [q] sentiments.

Angerona was the goddess that removed the [r] an-

[i] A carne. Vide Macrob. Saturn. l. 1.

[k] A nono die, qui fuit dies lustricus. Vide Macrob. Festum in voce lustricus.

[l] August. 4. c. 11.

[m] Plut. Quæst, Rom. 14.

[n] August. 4. c. 16.

[o] A medendo. Var. et Festus.

[p] A vitulando, id est, lætitia gestiendo.

[q] A sentiendo. Fest. Jul. Modest.

[r] Ut pelleret angores animi.

guishes of the mind: or was so named from [s] the squinancy, by which the cattle of the Romans were almost wholly destroyed; but they offered vows to her, and she removed the [t] plague.

Stata, or Statua Mater, was worshipped in the Forum, that it should not be burnt, or suffer damage from the frequent fires which happened there in the night.

The goddess Laverna was the protectress of thieves, who, from her, were named Laverniones: they worshipped her, that their designs and intrigues might be successful: [u] her image was a head without a body.

Volumnus and Volumna were so named, because, through their means, men [w] were willing to follow things that are good.

Aius Locutius was worshipped on this occasion: A common soldier reported, that in the night he heard a voice say, "The Gauls are coming." Nobody minded what he said, because he was a poor fellow. After the Gallic war, Camillus advised the Romans to expiate their offence in neglecting this nocturnal voice, which forewarned them of the Gallic war, and the ensuing destruction; upon which a temple was dedicated in Via Nova to Aius Locutius.

A particular god was assigned and ascribed to every member of the body of man.

The head was sacred to [x] Jupiter, the breast to Neptune, the waist to Mars, the forehead to Genius, the eyebrows to Juno, the eyes to Cupid, the ears to Memoria, the right hand to Fides, the back and the hinder parts to Pluto, the reins to Venus, the feet to Mercury, the knees to Misericordia, the ancles and soles of the feet to Thetis, and the fingers to Minerva.

The astrologers assign the parts of the body to the celestial constellations in another manner, thus: [y] The head they assign to Aries, the neck to Taurus, the shoulder to Gemini, the heart to Cancer, the breast to

[s] Ut arceret anginam.
[t] Fest. id. ib.
[u] Scalig. in Fest.
[w] A volendo, quòd ejus consilio bona vellent.
[x] Serv. in Geo.
[y] Firmic. et Manilius ap. Lil. Gyr. synt. 1.

Leo, the belly to Virgo, the reins to Libra, the secrets to Scorpio, the thighs to Sagittarius, the knees to Capricornus, the legs to Aquarius, and the feet to Pisces: hence the jargon found in Moore's and some other almanacs.

The chief of the funeral deities is Libitina, whom some account to be the same as Venus, since her name is derived [z] from lust or concupiscence; but others think that she was Proserpine. In her temple all things necessary for funerals were sold or let. Libitina sometimes signifies the grave, and Libitinarii, those men who were employed in burying the dead. Porta Libitina, at Rome, was that gate through which the dead bodies were carried to be burnt: and Rationes Libitinæ, in Suetonius, signifies those accounts which we call "the bills of mortality," or "the weekly bills."

QUESTIONS FOR EXAMINATION.

Who were Janus, Opis, Nascio, and Cunia?

What was the office of Levana?

What was the business of Carna, and what were the sacrifices offered to her?

Who was the goddess Nundina; and why was she so called?

What is the office of Juventus?

What are the duties of Horta and Quies?

Who was Vitula?

Who were Sentia and Angerona?

Why were Stata and Laverna worshipped?

From what did Volumnus and Volumna derive their names?

What is said of Aius Locutius?

What parts of the bodies were sacred to the gods?

How do the astrologers assign the parts of the body?

Who was the chief of the funeral deities?

[z] Ita dicta à libitu vel libidine.

PART VI.

OF THE

DII INDIGETES AND ADSCRIPTITII:

OR,

THE SEMI-DEI AND HEROES.

CHAPTER I.

HERCULES. HIS NAMES AND LABOURS.

IN the last division of the *Fabulous Panthèon*, are described the images of the Indigetes, or Semi-Dei, and the Heroes.

The Semi-Dei, Ημιθεοι [*Hemitheoi*], or Demi-Gods, were those who had human bodies, sacred minds, and celestial souls: they were born in this world for the good and safety of mankind. [a]Labeo, in St. Augustin, distinguishes them from the Heroes. He thinks that Heros was one of Juno's sons, and that the name Heros is derived from Ηρα [*Hera*], Juno's name in the Greek language. [b]Others think the word comes from ερα [*era*], "the earth;" because men owe their original to it. [c]Others again think it comes from ερως [*eros*], "love;" for heroes are the most illustrious product of love, and are themselves, as Hierocles observes, full of

[a] Lib. 10. c. 21. [b] Interp. Homeri ap. Lil. Gyr. synt. 1.
[c] Plat. in Cratylo.

love. But others think that this name is derived from ερεω [*ereo*], "to plead," and is given them because heroes are very elegant, and most powerful, and skilful in rhetoric. Or lastly, it is thought that the word comes from αρετη [*arete*], "virtue;" for heroes are endued with many virtues. But let us speak particularly concerning some of these heroes, of whom the most famous was Hercules.

There were many heroes called Hercules, but (as [d] Cicero says) the famous actions of them all are ascribed to him who was the son of Jupiter, by Alcmena, the wife of Amphytrio, king of Thebes.

When Amphytrio was absent, [e] Jupiter put on his shape and dress, and came to Alcmena; who, thinking that her husband was returned, entertained the deceitful god both at table and at bed, and had by him a son, whose limbs were so large, his constitution so robust, and every part of his body so full of vigour, that Jupiter was forced to join three nights together, and employ them all in producing a son of such marvellous strength. Before this, Alcmena had conceived a son by her husband. This son and Hercules were twins; his name was Iphiclus; [f] he was wonderfully swift in running.

When Juno had discovered Jupiter's adultery, she began to hate Hercules so violently, that she endeavoured to ruin him. First, she obtained an edict from Jupiter, which she endeavoured to turn to his utter destruction; for the wife of Sthenelus, king of Mycenæ, was pregnant with Euristheus at the same time when Alcmena was with Hercules. Jupiter ordained, that whichever of the two children was born first, he should be superior to the other: Juno accelerated Euristheus' birth, so that he was born after seven months, and came

[d] De Nat. Deor. 2. [e] Nat. Comes. Lil. Gyr.

[f] "Nam super extremas segetum currebat aristas,
Nec siccos fructus lædebat pondere plantæ."
Orph. in Hymn.

He over standing corn would run, and ne'er
In his swift motion bruise the tender ear.

into the world before Hercules. Again, she sent two vipers to destroy him when he lay crying in the cradle: but it was in vain; for the valiant infant griped them in his hands till they perished by his grasp, [g]as we are told by Ovid. [h]At length, by the mediation of Pallas, Juno was reconciled to the noble youth, and suckled him: but he drew the milk with such violence, that she violently put him away, and some of her milk was spilt; falling upon the sky, it made the Milky-way, which is in Greek called Γαλαξια [*Galaxia*]. Some of it passed through the clouds, and fell on the earth; and where it fell lilies sprang up: hence some call those flowers the [i]"roses of Juno."

He had two proper names, Hercules and Alcides; but his surnames are innumerable. His parents called him [k]Alcides, from his extraordinary strength, in which he greatly excelled all mankind. He was afterward called Hercules, [l]from the glory which Juno caused him: for when she exposed him to the greatest dangers, she rendered him most illustrious; and by enjoining him so many labours, she only exercised his patience and courage.

Hercules was subjected to Euristheus, not only by the edict of Jupiter and unkindness of Juno, but also because the oracle of Apollo at Delphi advised and persuaded him to submit himself, and obey Euristheus' commands; and especially, to undergo willingly the twelve labours which his master should lay upon him. Hercules obeyed the Fates, and served Euristheus twelve years: he performed the most dangerous and difficult commands with a suitable courage and success. Some say, that Hercules served him voluntarily, and per-

[g] "Tene ferunt geminos pressisse tenaciter angues,
Cum tener in cunis jam Jove dignus eras?" Epist.
You kill'd two serpents with your infant-hand,
Which then deserved Jove's sceptre to command?

[h] Eumolph. l. de Myst.

[i] Rosæ Junoniæ. Lil. Gyr.

[k] Ab ἀλκή robur.

[l] Juno Græcè dicitur ἥρα, et κλέος gloria, unde nomen Hercules.

formed those difficult tasks, to show how great love he bore Euristheus.

Though Hercules performed an infinite number of great and memorable actions, twelve are especially celebrated: and those twelve are comprised in as many [m] Latin verses, translated out of the Greek. The particular account of these twelve is this.

The first labour of Hercules was, that he tore in pieces, with his nails, [n] the lion in the wood of Nemæa, which some say fell from the orb of the moon, and was invulnerable by any weapon. This place was also named Cleone; from which the lion was also called Cleoneus. He afterwards skinned the lion, and with the skin made him a shield and breastplate.

2. There was a *hydra*, a serpent, in the lake Lerna, in the field of Argos, that had seven heads; some say nine, others fifty. When any of these heads were cut off, another presently sprang up in the place of it; unless the blood which issued from the wound was stopped

[m] "Prima Cleonei tolerata ærumna leonis.
Proxima Lernæam ferro et face contudit hydram.
Mox Erymantheum vis tertia perculit aprum.
Æripidis quarto tulit aurea cornua cervi.
Stymphalidas pepulit volucres discrimine quinto.
Threiciam sexto spoliavit Amazona baltheo.
Septima in Augeæ stabulis impensa laboris.
Octava expulso numeratur adorea tauro.
In Diomedis victor jam nona quadrigis.
Geryone extincto decimam dat iberia palmam.
Undecimum mala Hesperidum distracta triumphum.
Cerberus extremi suprema est meta laboris."
———— The Cleonian lion first he kills;
With fire and sword then Lerna's pest he quells:
Of the wild boar he clears th' Er'manthean fields;
The brass-foot stag with golden antlers yields:
He Stympha clears of man-devouring birds;
And next the bouncing Amazon ungirds;
The stables of king Augeas he cleans;
The Cretan bull he vanquishes and chains:
Diomedes' horses him their conqueror own;
Then he brings low three-headed Geryon:
Hesperian apples next his name sustains;
And his last labour Cerberus enchains.

[n] Eurip. in Herculo Infan.

by fire. Iolaus, the son of Iphiclus, procured for him lighted brands from the neighbouring wood, and with them Hercules stanched the blood issuing from the wounds he made. This seasonable assistance was not forgotten; for when Iolaus was grown to decrepid age, Hercules, [o] by his prayers, restored to him his youth again.

3. He bound the wild boar, whose fierceness and bigness were equally admirable, in the mountain Erymanthus of Arcadia; and afterward brought it to Euristheus.

4. He was ordered to bring to Mycenæ a hind, whose feet were brass, and horns gold. Nobody dared to wound her, because she was consecrated to Diana; nor could any body outrun her: yet Hercules hunted her a year on foot, caught her, and brought her away on his shoulders.

5. He partly killed and partly drove away the birds called Stymphalides, from the lake Stymphalus, which used to feed upon man's flesh.

6. He defeated the army of the Amazons, and took from Hippolyte, their queen, the finest belt in the world.

7. He in one day cleansed the stable of Augeas, by turning the course of a river into it. This stable had never been cleansed, although three thousand oxen stabled in it thirty years. Whence, when we would express a work of immense labour and toil, in proverbial speech, we call it "cleansing the Augean stable."

8. He tamed a great bull, that did innumerable mischiefs in the island Crete, and brought him bound to Euristheus.

9. He overcame Diomedes, the most cruel tyrant of Thrace, who fed his horses with the flesh of his guests. Hercules bound him, and threw him to be eaten by those horses to which the tyrant had exposed others.

10. He overcame in war Geryon, king of Spain, who

[o] Ovid. Met. 9.

had three bodies, and took his bay oxen that ate man's flesh, and brought them into Italy, when he had killed the dragon with seven heads, and the two-headed dog which guarded him.

11. He killed the dragon that watched, and then carried away the golden apples in the gardens of the Hesperides; whence perhaps he is called [p] Melius, and apples were offered up in his sacrifices. In Bœotia, when no bull (or sheep) could be procured at the time of sacrifice, they took an apple, and stuck into it four straws, which represented four legs, and two more for horns, with another for a tail, and offered Hercules this apple instead of a victim.

12. Lastly, he was commanded by Euristheus to go down into hell, and bring away thence the dog Cerberus. This he performed without delay, bound the three-headed monster in a triple chain, and by force brought with him up to the earth the dog, which strove and resisted in vain. When Cerberus saw the light, he vomited, and thence the poisonous herb [q] wolfsbane sprang. These are the twelve labours of Hercules.

13. He vanquished the cruel and enormous giant Antæus, the son of the earth, who was above sixty-four cubits high, and who forced strangers to wrestle with him. Hercules threw this giant down thrice, and perceiving that he recovered new strength as oft as he touched the earth, he lifted him in his arms from the ground, and then despatched him.

14. Busiris the tyrant used to sacrifice all the strangers that he caught to his father Neptune, till Hercules sacrificed both him and his son upon the same altar.

15. He killed the giants Albion and Bergeon, who intended to stop his journey: and when in the fight his arrows were consumed, so that he wanted arms, [r] he prayed to Jupiter, and obtained from him a shower of stones, with which he defeated and put to flight his ad-

[p] Μῆλον Græcè significat malum vel pomum.
[q] Aconitum.
[r] Cato in Orig.

versaries. This, they say, happened in that part of France [s] anciently called Gallia Narbonensis; which place is called the [t] Stony Plain.

16. When Atlas was weary of his burden, Hercules took the heavens upon his shoulders. He overcame the robber Cacus, who spit fire, and strangled him. He shot the eagle that devoured the liver of Prometheus, as he lay chained to the rock. And he slew Theodamus, the father of Hylas, because he denied him victuals: but he took care of Hylas, and was kind to him.

17. He delivered [u] Hesione, daughter of Laomedon, king of Troy, from the whale in this manner: He raised, on a sudden, a bank in the place where Hesione was to be devoured, and [w] stood armed before it: and when the whale came seeking his prey, Hercules leaped into his mouth, slided down into his belly, destroyed him, and came away safe. Laomedon, after this, broke his word, and refused to give Hercules the reward he promised; therefore he took it by force, and pillaged the city of Troy; giving to Telamon, who first mounted the wall, the lady Hesione, as a part of the booty.

18. In fighting for Deianira, Hercules overcame Achelous, the son of Oceanus and Terra, though Achelous first turned himself into a serpent, then into a bull. By plucking one of his horns off, he obliged him to yield; but Achelous purchased his horn again, giving Amalthæa's horn in its stead. The meaning of which is this: Achelous is a river of Greece, whose course winds like a serpent; its stream is so rapid, that it makes furrows where it flows, and a noise like the roaring of a bull; and indeed it is common among the poets to compare a river to a bull. This river divided itself into two streams, but Hercules forced it into one channel; that is, he broke off one of the horns or streams. The lands thus drained became fertile; so that Hercules is said to have received the horn of plenty.

[s] Mela. l. 26. Geog.
[t] Campus Lapideus.
[u] Ovid. Met. 11.
[w] Andrætus Tenedi in Navig. Prop.

19. Deianira was daughter of Oeneus, king of Ætolia. Hercules carried her to be married, and in their way they were stopped by a river; but the centaur Nessus offered to carry Deianira over upon his back. Nessus, when she was over, endeavoured to ravish her; which Hercules observing, while he swam, shot him with an arrow. When Nessus was dying, he gave Deianira his bloody coat, and told her, if a husband wore that coat, he would never follow unlawful amours. The credulous lady long after experienced the virtue of it, far otherwise than she expected. For Hercules, who had surmounted so many and so great labours, was at length overcome by the charms of Omphale, queen of Lydia, and, to gratify her, changed his club into a distaff, and his arrows into a spindle. His love also to Iole, daughter of Eurytus, king of Oechalia, brought on him destruction. For his wife Deianira, being desirous of turning him from unlawful amours, sent him Nessus' coat to put on when he went to sacrifice; which drove him into such distraction, that he burned himself on the pile he had raised, and was accounted among the number of the gods. The lines of Virgil, in praise of the hero, shall finish my description :-

——— " ut prima novercæ
Monstra manu, geminosque primus eliserit angues :
Ut bello egregias idem disjecerit urbes,
Trojamque Œchaliamque; ut duros mille labores
Rege sub Eurystheo, fatis Junonis iniquæ,
Pertulerit. Tu nubigenas, invicte bimembres,
Hylæumque, Pholumque, manu ; tu Cressia mactas
Prodigia, et vastum Nemeæ sub rupe leonem.
Te Stygii tremuere lacus : te janitor Orci,
Ossa super recubans antro semesa cruento.
Nec te ullæ facies, non terruit ipse Typhoëus,
Arduus, arma tenens : non te rationis egentem
Lernæus turba capitum circumstetit anguis.
Salve, vera Jovis proles, decus addite Divis :
Et nos, et tua dexter adi pede sacra secundo".
First, how the mighty babe, when swathed in bands,
The serpents strangled with his infant hands ;
Then, as in years and matchless force he grew,
Th' Œchalian walls and Trojan overthrew.

Pl. XXIII. p. 265.

H. Moses del. et sculp.

HERCULES

Publish'd by Wilkie & Robinson Paternoster Row May 1, 1810.

Besides a thousand hazards they relate,
Procured by Juno's and Euristheus' hate.
Thy hands, unconquer'd hero! could subdue
The cloud-born Centaurs, and the monster crew:
Nor thy resistless arm the bull withstood:
Nor he the roaring terror of the wood.
The triple porter of the Stygian seat,
With lolling tongue, lay fawning at thy feet,
And, seized with fear, forgot thy mangled meat.
Th' infernal waters trembled at thy sight:
Thee, god! no face of danger could affright;
Not huge Typhœus, nor th' unnumber'd snakes,
Increased with hissing heads in Lerna's lake.
Hail, Jove's undoubted son! an added grace
To heaven, and the great author of thy race.
Receive the grateful off'rings which we pay,
And smile propitious on thy solemn day.

QUESTIONS FOR EXAMINATION.

Who were the Semi-Dei?

What account is given of the Heroes?

Who was Hercules?

Who was the twin-brother of Hercules; and for what was he celebrated?

How did Juno act with regard to Hercules?

By whom was she reconciled; and what was the consequence of the reconciliation?

What were the proper names of Hercules, and how did he derive them?

Why was Hercules subject to Euristheus?

Repeat the Latin lines descriptive of Hercules' labours.

What was his first labour?

What was his second; third; fourth; fifth; sixth; seventh; eighth; ninth; tenth; eleventh; twelfth?

What did he do with regard to Antæus?

How did he act with Busiris?

Why did he kill the giants Albion and Bergeon?

What was his conduct with regard to Atlas, Cacus, Prometheus, and Theodamus?

How did he deliver Hesione?

What is the meaning of the fable of Achelous?

What is related of Deianira?

CHAPTER II.

JASON. THESEUS.

JASON, son of Æson, king of Thessalia, by Alcimede, was an infant when his father died, so that his uncle Pelius administered the government. When he came of age, he demanded possession of the crown; but Pelius advised him to go to Colchis, under pretence of gaining the Golden Fleece thence, though his real intention was to kill him with the labour and danger of the journey.

The Golden Fleece was the hide of a ram, of a white or a purple colour, which was given to Phryxus, son of Athamus and Nephele, by his mother. Phryxus and his sister Helle, fearing the designs of their stepmother Ino, got on a ram to save themselves by flight. But while they swam over the narrowest part of Pontus, Helle, affrighted at the tossing of the waves, fell down; whence the sea was named the Hellespont. Phryxus was carried over safe, and went to Æta, king of Colchis, a country of Asia, near the Pontus; where he was kindly received, and sacrificed the ram to Jupiter, or Mars, who afterward placed it among the constellations. Only his hide or fleece was hung up in a grove sacred to Mars. It was called the Golden Fleece, because it was of a golden colour; and it was guarded by bulls that breathed fire from their nostrils, and by a vast and watchful dragon, as a sacred and divine pledge, and as a thing of the greatest importance.

Jason went on board a ship called Argo, from the builder of that name; and chose forty-nine noble companions, who, from the ship, were called Argonautæ, among whom were Hercules, Orpheus, Castor, and Pollux. In his voyage, he visited Hipsyphile, queen of Lemnos, who had twins by him. Then, after a long voyage, and many dangers, he arrived at Colchis, and demanded the Golden Fleece of king Æta, who granted his request, on condition that he tamed the bulls which guarded it; killed the dragon, and sowed his teeth in the ground; and, lastly, destroyed the soldiers who sprang from the ground where these teeth were sown. Jason undertook the thing, and was delivered from manifest destruction by the assistance of Medea, the king's daughter, who was in love with him. For, observing her directions, he overcame the bulls, laid the dragon asleep, carried away the fleece, and fled by night, carrying Medea with him, whom he afterward married.

Æta pursued them, but his daughter, to stop his pursuit, tore her brother Absyrtus, who went with her, in pieces, and scattered the limbs on the road; that when her father saw the torn members of his son, he might stop to gather them up. So Jason and the Argonautæ returned to their own country, where Medea by her charms restored Jason's father, the old decrepid Æson, to youth again; though some say that Æson died before their return. After this, Jason divorcing himself from Medea, he married Creusa, the daughter of Creon, king of Corinth: and Medea, to revenge his perfidiousness, not only murdered the two children that she had by him in his own sight, but, in the next place, inclosed fire in a little box, and sent it to Creusa, who opened the box, and by the fire which burst out of it was burnt, together with the whole court. When she had done this, the admirable sorceress flew by magic art to Athens. Some write that she was reconciled afterward to Jason. But what has been said is enough for this hero; let us proceed to

Theseus, whose parents were Æthra and Ægeus, king of Athens. Minos, king of Crete, made war against Ægeus, because the Athenians had dishonourably and barbarously killed his son, who carried the prize in the games. When he had banished the Athenians, he imposed this severe condition upon them, that they should send seven of the most noble youths of their country into Crete by lot every year. In the fourth year the lot fell upon Theseus, which mightily grieved and troubled his father Ægeus. Theseus went on board a ship, whose sails and tackle were black, and received this command from his father: "If by the propitious providence of Heaven he escaped the dangers, and did return safe unto his own country again, that then he should change his black sails into white ones, that his father, being assured of his safety by that signal, might be sensible of his happiness as soon as might be."

The event was fortunate to Theseus; but very unfortunate to his father Ægeus: for when Theseus came to Crete, he was shut up in the Labyrinth; but he slew the Minotaur, and escaped out of that inextricable prison by the help of Ariadne. After this he set sail for Athens in the same mournful ship in which he came to Crete, but forgot to change his sails, according to the instructions which his father had given him; so that, when his father beheld from a watchtower the ship returning with black sails, he imagined that his son was dead, and cast himself headlong into the sea, which was afterward called [x] the Ægean Sea, from his name and destiny.

Ariadne was the daughter of Minos, king of Crete. She having delivered Theseus [y] out of the Labyrinth by the means of a thread, followed him in his return to the island of Naxus, where he perfidiously and ungratefully left her. But Bacchus, pitying her miserable condition, married her; and gave her a crown that was illuminated with seven stars, which he had before received from Venus. This crown was called Gnossia Corona, and Ariadne herself was surnamed Gnossis, from the city of that name in Crete. After the death of Ariadne, the same was carried among the stars, and made a constellation in the heavens. It was thought that Diana caused the death of Ariadne, because she preserved not her virginity.

The actions of Theseus were so famous, that they accounted him a Hercules. For, 1. He killed the

[x] Ægeum mare. [y] Propert. l. 3. el. 17.

Minotaur. 2. He overcame the Centaurs. 3. He vanquished the Thebans. 4. He defeated the Amazons. 5. He went down into hell; and returned back into the world again.

He and Pirithous, his most intimate friend, the lawful son of Ixion, agreed never to marry any women except Jupiter's daughters. Theseus married Helena, the daughter of Jupiter and Leda, and none of Jupiter's daughters remained on earth for Pirithous; therefore they both went down into hell to steal Proserpine away from her husband Pluto. As soon as they entered hell, Pirithous was unfortunately torn in pieces by the dog Cerberus; but Theseus came alive into the palace of Pluto, who fettered him, and kept him till Hercules was sent into hell by Euristheus to rescue him.

The Amazons were women animated with the souls and bravery of men; a military race, inhabiting that part of Scythia which is washed by the river Tanaïs: They were called Amazons, [z] either because they cut off one of their breasts, or [a] because they lived together without the society of men. They were a nation of women, who, that the country might have inhabitants, and not be depopulated when the present race of women died, admitted the embraces of the neighbouring men, and had children by them. They killed the boys at their birth, but brought up the girls. They cut off their right breast, that they might more conveniently use their hands in shooting their arrows, and brandish their weapons against their enemy. These female warriors, by their frequent excursions, became possessors of a great part of Asia, when Hercules, accompanied with Theseus, made war upon them, and defeated them; and taking Hippolyte, their queen, prisoner, he gave her in marriage to Theseus.

Theseus had by Hippolyte his son Hippolytus, who

[z] Ab α privativo et μαζὸς mamma.
[a] Ab ἅμα simul et ζῆν vivere.

was very beautiful, mightily addicted to hunting, and a remarkable lover of chastity: for when [b] Phædra his step-mother, the daughter of king Minos, whom Theseus had preferred to her sister Ariadne, solicited him, being grown a man, to commit wickedness, he refused to comply. This repulse provoked her so much, that when her husband returned, she accused him wrongfully, as if he had offered to ravish her. Theseus gave ear to the wicked woman, and believed her untruth against his son Hippolytus, who, perceiving it, fled away in his chariot. In his flight he met several monstrous sea-calves, which frighted his horses, so that they threw him out of his seat: his feet were entangled in the harness, and he was dragged through the thickets of a wood, and torn to pieces miserably. Æsculapius afterward, at the request of Diana, restored him to life again. But he, however, left Greece, and came into Italy, where he changed his name to Virbius, [c] because he had been a man twice. Phædra was gnawn with the stings of her own conscience, and hanged herself. And, not long after, Theseus, being banished from his country, ended an illustrious life with an obscure death.

QUESTIONS FOR EXAMINATION.

Who was Jason, and by whom was he sent to Colchis?

What is the story of the Golden Fleece?

How many companions had Jason in his expedition; what were they called, and why; and who were the principal?

Upon what condition did Jason obtain the Golden Fleece?

By what means did Medea stop the pursuit of her father?

What were the other acts of Medea?

Who were the parents of Theseus?

What circumstances attend the story of Theseus and his father Ægeus?

Who was Ariadne, and what is related of her?

What are mentioned as Theseus' actions?

[b] Ovid. in Ep. Phædr.

[c] Quod vir bis esset.

What agreement was made between Theseus and Pirithous; and what became of the latter?

Who were the Amazons; and what account is given of them?

What is the story of Hippolytus?

What became of Phædra and Theseus?

CHAPTER III.

CASTOR AND POLLUX.

CASTOR and Pollux are twin brothers, [d] the sons of Jupiter and Leda, who was the wife of Tyndarus, king of Laconia, whom Jupiter loved, but could not succeed in his amour till he changed himself into a swan; [e] which swan was afterward made a constellation. Leda brought forth two eggs, which were hatched, and produced the twin brothers. Out of the egg which Leda had conceived by Jupiter, came Pollux and Helena, who sprang from divine seed, and were therefore immortal. But out of the other, which she conceived by Tyndarus her husband, came [f] Castor and Clytemnestra, who were mortal, because they were begotten by a mortal father. Yet both Castor and Pollux are frequently called Tyndaridæ by the poets, as Helena is also called Tyndaris, from the same king Tyndarus.

Castor and Pollux accompanied Jason when he sailed to Colchis; and, when he returned thence, they recovered their sister Helena from Theseus, who had stolen her, by overcoming the Athenians that fought for him; to whom their clemency and humanity were so great after the defeat, that the Athenians called them [g] the sons of Jupiter; and hence white lambs were

[d] Pind. in Pythag. [e] Manil. 1 Astron. [f] Hor. Sat. 1.
[g] Διόσκουροι, id est, Jovis filii. Hom. in Hymn.

offered upon their altars. [h] But although they were both born at the same birth, and, as some think, out of the same egg, yet their tempers were different.

Castor being, as some say, a mortal person, was killed by Lynceus: upon which Pollux prayed to Jupiter to restore him to life again, and confer an immortality upon him. But this could not be granted. However, he obtained leave to divide his immortality between himself and his brother Castor: and thence it came to pass, [i] that they lived afterwards by turns every other day, or, as some say, every other fortnight. After the death of Castor, a kind of *pyrrhick*, or dance in armour, was instituted to his honour; which was performed by young men armed, and called [k] "Castor's dance."

At length they both were translated into heaven, and made a constellation, which is still called Gemini. Sailors esteem these stars lucky and prosperous to them, [l] because when the Argonauts were driven by a violent tempest, two lambent flames settled upon the heads of Castor and Pollux, and a calm immediately ensued: from which a virtue more than human was thought to be lodged in these youths. If only one flame appeared, they called it Helena, and it was esteemed fatal and destructive to mariners.

There was a famous temple dedicated to Castor and Pollux in the Forum at Rome; for it was believed, that in the dangerous battle of the Romans with the Latins, they assisted the Romans, riding upon white horses. And hence came that form of swearing by the temple of

[h] "Castor gaudet equis: Ovo prognatus eodem,
Pugnis: quot capitum vivunt, totidem in studiorum
Millia." Horat. Serm. 2. 1.
As many men, so many their delights.

[i] "Sic fratrem Pollux alterna morte redemit,
Itque reditque viam." Virg. Æn. 6.
Thus Pollux, offering his alternate life,
Could free his brother. They did daily go
By turns aloft, by turns descend below.

[k] Plin. l. 7. c. 5. 7. ap. Nat. Com. [l] Hor. Carm. 3.

Castor, which women only used, saying, [m] Æcastor: whereas, when men swore, they usually swore by Hercules, using the words [n] Hercule, Hercle, Hercules, Mehercules, Mehercule. But both men and women swore by the temple of Pollux, using the word Ædepol, an oath common to them both.

Clytemnestra was married to Agamemnon, whom, after his return from the siege of Troy, she killed, by the help of Ægisthus; with whom, in the mean time, she lived in adultery. She attempted also to kill his son Orestes, and would have done so, [o] if his sister Electra had not delivered him at the very point of destruction, sending him privately to Strophius, king of Phocis. After Orestes had lived there twelve years, he returned into his own country, and slew both Clytemnestra and Ægisthus. He killed also Pyrrhus, in the temple of Apollo, because he had carried away Hermione, the daughter of Menelaus, who was first betrothed to Orestes. Therefore the Furies tormented him, neither could he obtain deliverance from them, till he had expiated his wickedness at the altar of Diana Taurica, whither he was conducted by his friend Pylades, his perpetual companion and partner in all his dangers: [p] their friendship was so close and sacred, that either of them would die for the other.

The goddess Diana was worshipped in Taurica Chersonesus, or Cherronesus, a peninsula, so called from the Tauri, an ancient people of Scythia Europæa. [q] She was worshipped with human victims; the lives and the blood of men being sacrificed to her. When Orestes went thither, his sister Iphigenia, the daughter of Agamemnon, was priestess to Diana Taurica: she was made priestess on the following occasion.

Agamemnon, king of the Argivi, was, by the common consent of the Grecians, appointed general in their ex-

[m] Æcastor, et Ædepol, id est, per ædem Castoris et Pollucis.

[n] Passim apud Terent. Plaut. Cicer. &c.

[o] Soph. in Electr. Eurip. in Orest.

[p] Cic. de Amicit.

[q] Eurip. in Iphig. in Taur.

pedition against Troy; and, after his return home, was killed by his own wife Clytemnestra. This Agamemnon killed a deer by chance, in the country of Aulis, which belonged to Diana; the goddess was angry, and caused such a calm, that for want of wind the Grecian ships bound for Troy were fixed and immoveable: upon this they consulted the soothsayers, who answered, [r] That they must satisfy the winds, and Diana, with some of the blood of Agamemnon. Therefore Ulysses was forthwith sent to bring away Iphigenia, the daughter of Agamemnon, from her mother, by a trick, under the pretence of marrying her to Achilles. While the young lady stood at the altar to be sacrificed, the goddess pitied her, and substituted a hind in her stead, and sent her into Taurica Chersonesus; where, by the order of king Thoas, she presided over those sacrifices of the goddess which were solemnized with human blood. When Orestes was brought thither by the inhabitants to be sacrificed, he was known and preserved by his sister. After which Thoas was killed, and the image of Diana, which lay hidden among a bundle of sticks, was carried away; and hence Diana was called Fascelis, from *fascis*, a "bundle."

QUESTIONS FOR EXAMINATION.

Who were Castor and Pollux, and what was their origin?

Why were white lambs offered upon their altars?

What became of Castor, and what was granted to him at the request of his brother?

What do the sailors say of the stars Castor and Pollux?

What is related of the temple dedicated to them?

What is the story of Clytemnestra?

Who was Diana Taurica; how was she worshipped; and who was her priestess?

What is related of Agamemnon?

On what account was Diana called Fascelis?

[r] Eurip. in Iphig. in Taur.

CHAPTER IV.

PERSEUS. ÆSCULAPIUS.

PERSEUS was the son of Jupiter, by Danaë, the daughter of Acrisius, [s] who was shut up by her father in a very strong tower, where no man could come to her; because her father had been told by an oracle, that he should be killed by his own grandchild. But nothing is impregnable to love: for Jupiter, as we are told by [t] Horace, by changing himself into a shower of gold, descended through the tiles into the lady's bosom.

As soon as Acrisius had heard that his daughter had brought forth a son, he ordered that she and the infant should be shut up in a chest, and thrown into the sea: the chest was driven to the island Seriphus, where a fisherman found it, took them out, and presented them to king Polydectes; who became enamoured of Danaë, and brought up her son, whom he called Perseus.

Perseus, when he was grown a man, received from Mercury a sithe of adamant, and wings, which he fixed to his feet: Pluto gave him a helmet, and Minerva a shield of brass, so bright, that it reflected the images of

[s] Pausan. in Corinth.

[t] "Inclusam Danaën turris ahenea
Robustæque fores, et vigilum canum
Tristes excubiæ munierant satis
Nocturnis ab adulteris:
Si non Acrisium, virginis abditæ
Custodem pavidum, Jupiter et Venus
Risissent: fore enim tutum iter et patens,
Converso in pretium Deo." Carm. l. 3. 16.

Within a brazen tower immured,
By dogs and centinels secured,
From midnight revels and intrigues of love,
Fair Danaë was kept within her guardian's power:
But gentle Venus smiled, and amorous Jove
Knew he could soon unlock the door,
And by his art successful prove,
Changed to a golden shower.

things, like a looking-glass. His first exploit was the deliverance of Andromeda, the daughter of Cepheus king of Ethiopia, who was bound by the Nymphs to a rock, to be devoured by a sea-monster, because her mother Cassiope, or Cassiopeia, had proudly preferred her daughter's beauty to theirs; and when he had delivered her, he took her to wife. After which, both the mother and the daughter, and the son-in-law, were placed among the [u] celestial constellations. His next expedition was against the Gorgons, of whom we have spoken before: he encountered Medusa, their princess, whose head was supplied with snakes in the place of hair; he saw the image of her head by the brightness of his shield, and, by the favourable assistance of Minerva, struck it off: he then fixed it upon a shield, and, by showing it, afterward turned many persons into stone. Atlas was turned, by the sight of it, into the mountain in Mauritania of that name, because he rudely refused to entertain Perseus. When Medusa's head was cut off, the horse Pegasus sprang from the blood which fell on the ground: he was so called from πηγη [*pege*], "a fountain," [w] because he was produced near the fountains of the sea. This horse had wings; and flying over the mountain Helicon, he struck it with his hoof, and opened a fountain, which they call, in Greek, *Hippocrene;* and in Latin, *Fons Caballinus;* that is, the "horse-fountain." But afterward, while he drank at the fountain Pyrene in Corinth, where Bellerophon prepared himself for his expedition against the Chimæra, he was by him taken and kept.

Bellerophon's first name was Hipponus; [x] because he first taught the art of governing horses with a bridle: but when he had killed Bellerus, a king of Corinth, he was afterward called Bellerophontes. This Bellerophon, the son of Glaucus king of Ephyra, was equally beautiful and virtuous: he resisted all the temptations by

[u] Propert. l. 2. Hygin. de signis Cœlestibus, l. 2.
[w] Strabo, l. 8.
[x] Ita dictus ab equis fræno regendis.

which Sthenobæa, the wife of Prætus, enticed him to commit adultery; and his denial provoked her so, that in revenge she accused the innocent stranger to her husband. Prætus, however, would not violate the laws of hospitality with the blood of Bellerophon, but sent him into Lycia, to his father-in-law, Jobates, with letters, which desired him to punish Bellerophon, as his crime deserved. Jobates read the letters, and sent him to fight against the Solymi, that he might be killed in the battle: but he easily vanquished them, and in many other dangers, to which he was exposed, he always came off conqueror. At last, he was sent to kill the Chimæra; which he undertook, and performed, when he had procured the horse Pegasus, by the help of Neptune. [y] Therefore Jobates, admiring the bravery of the youth, gave him one of his daughters to wife, allotting him also a part of his kingdom. Sthenobæa killed herself when she heard this. This happy success so transported Bellerophon, that he endeavoured to fly upon Pegasus to heaven; for which Jupiter struck him with madness, and he fell from his horse into a field, called Aleius Campus, [z] because in that place Bellerophon wandered up and down blind, to the end of his life: but Pegasus was placed among the stars. Some say that this was the occasion of the fable of the Chimæra. There was a famous pirate, who used to sail in a ship in whose prow was painted a lion, in the stern a dragon, and by the body of the ship a goat was described; and this pirate was killed by Bellerophon, in a long boat that was called Pegasus. From the letters which Bellerophon carried to Jobates, [a] comes the proverb, "Bellerophon's letters;" when any one carries letters, which he imagines are wrote in his favour, but are sent to procure his ruin: and such letters are frequently called "Letters of Uriah," for the same reason.

Æsculapius is represented as a [b] bearded old man,

[y] Hom. Iliad. [z] Ab ἀλεύω erro. [a] Βελλεροφόντος γράμματα, *Bellerophontis literæ*, usitatius dictæ, *Literæ Uriæ*.
[b] Lucian. in Jove Trag.

leaning on his jointed cane, adorned with a crown of laurel, and encompassed with dogs. He is [c] the god of the physicians and physic, and the son of Apollo by the nymph Coronis. He improved the art of physic, which was before little understood; and for that reason they accounted him a god. [d] Apollo shot the nymph his mother when she was pregnant, because she admitted the embraces of another young man after he had enjoyed her. But he repented after he had killed her, and opening her body, took out the child alive, and delivered him to be educated by the physician Chiron, [e] who taught him his own art: the youth made so great a progress in it, that, because he restored health to the sick, and gave safety to those whose condition was desperate, he was thought to have a power of recalling the dead to life again. Upon this Pluto, the king of hell, [f] complained to Jupiter that his revenue was very much diminished, and his subjects taken from him, by means of Æsculapius; and at length by his persuasion Jupiter killed him with a stroke of thunder.

He wears a crown of laurel, [g] because that tree is powerful in curing many diseases. By the knots in his stuff, is signified the difficulty of the study of physic. He has dogs painted about him, and dogs in his temple; because many believe that he was born of uncertain parents, and exposed, and afterward nourished by a bitch. [h] Others say, that a goat, which was pursued by a dog, gave suck to the forsaken infant; and that the shepherds saw a lambent flame playing about his head, which was a prognostication of his future divinity. The Cyrenians used to offer a goat to him in the sacrifices; either because he was nourished by a goat, as was said, [i] or because a goat is always in a fever; and therefore a goat's constitution is very contrary to health. [k] Plato says,

[c] Cic. de Leg. 2. Corn. Celsus.
[d] Hom. in Hymn. [e] Ovid. Met. 1.
[f] Virg. Æn. 7. [g] Vide Festum.
[h] Lactant. de fals. Relig. Pausan. in Corinth.
[i] Didym. l. 3. ap. Nat. Com. [k] In Phædone.

that they used to sacrifice dunghill-cocks to him, which are deemed the most vigilant of all birds; for of all virtues, watchfulness is chiefly necessary to a physician.

Æsculapius was worshipped first at Epidaurus, [l] where he was born; afterward at Rome, because, on being sent for thither, he delivered the city from a dreadful pestilence. For which reason, [m] a temple was dedicated to him in an island in the mouth of the Tiber, where he was worshipped under the form of a great serpent; for when the Romans came to Epidaurus to transport the god thence, a great serpent entered into the ship, which they believed was Æsculapius, and brought it to Rome with them. Others tell the story thus: when the Romans were received by the people of Epidaurus with all kindness, and were carried into the temple of Æsculapius, the serpent, under whose image they worshipped that god, went voluntarily into the ship of the Romans.

I can tell you nothing of the children of Æsculapius, except their names. He had two sons, called Machaon and Podalirius, both famous physicians, who followed Agamemnon, the general of the Grecians, to the Trojan war, and were very serviceable among the soldiers; and two daughters, [n] Hygiœa (though some think this was his wife) and Jaso.

Chiron, his master, was a centaur, and the son of Saturn and Phillyra; for when Saturn embraced that nymph, he suddenly changed himself into a horse, [o] because his wife Ops came in. Phillyra was with child by him, and brought forth a creature, in its upper parts like a man, in its lower parts like a horse, and called it Chiron; who, when he grew up, betook himself into the woods; and there, learning the virtues of herbs, he became a most excellent physician. For his skill in physic, and for his other virtues, which were many, he was appointed tutor to Achilles; he also instructed Hercules

[l] Liv. l. 45. et l. 10. Flori Epitome, l. 11.
[m] Sueton. in Claud. c. 25.
[n] Hygiœa ab ὑγίεια sanitas, et Jaso derivatur ab ἰάομαι sano.
[o] Virg. Geo. 3.

in astronomy, and taught Æsculapius physic. At last, when he handled Hercules' arrows, one of them, dipped in the poisonous blood of the Lernæan hydra, fell upon his foot, and gave him a wound that was incurable, and pains that were intolerable; insomuch that he desired to die, but could not, because he was born of two immortal parents. Therefore at length the gods translated him into the firmament, where he now remains; for he became a constellation called Sagittarius, which is placed in the zodiac.

QUESTIONS FOR EXAMINATION.

Who was Perseus, and what is related of his mother?

How did Jupiter contrive to get at her?

Repeat the lines from Horace, and translation.

What order did Acrisius give with regard to his grandson, and how was the child saved?

What were the exploits of Perseus?

What is said of Medusa's head, and what happened when it was cut off?

How is Pegasus described?

For what was Bellerophon famous?

Give the circumstances attending his history.

What is meant by "Bellerophon's letters;" and what else are they called?

Who was Æsculapius?

What became of his mother?

Under whose care was Æsculapius brought up?

What complaint was made against him?

Why does he wear a crown of laurel; and what do the staff and dogs signify?

Why were goats and cocks sacrificed to him?

Where was he first worshipped; and why was he adored under the form of a serpent?

Who were Æsculapius's children?

What is the history of Chiron?

ÆSCULAPIUS

Publish'd by Wilkie & Robinson, Paternoster Row

CHAPTER V.

PROMETHEUS. ATLAS.

PROMETHEUS, the son of Japetes, [p] and the father of Deucalion, was the first, as we find in history, that formed man out of clay; which he did with such art and skill, that Minerva was amazed, and proffered to procure him any thing from heaven, which would complete his work. Prometheus answered, that he did not know what in heaven would be useful to him, since he had never seen heaven. Therefore Minerva carried him up into heaven, and showed him all its wonders. He observed that the heat of the sun would be very useful in animating the man which he had formed; therefore he lighted a stick by the wheel of the sun's chariot, and carried it lighted with him to the earth. This theft displeased Jupiter so much, that he sent Pandora into the world to Prometheus, with a box filled with all sorts of evils. Prometheus, fearing and suspecting the matter, refused to accept it: but his brother Epimetheus was not so cautious; for he took it and opened it, and all the evils that were in it flew abroad among mankind. When he perceived what he had done, he immediately shut the box again, and by good fortune hindered Hope from flying away, which stuck to the bottom of the box. You may remember how sweetly [q] Horace speaks of this theft of Prometheus.

[p] Vide Claud. Panegyr. de cons. Hon.

[q] "Audax omnia perpeti
Gens humana ruit per vetitum nefas.
Audax Japeti genus
Ignem fraude mala gentibus intulit:
Post ignem ætherea domo
Subductum, macies et nova febrium
Terris incubuit cohors:
Semotique prius tarda necessitas
Lethi corripuit gradum." Carm. l. 1.

Jupiter punished Prometheus in this manner: he commanded Mercury [r] to bind him to the mountain Caucasus; and then he sent an eagle to him there, which continually gnawed his liver. Yet some say, [s] that he was not punished because he stole fire from heaven, but because he had made a woman, which, they say, is the most pernicious creature in the world.

Prometheus had been serviceable to Jupiter, for he discovered to him his father Saturn's conspiracy, and prevented the marriage of Jupiter and Thetis, which he foresaw would be fatal; therefore Jupiter suffered Hercules to shoot the eagle, and set Prometheus at liberty.

This, perhaps, is the meaning of this fable: Prometheus, whose name is derived [t] from a word denoting foresight and providence, was a very prudent person; and because he reduced men, who before were rude and savage, to the precepts of humanity, he was feigned thence to have made men out of the dirt: and because he was diligent in observing the motions of the stars from the mountain Caucasus, therefore they said that he was chained there. To which they added that he stole fire from the gods, because he invented the way of striking fire by means of the flint; or was the first that discovered the nature of lightning. And lastly, because he applied his mind to study with great care and solicitude, [u] therefore they imagined an eagle preying upon his liver continually.

We have said that Prometheus was the father of

> No power the pride of mortals can control:
>   Prone to new crimes, by strong presumption driven,
> With sacrilegious hands Prometheus stole
>   Celestial fire, and bore it down from heaven:
> The fatal present brought on mortal race
>   An army of diseases; death began
> With vigour then to mend its halting pace,
>   And found a more compendious way to man.

[r] Hesiod. in Theog. [s] Menander Poëta.
[t] Ἀπὸ τῆς προμηθίας, id est, providentiâ. Pausan. in Eliac.
[u] Apoll. l. 3.

Deucalion, who was king of Thessaly. During his reign, there was so great a deluge, that the whole earth was overflowed by it, and all mankind entirely destroyed, excepting only Deucalion and Pyrrha his wife, who were carried in a ship upon the mountain Parnassus; and when the waters were abated, they consulted the oracle of Themis, to know by what means mankind should again be restored. The oracle answered, that mankind would be restored, if they cast the bones of their great mother behind them. By *great mother*, the oracle meant the *earth;* and by her *bones*, the *stones:* therefore casting the stones behind their back, a prodigious miracle ensued; [w] for those stones that were thrown by Deucalion became men, and those that were thrown by Pyrrha became women. The occasion of which fable was this: Deucalion and his wife were very pious, and by the example of their lives, and the sanctity of their manners, they softened the men and women, who before were fierce and hard like stones, into such gentleness and mildness, that they observed the rules of civil society and good behaviour.

Atlas, king of Mauritania, the son of Japetus, and brother of Prometheus, is represented as sustaining the heavens on his shoulders. He was forewarned by an oracle that he would be almost ruined by one of the sons of Jupiter, and therefore resolved to give entertainment to no stranger at all. At last Perseus, who was begotten by Jupiter, travelled by chance through Atlas' dominions, and designed, in civility, to visit him. But the king excluded him the court; which inhumanity provoked him so much, that, putting his shield

[w] ——————— "Saxa
Missa viri manibus faciem traxere virilem;
Et de fœmineo reparata est fœmina jactu.
Inde genus durum sumus, experiensque laborum;
Et documenta damus, quâ simus origine nati." Ov. Met. 1.

——— ——————— And of the stones
Those thrown by th' man the form of men endue;
And those were women which the woman threw.
Hence we, a hardy race, inured to pain;
Our actions our original explain.

before the eyes of Atlas, and showing him the head of Medusa, he turned him into the mountain of his own name; which is of so great height that it is believed to touch the [x] heavens. Virgil makes mention of him [y] in the fourth book of his Æneid.

The reason why the poets feigned that Atlas sustained the heavens on his shoulders, was this: Atlas was a very famous astronomer, and the first person who understood and taught the doctrine of the sphere; and on the same account the poets tell us, that his daughters were turned into stars.

By his wife Pelione [z] he had seven daughters, whose names were Electra, Halcyone, Celæno, Maia, Asterope, Taygete, and Merope; and they were called by one common name, Pleiades; and by his wife Æthra [a] he had seven other daughters, whose names were Ambrosia, Eulora, Pasithoe, Coronis, Plexaris, Pytho, and Tyche; and these were called by one common name, Hyades, from [b] a word which in the Greek language signifies "to rain," because when they rise or set they are supposed to cause great rain; and therefore the Latins called them [c] *Suculæ*, that is, "Swine," because the continual rain that they cause makes the roads so muddy, that they seem to delight in dirt, like swine. [d] Others

x Herod. in Melpom.

y —— "Jamque volans apicem et latera ardua cernit
Atlantis duri, cœlumque vertice fulcit:
Atlantis, cinctum assidue cui nubibus atris
Piniferum caput, et vento pulsatur et imbri:
Nix humeros infusa tegit; tum flumina mento
Præcipitant senis, et glacie riget horrida barba."
Now sees the top of Atlas as he flies,
Whose brawny back supports the starry skies:
Atlas, whose head with piny forests crown'd
Is beaten by the winds, with foggy vapours bound:
Snows hide his shoulders; from beneath his chin
The founts of rolling streams their race begin.

z Ovid. Fast. 5. a Aratus in Astron.

b "Ἀπὸ τοῦ ὕειν, id est, pluere.
Navita quas Hyades Graius ab imbre vocat."
From rain the sailors call them Hyades.

c Suculæ, quemadmodum eas Græci vocant ὗες, id est, sues. Aulus Gell. l. 13. c. 19. d Eurip. in Jove.

derive their names from Hyas their brother, who was devoured by a lion: his sisters were so immoderately afflicted and grieved at his death, that Jupiter in compassion changed them into seven stars, which appear in the head of Taurus. And they are justly called Hyades, [e] because showers of tears flow from their eyes to this day.

The Pleiades derive their name from a Greek word signifying [f] "sailing." For when these stars rise, they portend good weather to navigators. Because they rise in the [g] spring-time, the Romans call them Vergiliæ. Yet others think that they are called Pleiades [h] from their number, since they never appear single, but all together, except Merope, who is scarcely ever seen; for she is ashamed that she married Sisyphus, a mortal man, when all the rest of the sisters married gods: [i] others call this obscure star Electra, because she held her hand before her eyes, and would not look upon the destruction of Troy. The Hyades were placed among the stars because they bewailed immoderately the death of their brother Hyas; and the Pleiades were translated into heaven, because they incessantly lamented the hard fate of their father Atlas, who was converted into a mountain. But let us speak a little about their uncle Hesperus.

Hesperus was the brother of Atlas, and because he lived some time in Italy, that country was called anciently Hesperia, from him. He frequently went up to the top of the mountain Atlas to view the stars. At last he went up, and came down from the mountain no more. This made the people imagine that he was carried up into heaven; upon which they worshipped him as a god, and called a very bright star from his name Hesperus, Hesper, Hesperugo, Vesper, and Vesperugo,

[e] Hesiod. in Theog.

[f] Ἀπὸ τοῦ πλέειν à navigando, commodum enim tempus navigationi ostendunt.

[g] Vergiliæ dictæ à verno tempore quod exoriuntur.

[h] Quasi πλείονες, hoc est, plures, quòd numquam singulæ appareant, sed omnes simul.

[i] Ovid. Fast. 4.

which is called the evening star, when it sets after the sun; but when it rises before the sun, it is called φωσφορος [*Phosphorus*], or Lucifer; that is, the morning star. Further, this Hesperus had three daughters, Egle, Prethusa, and Hesperethusa; who in general were called the Hesperides. It was said, that in their gardens trees were planted that bore golden fruit; and that these trees were guarded by a watchful dragon, which Hercules killed, and then carried away the golden apples. Hence the phrase, [k] To give some of the apples of the Hesperides; that is, to give a great and splendid gift.

QUESTIONS FOR EXAMINATION.

Who was Prometheus?

What did he bring from heaven?

What did Jupiter do in consequence?

Repeat the lines of Horace, and translation.

How did Jupiter punish Prometheus?

Why did he set him at liberty?

From what is the name of Prometheus derived, and what is the meaning of the fable?

What is the story of Deucalion?

How is Atlas represented, and how was he changed into a mountain?

Repeat the lines from Virgil.

Why has Atlas the world on his shoulders?

Who were his daughters?

From what do the Hyades derive their name?

Whence are the Pleiades named?

What is said of Hesperus?

[k] Μῆλα Ἑσπεριδῶν δωρῆσαι, id est, mala Hesperidum largiri.

CHAPTER VI.

ORPHEUS AND AMPHION. ACHILLES.

ORPHEUS and Amphion are drawn in the same manner, and almost in the same colours, because they both excelled in the same art, namely, in music; in which they were so skilful, that by playing on the harp they moved not only men, but beasts, and the very stones themselves.

Orpheus, the son of Apollo by Calliope the Muse, with the harp that he received from his father, played and sang so sweetly, that he tamed wild beasts, stayed the course of rivers, and made whole woods follow him. [1] He descended with the same harp into hell, to recover, from Pluto and Proserpine, his wife Eurydice, who had been killed by a serpent, when she fled from the violence of Aristæus. Here he so charmed both the king and queen with the sweetness of his music, that they permitted his wife to return to life again, upon this condition, that they should not look upon her till they were both arrived upon the earth: but so impatient and eager was the love of Orpheus, that he could not perform the condition; therefore she was taken back into hell again. Upon this, Orpheus resolved for the future to live a widower: and with his example alienated the minds of many others from the love of women. This so provoked the Mænades and Bacchæ, that they tore him in pieces: though others assign another reason of his death, which is this: the women, by the instigation of Venus, were so inflamed with the love of him, that, quarrelling with one another who should have him, they tore him in pieces. His bones were afterward gathered by the Muses, and re-

[1] Apoll. l. 1. Argo.

posed in a sepulchre, not without tears; and his harp was made the constellation Lyra.

Amphion was the son of Jupiter by Antiope. He received his lute and harp from Mercury; and [m] with the sound thereof moved the stones so regularly, that they composed the walls of the city of Thebes.

The occasion of which fable was this: Orpheus and Amphion were both men so eloquent, that they persuaded those who lived a wild and savage life before to embrace the rules and manners of civil society.

Arion is a proper companion for these two musicians, for he was a lyric poet of Methymna, in the island of Lesbos, and gained immense riches by his art. [n] When he was travelling from Lesbos into Italy, his companions assaulted him, to rob him of his wealth; but he entreated the seamen to suffer him to play on his harp before they cast him into the sea: [o] he played sweetly, and then threw himself into the sea; where a dolphin, drawn thither by the sweetness of his music, received him on his back, [p] and carried him to Tenedos. The dolphin for this kindness was carried into heaven, and made a constellation.

Achilles was the son of Peleus by Thetis. His mother plunged him in the Stygian waters when he was an infant; which made his whole body ever after invulnerable, excepting that part of his foot by which he was held when he was washed. Others say, that Thetis

[m] "Dictus et Amphion, Thebanæ conditor urbis,
Saxa movere sono testudinis, et prece blanda
Ducere quo vellet." — Hor. Arte Poet.

Amphion too, as story goes, could call
Obedient stones to make the Theban wall.
He led them as he pleased; the rocks obey'd,
And danced in order to the tunes he play'd.

[n] Paus. in Bœotic. [o] Herod. in Clio.

[p] "Ille sedet, citharamque tenet, pretiumque vehendi
Cantat, et æquoreas carmine mulcet aquas." Ov. Fast. 2.

He on his crouching back sits all at ease
With harp in hand, by which he calms the seas,
And for his passage with a song he pays.

hid him in the night under a fire, [q]after she had anointed him in the day with ambrosia; whence at first he was called Pyrisous, because he escaped safe from the fire; and afterward Achilles, [r]because he had but one lip, for he licked the ambrosia from his other lip, so that the fire had power to burn it off. Others again report, [s]that he was brought up by Chiron the Centaur, and fed, instead of milk, with the entrails of lions, and the marrow of boars and bears: so that by that means he received immense greatness of soul, and mighty strength of body. From him, those who greatly excelled in strength were called Achilles; [t]and an argument is called Achilleum, when no objection can weaken or disprove it.

Thetis, his mother, had heard from an oracle, that he should be killed in the expedition against Troy. On the other hand, Calchas the diviner had declared, that Troy could not be taken without him. By the cunning of Ulysses he was forced to go: for when his mother Thetis hid him in a boarding-school (in Gynecæo) in the island Scyros, one of the Cyclades, in the habit of a virgin, among the daughters of king Lycomedes, Ulysses discovered the trick: he went thither in the disguise of a merchant, and took with him several goods to sell. The king's daughters began to view and handle curiously the bracelets, the glasses, the necklaces, and such like women's ornaments; but Achilles, on the contrary, laid hold of the targets, and fitted the helmets to his head, and brandished the swords, and placed them to his side. Thus Ulysses plainly discovered Achilles from the virgins, and compelled him to go to the war; after that Vulcan, by Thetis' entreaty, had given him impenetrable armour. Achilles at Troy killed Hector, the son of Priamus; and was killed himself by Paris, by a trick of Polyxena: [u]and

[q] Apoll 4. Argon. [r] Ab α priv. et χεῖλος, labrum; quasi sine labro. [s] Apoll. l. 3. Eurip. in Iphig.
[t] Gell. l. 2. c. 11. [u] Lycophron. in Alexand.

all the Nymphs and Muses are said to have lamented his death.

This Polyxena was the daughter of Priamus, king of Troy, a virgin of extraordinary beauty. Achilles by chance saw her upon the walls of the city, and fell in love with her, and desired to marry her. Priamus consented. They met in the temple of Apollo to solemnize the marriage; where Paris, the brother of Hector, coming in privately, and lurking behind Apollo's image, shot Achilles suddenly with an arrow, in that part of his foot in which only he was vulnerable. After this Troy was taken, and the ghost of Achilles demanded satisfaction for the murder, which the Grecians appeased by offering the blood of Polyxena.

QUESTIONS FOR EXAMINATION.

Who were Orpheus and Amphion, and in what did they excel?

What is related of Orpheus?

Who was Amphion, and what was the occasion of the fable?

Who was Arion, and what is related of him?

Who was Achilles, and what is reported of him during his infancy?

In what did Achilles excel; and what is the nature of the argument named after him?

Why and how was he forced into the Trojan war?

What hero did he kill, and by whom was he slain?

How was he killed, and what did the Grecians do to appease his ghost?

CHAPTER VII.

ULYSSES. ORION.

Ulysses was so named, because when his mother was travelling, as some say, in the island Ithaca, as others say, in Bœotia, she fell down on the [w] road, and brought him

[w] Græcè 'Οδυσσεύς, ab ὁδὸς via; quòd in ipsâ viâ ejus mater iter faciens lapsa illum peperit. Vide Nat. Com. et Hom. in Odyss.

into the world. He was the son of Laertes and Anticlea. His wife was Penelope, a lady highly famed for her prudence and virtue. He was unwilling that the Trojan war should part him and his dear wife; therefore, to avoid the expedition, he pretended to be mad, joining the different beasts to the same plough, and sowing the furrows with salt. But this pretence was detected by Palamedes, who laid his infant son in the furrow, while Ulysses was ploughing, to see whether he would suffer the ploughshare to wound him or not. When Ulysses came where his son lay, he turned the plough; and thus it was discovered that he was not a madman, and he was compelled to go to the war. There he was mightily serviceable to the Grecians, and was almost the sole occasion of taking the town. He forced Achilles from his retreat, and obtained the arrows of Hercules from Philoctetes, which he brought against Troy. He took away the ashes of Laomedon, which were preserved upon the gate Scæa in Troy. He stole the Palladium from the city; killed Rhœsus, king of Thrace, and took his horses, before they had tasted the water of the river Xanthus. In which things the destiny of Troy was wrapped up: for if the Trojans had preserved them, the town could never have been conquered. He contended with Ajax the son of Telamon and Hesione, who was the stoutest of all the Grecians except Achilles, before judges, for the arms of Achilles. The judges were persuaded by the eloquence of Ulysses, gave sentence in his favour, and assigned the arms to him. This disappointment made Ajax mad, upon which he killed himself, and his blood was turned into the violet.

When Ulysses departed from Troy to return home, he sailed backward and forward ten years; for contrary winds and bad weather hindered him from getting home. During which time, 1. He put out the eye of Polyphemus with a firebrand; and then sailing to Æölia, he there obtained from Æölus all the winds which were contrary to him, and put them into leathern bags. His companions, believing that the bags were filled with money, and not with wind, intended to rob him; therefore, when they came almost to Ithaca, they untied the bags, and the winds gushed out, and blew him back to Æölia again. 2. When Circe had turned his companions into beasts, he first fortified himself against her charms with the antidote that Mercury had given him, and then ran into her cave with his sword drawn, and forced her to restore his companions to their former shapes again; after which, Circe and he were reconciled, and he had by her Telegonus. 3. He went down into hell, to know his future fortune from the prophet Tiresias. 4. When he sailed to the islands of the Sirens, he stopped the ears of his companions, and bound himself with strong ropes to the ship's mast: by these means he avoided the dangerous snares into which, by their charming voices, they led men. 5. And lastly, after his ship was broken and wrecked by the waves, he escaped by swimming; and came naked and alone to the port of Phæacia, where Nausica, the daughter of king Alcinous, found him hidden among the young trees, and entertained him civilly. When his companions were found, and the ship refitted, he was sent asleep into Ithaca, where Pallas awaked him, and advised him to put on the habit of a beggar. Then he went to his neatherds, where he found his son Telemachus; and from them he went home in a disguise; where, after he had received several affronts from the wooers of Penelope, by the assistance of the neat-herds, and his son, to whom he discovered himself, he set upon them, and killed them every one; and then received his Penelope.

Penelope, the daughter of Icarus, was a rare and perfect example of chastity. For though it was generally thought that her husband Ulysses was dead, since he had been absent from her twenty years; yet, neither the desires of her parents, nor the solicitations of her lovers, could prevail on her to marry another man, and to violate the promises of constancy which she gave to her husband when he departed. And when many noblemen courted her, and even threatened her with ruin unless she declared which of them should marry her, she desired that the choice might be deferred till she had finished the piece of needle-work about which she was then employed: but undoing by night what she had worked by day, she delayed them till Ulysses returned and killed them all. Hence came the proverb, [x] "To weave Penelope's web;" that is, to labour in vain; when one hand destroys what the other has wrought.

Orion, when young, was a constant companion of Diana: but because his love to the goddess exceeded the bounds of modesty, or because, as some say, he extolled the strength of his own body very indecently, and boasted that he could outrun and subdue the wildest and fiercest beasts, his arrogance grievously displeased the Earth; therefore she sent a scorpion, which killed him. He was afterward carried to the heavens, and there made a constellation; which is thought to predict foul weather when it does not appear, and fair weather when it is visible; whence the poets call him [y] tempestuous, or stormy Orion.

QUESTIONS FOR EXAMINATION.

From what did Ulysses derive his name?

How did he excuse himself from going to the Trojan war, and how was the artifice detected?

What exploits did he perform at Troy?

What was the contention between him and Ajax, and what was the consequence of it?

What acts did he perform during his return?

What happened to him in Ithaca?

What is said of Penelope; and whence is the origin of the phrase, "To weave Penelope's web?"

What is said of Orion?

What does the constellation predict?

[x] *Penelopes telam texere,* id est, inanem operam sumere. Vid. Erasm. Adag.

[y] Nimbosus Orion. Virg. Æn. nam ὀρίνω significat *turbo, moveo,* unde etiam ipse nomen sumpsisse à nonnullis judicatur.

CHAPTER VIII.

OSIRIS, APIS, SERAPIS.

Osiris, Apis, and Serapis, are three different names of one and the same god. Osiris was the son of Jupiter, by Niobe, the daughter of Phoroneus; and was king of the Argives many years. He was stirred up, by the desire of glory, to leave his kingdom to his brother Ægialus, and to sail into Egypt, to seek a new name and new kingdoms. The Egyptians were not so much overcome by his arms, as obliged to him by his courtesies and kindness. After this, he married Io, the daughter of Inachus, whom Jupiter formerly turned into a cow; but, when by her distraction she was driven into Egypt, her former shape was again restored, and she married Osiris, and instructed the Egyptians in letters. Therefore, both she and her husband attained to divine honours, and were thought immortal by that people. But Osiris showed that he was mortal; for he was killed by his brother Typhon. Io (afterward called Isis) sought him a great while; and when she had found him at last in a chest, she laid him in a monument in an island near to Memphis, which island is encompassed by that sad and fatal lake, the Styx. And because when she sought him she had used dogs, who by their excellent virtue of smelling might discover where he was hidden, thence the ancient custom came, [1] that dogs went first in an anniversary procession in honour of Isis. And the people carefully and religiously worshipped a god with a dog's head, called Anubis; which god the poets commonly call [a] Barker, "a god half a dog, a dog half a [b] man." He is also called [c] Hermanubis; because his sagacity is so great, that some

[1] Ex. Gyr. synt. 9. [a] Latratorem, semicanem Deum, Virg. Æn. 8. [b] Semi-hominem canem. Ovid. Met. 9. Lucan, seduli. [c] Plut. in Osiride. Serv. in Æn. 8.

think him to be the same with Mercury. But let us return to Osiris and Isis.

After the body of Osiris was interred, there appeared to the Egyptians a stately, beautiful ox; the Egyptians thought that it was Osiris, therefore they worshipped it, and called it Apis, which in the Egyptian language signifies an "ox." But because the body, after his death, was found shut up in a [d] chest, he was afterward from this called Sorapis, and by the change of a letter Serapis; as we shall see more clearly and particularly by and by, when I have observed what Plutarch says, that Osiris was thought to be the Sun. His name comes from *os*, which in the Egyptian language signifies "much," and *iris*, an "eye;" and his image was a sceptre, in which was placed an eye. So that Osiris signifies the same as πολυοφθαλμος [*polyophthalmos*], "many-eyed," which agrees very well to the Sun, who seems to have so many eyes as he has rays, by which he sees, and makes all things visible.

Some say that Isis is Pallas, others Terra, others Ceres, and many the Moon; for she is painted sometimes [e] horned, as the moon appears in the increase, and wears black garments; because the moon shines in the night. In her right hand she held a cymbal, and in her left a bucket. Her head was crowned with the feathers of a vulture; for among the Egyptians that bird is sacred to Juno; and therefore they adorned the tops of their porches with the feathers of a vulture. The priests of Isis, called after her own name Isiaci, [f] abstained from the flesh of swine and sheep; they used no [g] salt to their meat, lest they should violate their chastity. [h] They shaved their heads, [i] they wore paper shoes, and a [k] linen vest, because Isis first taught the use

[d] Σορὸς significat arcam, in qua inventum est illius corpus inclusum.

[e] Κεραοφόρος, id est, cornigera, affingebatur, ad Lunæ crescentis similitudinem, et μελανόστολος, nigris vestibus induta, quòd luna luceat in tenebris. Vide Serv. in Æn. 8.

[f] Ælian. de Anim. Herodot. l. 2.

[g] Plut. symp. 5. c. 10.

[h] Cœl. Rhodigin. 5. c. 12.

[i] Herodot. l. 1.

[k] Claud. 4. Hon. cons.

of flax; and hence she is called [l] Linigera, and also [m] Inachis, from Inachus, her father. By the name of Isis is usually understood "wisdom;" and accordingly, upon the pavement of the temple, there was this inscription: [n] "I am every thing that hath been, and is, and shall be; nor hath any mortal opened my veil."

By the means of this Isis, [o] Iphis, a young virgin of Crete, the daughter of Lygdus and Telethusa, was changed into a man. For when Lygdus went a journey, he enjoined his wife, who was then pregnant, if she brought a daughter, that she should not educate her, but leave her exposed in the fields to perish by want. Telethusa brought forth a daughter, but was very unwilling to lose her child; therefore she dressed it in a boy's habit, and called it Iphis, which is a common name to boys and girls. The father returned from his journey, and believed both his wife and his daughter, who personated a son: and as soon as she was marriageable, her father, who still thought that she was a man, married her to the beautiful Ianthe. As they went to the temple to celebrate the marriage, the mother was mightily concerned; and she begged the favourable assistance of Isis, who heard her prayers, and changed the virgin Iphis into a most beautiful young man. Now let us come to Serapis and Apis again.

Though Serapis, of whose name we gave the etymology before, was the god of the Egyptians, yet he was worshipped in Greece, [p] especially at Athens, [q] and also at Rome. Among different nations he had different names: for he was called sometimes [r] Jupiter Ammon, sometimes Pluto, Bacchus, Æsculapius, and sometimes Osiris. His name was reckoned abominable by the Grecians; [s] for all names of seven letters, *επταγραμματα*

[l] Ovid. de Pon. el. 1. [m] Propert. l. 1. et 2.

[n] Ἐγώ εἰμι πᾶν τὸ γεγονός, καὶ ὄν, καὶ ἐσόμενον καὶ τὸ ἐμὸν πέπλον οὐδεὶς τῶν θνητῶν ἀπεκάλυψεν. Ego sum quicquid fuit, est, erit; nec meum quisquam mortalium peplum retexit. Plut. in Iside.

[o] Ovid. Met. 9. [p] Pausan. in Attic. [q] Publ. Victor.

[r] Tacitus, l. 20. Plut. de Osiride. [s] Porphyrius.

[*heptagrammata*] are by them esteemed infamous. Some say that Ptolemy, the son of Lagus, procured the effigies of him at Pontus, from the king of Sinope, and dedicated a magnificent temple to him at Alexandria. Eusebius calls him the [t] "Prince of evil dæmons:" a flasket was placed [u] upon his head, and near him lay a creature with three heads; a dog's on the right side, a wolf's on the left side, and a lion's head in the middle: a snake with his fold encompassed them, whose head hung down unto the god's right hand, with which he bridled the terrible monster.

Apis [w] was king of the Argivi, and being transported thence into Egypt, he became Serapis, or the greatest of all the gods of Egypt. After the death of Serapis, the ox that we mentioned a little before succeeded in his place. [x] Pliny describes the form and quality of this ox, thus: An ox, in Egypt, is worshipped as a god: they call him Apis. He is thus marked: there is a white shining spot upon his right side, horns like the moon in its increase, and a nose under its tongue, which they call *cantharus*. His body, [y] says Herodotus, was all black: in his forehead he had a white square shining figure; the effigies of an eagle in his back; and beside the *cantharus* in his mouth, he had hair of two sorts in his tail. But Pliny goes on: If he lives beyond an appointed period of time, they drown him in the priests' fountain; then the priests shave their heads, mourn and lament, and seek another to substitute in his room. When they have found one, he is brought by the priests to Memphis. He hath two chapels, or chambers, which are the oracles of the people; in one of them he foretels good, in the other ill.

[t] Præp. Evang. 4.
[u] Macrob. in Saturn.
[w] Aug. de Civ. Dei, 18.
[x] Plin. Hist. Nat. l. 8. c. 40.
[y] Herodot. l. 3.

QUESTIONS FOR EXAMINATION.

Who was Osiris; whom did he marry; and what is told of his wife?

What was Io afterwards called, and why did dogs go first in the procession devoted to her?

Who was Anubis?

What was Apis; why was the name of Osiris changed to Serapis; and what does Osiris signify?

Who was Isis; what is said of her; and what is signified by the name?

How was Iphis changed into a man, and what was the cause of this metamorphosis?

Under what name has Serapis been worshipped?

How is he denominated by Eusebius; and what symbols are connected with him?

Who was Apis; and how is he described by Pliny?

APPENDIX.

OF THE VIRTUES AND VICES WHICH HAVE BEEN DEIFIED.

CHAPTER I.

THE VIRTUES AND GOOD DEITIES.

THE ancients not only worshipped the several species of virtues, but also Virtue herself, as a goddess. Therefore, first of her, and then of the others.

Virtue derives her name from *vir*, because virtue is the most manly ornament. [a] She was esteemed a goddess, [b] and worshipped in the habit of an elderly matron sitting upon a square stone. [c] M. Marcellus dedicated a temple to her; and hard by placed another, that was dedicated to Honour: the temple of Virtue was the passage to the temple of Honour; hence by Virtue alone true honour is attained. The priests sacrificed to Honour with bare heads, and we usually uncover our heads when we see honourable and worthy men; and since honour itself is valuable and estimable, it is no wonder if such respect is shown in celebrating its sacrifices.

Fides had a temple at Rome, near the Capitol, which

[a] Cic. Quæst. Tusc. 2. [b] Aug. de Civ. Dei, 4. [c] Liv. l. 2.

[d] Numa Pompilius, it is said, first consecrated to her. [e] Her sacrifices were performed without slaughter, or blood. The heads and hands of the priests were covered with a white cloth when they sacrificed, because faith ought to be close and secret. Virgil calls her [f] Cana Fides, either from the candour of the mind, whence fidelity proceeds, or because faith is chiefly observed by aged persons. The symbol of this goddess was a white dog, which is a faithful creature. [g] Another symbol was two hands joined, or two young ladies shaking hands: for, [h] by giving the right hand, they engaged their faith for their future friendship.

Hope had a temple at Rome, in the herb-market, which was unfortunately burnt down with lightning. [i] Giraldus says, that he has seen her effigies in a golden coin of the emperor Adrian. She was described in the form of a woman standing; her left hand lightly held up the skirts of her garments; she leaned on her elbow; and in her right hand held a plate, on which was placed a *ciberium*, a sort of a cup, fashioned to the likeness of a flower, with this inscription, SPES, P. R. "The Hope of the People of Rome." We have already related in what manner Hope was left and preserved in the bottom of Pandora's box.

Justice was described like a virgin, with a piercing, stedfast eye, a severe brow, her aspect awful, noble, and venerable. Alexander says, that among the Egyptians she had no head, and that her left hand was stretched forth, and open. The Greeks called her Astrea.

Attilius, the duumvir, dedicated a chapel to Piety at Rome, in the place where that woman lived, who fed her mother in prison with the milk of her breasts. The story is this: [k] The mother was punished with imprisonment; her daughter, who was an ordinary woman, then gave suck; she came to the prison frequently, and

[d] Cic. de Officiis. [e] Dion. Halicarn. l. 2. [f] Serv. in l. et 8. Æn. [g] Stat. Theb. l. [h] Dextrâ datâ fidem futuræ amicitiæ sancibant. Liv. l. 21. [i] Syntagm. l. 1.
[k] Plin. Hist. Nat. l. 7. c. 36.

the gaoler always searched her, to see that she carried no food to her mother: at last she was found giving suck to her mother with her breasts. This extraordinary piety of the daughter gained the mother's freedom; and they both were afterward maintained at the public charge; and the place was consecrated to the goddess Piety. There is a like example in the [l] Grecian history, of a woman, who by her breasts nourished Cymon, her aged father, who was imprisoned, and supported him with her own milk.

The Athenians erected an altar to *Misericordia*, "Mercy;" [m] where was first established an asylum, a place of common refuge to the miserable and unfortunate. It was not lawful to force any one from thence. When Hercules died, [n] his kindred feared some mischief from those whom he had afflicted; therefore they erected an asylum, or temple of mercy, at Athens.

Nothing memorable occurs concerning the goddess Clemency, unless that there was a temple erected to Clementia Cæsaris, "The Clemency of Cæsar," as we read in [o] Plutarch.

Two temples at Rome were dedicated to Chastity; the one to Pudicitia Patricia, which stood in the ox-market; the other to Pudicitia Plebeia, built by Virginia, the daughter of Aulus: for when she, who was born of a patrician family, [p] had married a plebeian, the noble ladies were mightily incensed, and banished her from their sacrifices, and would not suffer her to enter into the temple of Pudicitia, into which senatorian families only were permitted entrance. A quarrel arose upon this among the women, and a great breach was made between them. This induced Virginia, by some extraordinary action, to blot out the disgrace she had received; and therefore she built a chapel in the long street where she lived, and adorned it with an altar, to which she invited the plebeian matrons; and complaining to them

[l] Val. Max. l. 5. [m] Pausan. in Attic. [n] Serv. in Æn. 8.
[o] In Vitâ Cæsaris. [p] Liv. l. 10.

that the ladies of quality had used her so barbarously: "I dedicate," says she, "this altar to Pudicitia Plebeia; and I desire of you that you will as much adore Chastity as the men do Honour; that this altar may be followed by purer and more chaste votaries than the altar of Pudicitia Patricia, if it be possible." It is said in history, that the women, who were contented with one marriage, were usually rewarded with a [q]crown of chastity.

Truth, the mother of Virtue, [r]is painted in garments as white as snow; her looks are serene, pleasant, courteous, cheerful, and yet modest; she is the pledge of all honesty, the bulwark of honour, the light and joy of human society. [s]She is commonly accounted the daughter of Time, or Saturn; because truth is discovered in the course of time: but Democritus feigns that she lies hidden in the bottom of a well.

Good Sense, or Understanding (*mens*), was made a goddess by the Romans, [t]that they might obtain a sound mind. [u]An altar was built to her in the Capitol, by M. Æmilius. [w]The prætor Attilius vowed to build a chapel to her; which he performed when he was created duumvir.

We shall find by [x]the concurrent testimony of many, that the goddess Concordia had many altars at several times dedicated to her; but she was especially worshipped by the ancient Romans. Her image held a bowl in her right hand, and a horn of plenty, or a sceptre from which fruit seemed to sprout forth, in her left. [y]The symbol of Concord was two right hands joined together, and a pomegranate.

Pax was honoured formerly at Athens with an altar, [z]as Plutarch tells us. At Rome she had a most magnificent temple in the Forum, begun by Claudius, and

[q] Corona pudicitiæ. Val. Max. l. 2.
[r] Philost. in Heroic. et Amp.
[s] Plut. in Quæst.
[t] Aug. de Civ. Dei, 2.
[u] Cic. Nat. Deor. 2.
[w] Liv. 22 et 23.
[x] Liv. l. 9. Plut. in C. Gracch. Suet. in Tib.
[y] Lil. Gyr. synt. 1.
[z] Plut. in Cimon.

SALUS

Publish'd by Wilkie & Robinson Paternoster Row May 1 1810.

finished by Vespasian; [a] which was afterward consumed in a fire under Emperor Commodus. She was described in the form of a matron, holding forth ears of corn in her hands, and crowned with olives and laurel, or sometimes roses. Her particular symbol was a *caduceus*, a white staff borne by ambassadors when they go to treat of peace.

The goddess Salus was so much honoured by the Romans, that anciently several holy days were appointed in which they worshipped her. [b] There was a gate at Rome called Porta Salutaris, because it was near to the temple of Salus. Her image was the figure of a woman sitting on a throne, and holding a bowl in her right hand. Hard by stood her altar, a snake twining round it, and lifting up his head toward it. The Augurium Salutis was formerly celebrated in the same place. [c] It was a kind of divination, by which they begged leave of the gods that the people might pray for peace.

Fidelity, [d] says St. Augustin, had her temple and altar, and sacrifices were performed to her. They represented her like a venerable matron sitting upon a throne, holding a [e] white rod in her right hand, and a great horn of plenty in her left.

As the Romans were, above all things, careful of their liberty, especially after the expulsion of the kings, when they set themselves at liberty, [f] so they built a temple to Liberty, among the number of their other goddesses. And Cicero tells us, that Clodius consecrated his house to her.

The Romans invoked Pecunia as a goddess, that they might be rich. They worshipped the god Æsculanus and his son Argentinus, that they might have plenty of brass and silver; and esteemed Æsculanus, the father of Argentinus, because brass money was used before silver. "I wonder," [g] says St. Augustin, "that Aurinus was not

[a] Herodot. l. 2. [b] Macrob. Saturn. l. c. 16.
[c] Dion. l. 27. Aug. Pollutian. Miscel. c. 12.
[d] De Civ. Dei, 4. [e] Caduceus. [f] Lil. Gyr.
[g] Miror autem quòd Argentinus non genùit Aurinum, quia et aurea pecunia subsecuta est. De Civ. Dei, l. 4.

made a god after Argentinus, because silver money was followed by gold." To this goddess, Money, O how many apply their devotions to this day! what vows do they make, and at what altars do they importune, that they may fill their coffers! "If you have those gods," [h] says Menander, "gold and silver, at home, ask whatever you please, you shall have it; the very gods themselves will be at your service."

Lycurgus ridiculously erected an image, among the [i] Lacedæmonians, to the god Risus. The Thessalonians, of the city of Hypata, every year sacrificed to this god with great jollity.

The god [k] Bonus Genius had a temple in the way that leads to the mountain Mænalus, as says Pausanias. At the end of the supper, they offered a cup to him, filled with wine and water, which was called [l] "The grace cup." Some say that the cup had more water than wine; others say the contrary.

QUESTIONS FOR EXAMINATION.

From what does the goddess Virtue derive her name?

To what does the temple of Virtue lead?

In what way did the priests sacrifice to Honour?

Where was the temple of Fides, and how were her sacrifices performed?

What were the usual symbols of Fides?

How is Hope described, and where was her temple?

How was Hope preserved to the inhabitants of the earth?

How is Justice described?

Where was there a chapel dedicated to Piety, and what was the cause of it?

What temples were dedicated to Chastity?

How is Truth painted; whose daughter is she; and why?

Why was *mens* made a goddess?

How is Concordia described, and by what symbol is she known?

Where was Pax honoured, how is she described, and what is her peculiar symbol?

[h] Hos deos Aurum et Argentum si domi habeas, quicquid voles, roga, tibi omnia aderunt, ipsos habebis vel ministrantes deos. Ap. Stob. or. de laude auri.

[i] Plut. in Lycurgo.

[k] Ἀγαθὸς Θεός.

[l] Ἀγαθοῦ Δαίμονος, poculum boni Genii.

What is said of the goddess Salus?

How is Fidelity represented?

What is said of Liberty?

Why did the Romans invoke Pecunia as a goddess?

What was the saying of Menander?

Who sacrificed to Risus?

Where was there a temple dedicated to Bonus Genius, and what was offered this god?

CHAPTER II.

THE VICES AND EVIL DEITIES.

I CALL those Evil Deities which oppose our happiness, and many times do us mischief. And first, of the Vices to which temples have been consecrated.

That Envy is a goddess appears by the confession of Pallas, who owned that she was assisted by her to infect a young lady, called Aglauros, with her poison. Ovid describes the [m] house where she dwells in very elegant verse, and afterward gives a most beautiful description of [n] Envy herself.

m "Protinus Invidiæ nigro squallentia tabo
Tecta petit. Domus est imis in vallibus antri
Abdita, sole carens, nec ulli pervia vento;
Tristis, et ignavi plenissima frigoris; et quæ
Igne vacet semper, caligine semper abundet." Met. 2.

Then straight to Envy's cell she bends her way,
Which all with putrid gore infected lay.
Deep in a gloomy cave's obscure recess,
No beams could e'er that horrid mansion bless;
No breeze e'er fann'd it; but about it roll'd
Eternal woes, and ever lazy cold;
No spark shone there, but everlasting gloom,
Impenetrably dark, obscured the room.

n "Pallor in ore sedet; macies in corpore toto;
Nusquam recta acies; livent rubigine dentes;
Pectora felle virent; lingua est suffusa veneno;
Risus abest, nisi quem visi movere dolores.

The vices Contumely and Impudence were both adored as deities by the [o] Athenians: and particularly, it is said, they were represented by a partridge; which is esteemed a very impudent bird.

The Athenians erected an altar to Calumny. [p] Apelles painted her thus: [q] There sits a man with great and open ears, inviting Calumny, with his hand held out, to come to him; and two women, Ignorance and Suspicion, stand near him. Calumny breaks out in a fury; her countenance is comely and beautiful, her eyes sparkle like fire, and her face is inflamed with anger; she holds a lighted torch in her left hand, and with her right twists a young man's neck, who holds up his hands in prayer to the gods. Before her goes Envy, pale and nasty; on her side are Fraud and Conspiracy; behind her follows Repentance, clad in mourning and her clothes torn, with her head turned backward, as if she looked for Truth, who comes slowly after.

Fraud [r] was described with a human face, and with a serpent's body: in the end of her tail was a scorpion's sting: she swims through the river Cocytus, and nothing appears above water but her head.

> Nec fruitur somno, vigilantibus excita curis;
> Sed videt ingratos, intabescitque videndo,
> Successus hominum: carpitque, et carpitur unà;
> Suppliciumque suum est." Met. 2.
> A deadly paleness in her cheeks was seen;
> Her meagre skeleton scarce cased with skin;
> Her looks awry; an everlasting scowl
> Sits on her brows; her teeth deform'd and foul;
> Her breast had gall more than her breast could hold;
> Beneath her tongue black coats of poison roll'd;
> No smiles e'er smooth'd her furrow'd brows, but those
> Which rise from common mischiefs, plagues, and woes:
> Her eyes, mere strangers to the sweets of sleep,
> Devouring spite for ever waking keep;
> She sees bless'd men with vast successes crown'd,
> Their joys distract her, and their glories wound:
> She kills abroad, herself's consumed at home,
> And her own crimes are her perpetual martyrdom.

[o] Pausan. in Attic. Cic. de Leg. 2. Theophr. de Leg. [p] Idem apud Diogen. [q] Lucian. lib. de non temerè credendis calumniis.
[r] Bocat. in Gen. Deor.

Petronius Arbiter, where he treats of the civil war between Pompey and Cæsar, has given a [s] beautiful description of the goddess Discordia.

Fury is described sometimes chained, sometimes raging and revelling with her chains broke: but [t] Virgil chooses to describe her bound in chains, although [u] Petronius describes her at liberty, unbound.

[w] Pausanias and [x] Plutarch say, that there were temples dedicated to Fame. She is finely and delicately described by Virgil, which description I will [y] subjoin.

[s] "Intremuere tubæ, ac scisso Discordia crine
Extulit ad superos Stygium caput. Hujus in ore
Concretus sanguis, comusaque lumina flebant;
Stabant ærata scabrâ rubigine dentes;
Tabo lingua fluens, obsessa draconibus ora:
Atque inter toto laceratam pectore vestem,
Sanguineam tremula quatiebat lampada dextra."
The trumpets sound, and with a dismal yell
Wild Discord rises from the vale of hell.
From her swell'd eyes there ran a briny flood,
And clotted gore upon her visage stood;
Around her head serpentine elf-locks hung,
And streams of blood flow'd from her sable tongue:
Her tatter'd clothes her yellow skin betray
(An emblem of the breast on which they lay);
And brandish'd flames her trembling hand obey.

[t] ———————"Furor impius intus
Sæva sedens super arma, et centum vinctus ahenis
Post tergum nodis, fremit horridus ore cruento." Æn. 1.
——————— Within sits impious War
On cursed arms, bound with a thousand chains,
And, horrid with a bloody mouth, complains.

[u] ——————"Furor abruptis, ceu liber, habenis
Sanguineum late tollit caput; oraque mille
Vulneribus confossa cruenta casside velat.
Hæret detritus lævæ Mavortius umbo
Innumerabilibus telis gravis, atque flagranti
Stipite dextrâ minax terris incendia portat."
Disorder'd Rage, from brazen fetters freed,
Ascends to earth with an impetuous speed:
Her wounded face a bloody helmet hides,
And her left arm a batter'd target guides;
Red brands of fire, supported in her right,
The impious world with flames and ruin fright.

[w] Pausan. in Attic. [x] Plut. in Camillo.

[y] "Fama, malum quo non aliud velocius ullum,
Mobilitate viget, viresque acquirit eundo;

Why was Fortune made a goddess, says [z] St. Augustin, since she comes to the good and bad without any judgment? She is so blind, that without distinction she runs to any body; and many times she passes by those that admire her, and sticks to those that despise her. So that [a] Juvenal had reason to speak in the manner he does of her. Yet the temples that have been conse-

Parva metu primo; mox sese attollit in auras,
Ingrediturque solo, et caput inter nubila condit.
Illam terra parens, ira irritata deorum,
Extremam (ut perhibent) Cæo Enceladoque sororem
Progenuit; pedibus celerem et pernicibus alis:
Monstrum horrendum, ingens; cui quot sunt corpore plumæ.
Tot vigiles oculi subter (mirabile dictu)
Tot linguæ, totidem ora sonant, tot subrigit aures.
Nocte volat cœli medio terræque, per umbram
Stridens, nec dulci declinat lumina somno.
Luce sedet custos, aut summi culmine tecti,
Turribus aut altis, et magnas territat urbes:
Tam ficti pravique tenax, quam nuncia veri." Æn. 4.
Fame, the great ill, from small beginnings grows,
Swift from the first, and every moment brings
New vigour to her flights, new pinions to her wings.
Soon grows the pigmy to gigantic size,
Her feet on earth, her forehead in the skies.
Enraged against the gods, revengeful Earth
Produced her last of the Titanian birth.
Swift is her walk, more swift her winged haste,
A monstrous phantom, horrible and vast;
As many plumes as raise her lofty flight,
So many piercing eyes enlarge her sight;
Millions of opening mouths to Fame belong,
And every mouth is furnish'd with a tongue;
And round with listening ears the flying plague is hung.
She fills the peaceful universe with cries;
No slumbers ever close her wakeful eyes;
By day from lofty towers her head she shows,
And spreads through trembling crowds disastrous news.
With court-informers' haunts, and royal spies,
Things done relates, not done she feigns, and mingles truth with lies:
Talk is her business, and her chief delight
To tell of prodigies, and cause affright.

[z] Aug. de Civ. Dei, 1.

[a] "Nullum numen abest si sit prudentia; sed te
Nos facimus, Fortuna, Deam, cœloque locamus." Sat. 20.
Fortune is never worshipp'd by the wise;
But she, by fools set up, usurps the skies.

FORTUNE

Publish'd by Wilkie & Robinson Paternoster Row May 1 1810.

crated to her, and the names that she has had, are innumerable: the chief of them I will point out to you.

She was styled Aurea, or Regia Fortuna, and [b] an image of her so called was usually kept in the emperor's chamber; and when one died, it was removed to the palace of his successor.

She is also called Cæca, "blind." Neither is she only, says [c] Cicero, blind herself, but she many times makes those blind that enjoy her.

She was called Muliebris, because the mother and the wife of Coriolanus saved the city of Rome. And when her image was consecrated in their presence, [d] it spoke these words twice: "Ladies, you have dedicated me as you should do."

Servius Tullius dedicated a temple to Fortuna Obsequens, because she obeys the wishes of men. The same prince worshipped her, and built her chapels; where she was called Primigenia, [e] because both the city and the empire received their origin from her; also Privata or [f] Propria, because she had a chapel in the court, which that prince used so familiarly, that she was thought to go down through a little window into his house.

Lastly, she was called [g] Viscata, Viscosa, because we are caught by her, as birds are with birdlime; in which sense, Seneca says, [h] "kindnesses are birdlime."

Febris, Fever, had her altars and temples in the palace. [i] She was worshipped that she should not hurt: and for the same reason they worshipped all the other gods and goddesses of this kind.

Fear and Paleness were supposed to be gods, [k] and worshipped by Tullus Hostilius, [l] when in the battle between the Romans and the Vejentes it was told him,

[b] Spart. in Severo. Gyr. synt. 15.
[c] De Amicitia. [d] Rite me, Matronæ, dedicastis. Aug. de Civ. Dei, 4. Val. Max. l. 2. [e] Plutarch. [f] Ibid.
[g] Plutarch. in Quæst. [h] Beneficia sunt viscosa. De Beneficiis.
[i] Cic. 3 de Nat. et 2 de Leg. [k] Aug. de Civ. Dei, 4.
[l] Liv. l. 1.

that the Albans had revolted, and the Romans grew afraid and pale; for in this doubtful conjuncture he vowed a temple to Pallor and Pavor.

The people of Gadara [m] made Poverty and Art goddesses; because the first whets the wit for the discovery of the other.

Necessity and Violence had their chapel upon the Acro-Corinthus: but it was a crime to enter into it.

M. Marcellus dedicated a chapel to Tempestas, without the gate of Capena, after he had escaped a severe tempest in a voyage to the island of Sicily.

Both the Romans and Egyptians worshipped the gods and goddesses of Silence. The Latins particularly worshipped [n] Ageronia and Tacita, whose image, they say, stood upon the altar of the goddess Volupia, with its mouth tied up and sealed; [o] because they who endure their cares with silence and patience do by that means procure to themselves the greatest pleasure.

The Egyptians worshipped Harpocrates, as the "god of silence," [p] after the death of Osiris. He was the son of Isis. They offered the first fruits of the lentils and pulse to him. They consecrated the tree *persea* to him, because the leaves of it were shaped like a tongue, and the fruit like a heart. He was painted naked, in the figure of a boy, crowned with an Egyptian mitre, which ended at the points as it were in two buds; he held in his left hand a horn of plenty, while a finger of his right hand was upon his lip, thereby commanding silence. And therefore I say no more; neither can I better be silent, than when a god commands me to be so.

QUESTIONS FOR EXAMINATION.

How are the evil deities described?

How is it ascertained that Envy is a goddess?

[m] Arrian apud Gyr. synt. 4.

[n] Macrob. Sat. Plut. in Numa. Plin. l. 3. Quòd, qui suos angores (unde Angeronia dicta est) æquo animo ferunt, perveniunt ad maximam voluptatem. [p] Epiph. 3. contra Hæreses.

Repeat the lines descriptive of her house.
Give Ovid's description of Envy herself.
Whom did the Athenians adore as deities?
How is Calumny painted by Apelles?
How was Fraud described?
Repeat the lines descriptive of Discord.
How is Fury described by Virgil?
What are the lines by Petronius?
Give me Virgil's fine description of Fame.
How is Fortune described?
What does Juvenal say of her?
How is she described by Cicero?
What did Servius Tullius do with respect to Fortune?
Why was Fortune called Viscosa, and what was Seneca's phrase?
Why was Febris worshipped?
By whom were Fear and Paleness worshipped?
Why, and by whom were Poverty and Art deified?
What is said of Necessity and Violence?
Who dedicated a temple to Tempestas; and why did he do so?
Who worshipped the gods and goddesses of Silence?
Whom did the Latins worship, and why?
Whom did the Egyptians worship?
How is Harpocrates painted?

INDEX.

INDEX.

B.

D.

INDEX.

Q.

THE END.

LONDON:
PRINTED BY THOMAS DAVISON, WHITEFRIARS.

TO BE HAD OF THE SAME PUBLISHERS.

In seven volumes 8vo. price 3*l.* 13*s.* 6*d.*

THE HISTORY OF MODERN EUROPE; with an Account of the Decline and Fall of the Roman Empire, and a View of the Progress of Society from the Rise of the Modern Kingdoms to the Peace of Paris, in 1763: in a Series of Letters from a Nobleman to his Son. A new Edition, with a Continuation, terminating at the Pacification of Paris, in 1815. By CHARLES COOTE, LL. D.

The sixth and seventh volumes may be had separately, price 12*s.* each volume.

Of whom may also be had, the HISTORY OF ANCIENT EUROPE, by the same, in 3 vols. 8vo. price 2*l.* 2*s.* boards.

THE UNION DICTIONARY; containing all that is truly useful in the Dictionaries of Johnson, Sheridan, and Walker; the Orthography and explanatory Matter selected from Dr. Johnson, the Pronunciation adjusted according to Mr. Walker, with the Addition of Mr. Sheridan's Pronunciation of those Words wherein these two eminent Orthoëpists differ. With a Mythological and Historical Appendix of proper Names, deduced from the best Authorities. By THOMAS BROWNE, LL. D. Author of a "New Classical Dictionary." In one vol. crown octavo, price 10*s.* 6*d.* bound. The 3d edition.

THE COMPLETE PRACTICAL ARITHMETICIAN; containing several new and useful Improvements, adapted to the Use of Schools and Private Tuition. By THOMAS KEITH. Revised and Corrected. Seventh edition. Price 4*s.* 6*d.* bound.

THE HISTORY OF ENGLAND; from the earliest Times to the Death of George II. By OLIVER GOLDSMITH, M.B. With a Continuation to the Peace of Paris, 1815. By CHARLES COOTE, LL. D. In four vols. 8vo. Price 1*l.* 12*s.* boards. New edition.

AN ABRIDGMENT OF THE ABOVE; in one vol. 12mo. Price 3*s.* 6*d.* bound.

THE HISTORY OF ROME; from the Foundation of the City of Rome to the Destruction of the Western Empire. By OLIVER GOLDSMITH, M. B. In two vols. 8vo. Price 14*s.* boards.

AN ABRIDGMENT OF THE ABOVE; in one vol. 12mo. Price 3*s.* 6*d.* bound.

THE HISTORY OF GREECE; from the earliest State to the Death of Alexander the Great. By OLIVER GOLDSMITH, M. B. To which is added, a summary Account of the Affairs of Greece, from that Period to the Sacking of Constantinople by the Ottomans. In 2 vols. 8vo. Price 14*s.* in boards.

AN ABRIDGMENT OF THE ABOVE; in one vol. 12mo. Price 3*s.* 6*d.* bound.

THE LIFE OF M. TULLIUS CICERO. By CONYERS MIDDLETON, D.D. principal Librarian to the University of Cambridge. In two vols. 8vo. price 18*s.* boards,

EVERY MAN HIS OWN GARDENER; being a new and much more complete Gardener's Calendar and General Directory than any one hitherto published. By THOMAS MAWE, and JOHN ABERCROMBIE. The twenty-first edition, with great Improvements, and the whole Art brought down to the present State of Horticultural Knowledge. In one thick volume, 12mo. Price 8*s.* bound.

A DICTIONARY OF QUOTATIONS, in most frequent Use, taken chiefly from the Latin and French, but comprising many from the Greek, Spanish, and Italian Languages, translated into English; with Illustrations historical and idiomatic. By D. E. MACDONNEL, of the Middle Temple. The Seventh Edition, revised and corrected. Price 7*s.* 6*d.* boards.

SHORT GREEK EXERCISES, on an improved Plan; containing the most useful Rules in Syntax: being a concise Introduction to the Writing of Greek. By the Rev. J. PICQUOT. Price 3*s.* boards. A Key to the above, price 1*s.* 6*d.* sewed.

Lightning Source UK Ltd.
Milton Keynes UK
UKHW021137070819
347556UK00004B/716/P